ITEM 023 269 217

edexcel
advancing learning, changing lives

Edexcel AS PE

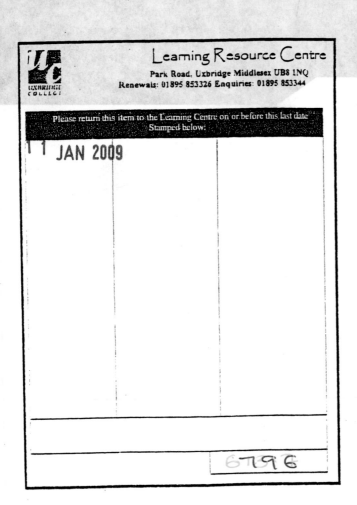

UXBRIDGE COLLEGE

Learning Resource Centre
Park Road, Uxbridge Middlesex UB8 1NQ
Renewals: 01895 853326 Enquiries: 01895 853344

Please return this item to the Learning Centre on or before this last date
Stamped below:

1 1 JAN 2009

6796

Mike Hill

Colin Maskery

Gavin Roberts

D0709750

A PEARSON COMPANY

Published by Pearson Education Limited, a company incorporated in England and Wales, having its registered office at Edinburgh Gate, Harlow, Essex, CM20 2JE. Registered company number: 872828

Edexcel is a registered trademark of Edexcel Limited

Text © Pearson Education Limited 2008

First published 2008

12 11 10 09 08
10 9 8 7 6 5 4 3 2

British Library Cataloguing in Publication Data is available from the British Library on request.

ISBN 978 0 43550050 4

Copyright notice
All rights reserved. No part of this publication may be reproduced in any form or by any means (including photocopying or storing it in any medium by electronic means and whether or not transiently or incidentally to some other use of this publication) without the written permission of the copyright owner, except in accordance with the provisions of the Copyright, Designs and Patents Act 1988 or under the terms of a licence issued by the Copyright Licensing Agency, Saffron House, 6–10 Kirby Street, London EC1N 8TS (www.cla.co.uk). Applications for the copyright owner's written permission should be addressed to the publisher.

Designed by Wooden Ark Studios
Typeset by Pentacorbig
Original illustrations © Pearson Education Limited 2008
Cover design by Wooden Ark Studios
Cover photo by ©Mike Powell/Getty Images
Printed in China (GCC/02)

Websites
The websites used in this book were correct and up-to-date at the time of publication. It is essential for tutors to preview each website before using it in class so as to ensure that the URL is still accurate, relevant and appropriate. We suggest that tutors bookmark useful websites and consider enabling students to access them through the school/college intranet.

CONTENTS

INTRODUCTION

UNITS 1 AND 2

Your AS Physical Education course is divided into two units:

- *Participation in Sport and Recreation* and
- *The Critical Sports Performer*.

This Student Book provides an exact match to the Edexcel specification and as well as teaching and learning material it includes features such as suggested tasks, examiner tips and extension opportunities.

The AS PE for Edexcel student book is divided into three sections:

- Unit 1 Participation in Sport and Recreation Part A Healthy and Active Lifestyles
- Unit 1 Participation in Sport and Recreation Part B Opportunities and Pathways
- Unit 2 The Critical Sports Performer.

The first two sections cover the part of your qualification that is assessed by examination and the third section the part that is assessed by coursework.

Unit 1 Part A is worth 25 per cent of the Advanced Subsidiary award and is marked out of a total of 45

Unit 1 Part B is worth 25 per cent of the Advanced Subsidiary award and is marked out of a total of 45

Together, Part A and Part B are 50 per cent of the total Advanced Subsidiary and 25 per cent of the General Certificate of Education mark.

Unit 2 is worth 50 per cent of the Advanced Subsidiary award and is marked out of a total of 90.

LEARNING STYLES

The key to success at AS level is to understand that you need to learn the concepts, definitions and examples required to answer the questions in the exam. The information you are given in your lessons and the words and case studies presented in the text are only that – information. You will need to go over the chapters several times and attempt all the tasks if you really want to learn the information. It is also important to find out what is the best way for you to learn. We have offered a range of tasks and activities in the text book and you may find some are easier to complete than others.

Generally each person will have a preferred style of learning and research suggests that there are three main types of learning:

- through sight (visually)
- through sound (auditory)
- through physical movement (kinaesthetic).

If you are not sure which is your preferred learning style there is a range of short online tests that you can do to identify your preferred style.

Learning style	Strategies for revision
Visual style	Use tables and diagrams to summarise key points Use colour or highlighters to reinforce the most important points Use the pictures and photos in the book to create a 'visual' case study Put information into timelines or picture boards to help understand the links between concepts
Auditory style	Where possible discuss the topics you are learning with friends Record lessons or notes on an MP3 player for re-listening later and repeat/chant facts/information/examples over and over to retain
Kinaesthetic style	Write out notes several times – each time try to reduce the number of words you are using Make your own charts and tables Trace keywords and phrase with your fingers Try to do things with your hands while you are revising – squeezing a squash or tennis ball, for example

Although using your preferred style of learning will help you revise for exams most effectively it is equally important to try lots of different techniques. If we can use all three styles of learning we will be able to learn more effectively, retaining up to 90 per cent of information presented. Compare that to 60 per cent if doing solely practical activities, 50 per cent using solely visual stimuli or 20 per cent using solely auditory cues.

So when learning or revising make sure you try to present the information in the following ways:

- **Draw it!** (visual) – use mind maps and posters
- **Describe it!** out loud if necessary (auditory) – use audio tapes, podcasts and mnemonics
- **Do it!** (kinaesthetic) – make models, role-play or even move around while learning.

HABITS FOR SUCCESS

Here are the 12 'habits of success' with some ideas on how to apply them to your study of Physical Education.

What's the habit	Apply the habit	Top tip
Take responsibility for yourself	Be proactive and take responsibility for your life. Only you can change your studying behaviour	If it's to be, it's up to me
Be resilient and persistent	Never give up, always keep trying even if things are hard	
Learn from your mistakes	If at first you don't succeed try, try and try again	
There's no such thing as failure, only feedback! (Don't forget to ask for it if it's not forthcoming)		
Be optimistic	Look for the positive outcomes from all actions	Always look on the bright side of life!
Have confidence and self-belief	Believe in yourself and your talents	Say to yourself, 'I'm brilliant!'
Have self-discipline	Learn to wait for things you want (delayed gratification)	No pain, no gain!
Take some risks	Stretch yourself. It's good to venture outside your comfort zone	Challenge yourself
Set yourself some learning goals	Write down your goals and keep a note of your progress towards them	Don't forget your goals need to be SMART (specific, measurable, agreed, realistic and time-bound).
Make a plan and prioritise tasks	Be organised and make a list of what you need to get done	Never put off till tomorrow what can be done today
Work with others	Take notice of what successful students do and copy them!	Listen and learn
Be good to yourself	Get enough sleep and don't party too hard! Exercise and eat well	A healthy body makes for a healthy mind

FEATURES OF THE BOOK

Learning outcomes

These help to ensure you understand fully the content of the chapter. When you have completed a particular topic area, make sure you can achieve each learning objective stated. When preparing for your examination you should collate all the learning objectives from the beginning of the chapters and tick them off as you prepare.

Key terms

Throughout the text you will find explanations of important key terms and concepts that may be new to you. These are a useful reference source. You should aim to use these in your written answers.

Tasks

You will find a range of motivating activities to help you practise what you are learning, including opportunities for small-group discussions. These also help to reinforce learning.

Remember

These features will help to highlight key concepts.

Apply it!

These activities will encourage the application of concepts to real-life contexts. They will reinforce how theory is used in practice.

Hotlinks

Website-related activities throughout the text will direct you to additional exciting resources and encourage further research on topics.

Take it further

These activities will provide opportunities for you to undertake further work on a topic and strengthen your understanding.

LEARNING OUTCOMES

By working through this chapter, you should:
■ know the four basic requirements for physical activity...

KEY TERM
health-related fitness
a basic level of physical fitness components...

TASK
Record your daily activities in a diary...

REMEMBER
■ A high risk profile for diabetes is an inactive, overweight individual...

APPLY IT!
Vigorous cycling will burn between 500 and 700 calories per hour...

HOTLINKS
Research osteoporosis at **www.nos.org.uk**...

TAKE IT FURTHER
If your weighing scales say that you have lost '6 pounds of weight this week'...

Case studies

New and up-to-date case studies provide real-life examples of the topics you are studying. Questions on the case studies will enable you to explore the topic further, understand the key issues and deepen your knowledge of the topic.

Exam tips

Essential bits of exam technique and advice that should help you gain all potential marks.

EXAMCAFÉ

In our unique ExamCafé you'll find lots of ideas to help you prepare for your Unit 1 Examinations, as well as your Unit 2 Coursework. For example, there is handy advice on **Getting started** with **Revision checklists** at the end of each chapter to check that you have taken on board all the concepts within the chapter and are aware of what you need to know and understand, and **Get the result** that gives you sample questions and answers accompanied by examiners' tips. These sections have been specifically written to help you improve your examination performance so make full use of them.

**CASE STUDY
NOTATION IN TENNIS**

Let's look at the data collected...

EXAM TIP

When presenting your coursework for final submission...

Exam**Café**
Relax, refresh, result!

ExamCafé
Relax, refresh, result!

Relax and prepare

Student tips

Kesia

'When people said that AS was harder than GCSE, I guess I didn't really believe them. Most things in class were okay. I didn't do much work outside of lessons. When I came to revise a couple of days before the exams, I found that I couldn't remember half the stuff. So on the day of the exam I went into college an hour early to get help from my teacher but she wasn't there. I had stopped writing before the half way point of the exam.

Maneno

'You should start revising well in advance and read around the subject every evening. Hand in your coursework early so you have time to make amendments. If you get stuck in a lesson do not hold back. Ask for help. Otherwise when you come to the exams you will be stuck. Teachers are there to help you so use them as a resource.'

Tim

'From my experience doing your coursework early is the best way as your teacher can correct it with time for you to make amendments. Doing good coursework is the easiest way to get good grades as you have loads of time and help so there is no excuse for poor work. My teacher said something about not being organised.'

Getting started ...

What's so different about AS?

It is harder than GCSE: You might find yourself tempted to put in minimal effort particularly if you did okay in your GCSEs by not revising.

It is not a memory test: While it is true that you will need to remember a lot of information, the exams are testing whether you can apply the relevant information in answering the question.

It requires longer answers: The questions can require an essay-style answer and although you could give quite brief answers to some questions, you might not fully answer the question (and hence not get good marks) unless you give an extended detailed response.

Get the result !

Before answering the question make sure you read the question two or three times first. When you are happy that you know what the question is asking underline or highlight all the question cues and key words; only then should you put pen to paper and attempt an answer. The table below lists some common question cues, or doing words, together with an idea of the requirements from the candidate in their answer.

Question cues doing word(s)	What you need to do ...
Account for	Explain, clarify, give reasons
Analyse	Resolve into its component parts, examine critically
Assess	Determine the value of, weigh up
Compare	Look for similarities and differences between examples perhaps reach conclusion about which is preferable and justify this clearly
Contrast	Set in opposition in order to bring out the differences sharply
Compare and contrast	Find some points of common ground between x and y and show where or how they differ
Criticise	Make a judgement backed by a discussion of the evidence of reasoning involved, about the merit of theories or opinions or about the truth assertions
Define	State the exact meaning of a word or phrase, in some cases it may be necessary or desirable to examine different possible or often used definitions
Describe	Give a detailed account of
Discuss	Explain, then give two sides of the issue and any implications
Distinguish/ Differentiate between	Look for differences between

Evaluate	Make an appraisal of the worth/validity/effectiveness of something in the light of its truth or usefulness
Explain	Give details about how and why something is so
To what extent	Usually involves looking at evidence/ arguments for and against and weighing them up
Illustrate	Make clear and explicit, usually requires the use of carefully chosen examples
Justify	Show adequate grounds for decisions or conclusions and answer the main objections likely to be made about them
Outline	Give the main features or general principles of a subject, omitting minor details and emphasising structure and arrangement
State	Present in a brief, clear form
Summarise	Give a concise, clear explanation or account of the topic, presenting the chief factors and omitting minor details and examples
What arguments can be made for and against this view	Look at both sides of this argument

examiner's tips

- When drawing diagrams or graphs in your written examination make sure that you draw the images sufficiently large to show the necessary detail clearly and that you label all the parts fully and clearly. Some diagrams may benefit from a key which should be easy to follow. Draw your diagrams and graphs with a pencil and do not use any colours other than blue or black ink to label them.

- If you are asked to sketch a graph then this can be done with an approximate calibration of axes. However if you are required to plot a graph then a more accurate interpretation of data is needed using graph paper and fully calibrated axes.

examiner's tips

- Read the questions thoroughly so that you understand what they are asking you and what you have to do.

- Relate your answer to the number of marks available for that question. Remember that you usually have to make one point in your answer for each mark that is available.

- Wherever possible, apply theory to a practical activity and make sure that you name that activity.

- Make sure that in your anatomy and physiology, and skill answers you use the appropriate technical terms.

- Make sure that you plan the use of your time properly.

- Make sure that you revise all aspects of each area. Do not think that just because a topic was in a previous exam it will not be in yours.

UNIT 1
PARTICIPATION IN SPORT AND RECREATION

PART A
HEALTHY AND ACTIVE LIFESTYLES

In this first section we will look at the concepts and understanding necessary to pursue a healthy and active lifestyle. This will include an examination of the need to be healthy with seemingly increasing political and social pressure as well as those pressures we apply personally to ourselves. We will look at factors that contribute to providing a healthy lifestyle before exploring the reasons why the body responds and then adapts to a changing environment. Then we will explore how we can use this knowledge to improve our health or fitness, or maintain what we already have.

CHAPTER 1 THE DEVELOPMENT OF ACTIVE LEISURE AND RECREATION

LEARNING OUTCOMES

By working through this chapter, you should:

■ know and understand the four basic requirements for physical activity

■ define the concepts of leisure and recreation

■ know the current trends in terms of active leisure and recreation and factors that affect them

■ know the initiatives designed by the various governing and sporting bodies to increase grass roots mass participation

■ know the main contemporary concerns

TASK

Record your daily activities in a diary, include everything that you do! Balance out the activities into two columns: those that contribute to good health and those that contribute to worsening your health. How does it read?

Here we will look at the development of active leisure and recreation within the UK. This includes the *requirements necessary* to enable an active and healthy lifestyle as well as developing a clear understanding of the *concepts of recreation and active leisure*. Then the need for a less sedentary society will be explored through issues of *contemporary concern*.

Within the context of healthy and active lifestyles there are several requirements, all of which seem basic and essential to the point of being obvious. However, the fact that ways to increase the pursuit of an active lifestyle exist, and are increasing, would suggest that these requirements (fitness, ability, resources and time) are not basic, not obvious or alternatively not easily achieved.

Military generals complained that recruits are 'not as fit and healthy as they used to be'. This is not an unfamiliar statement; however, it was not made recently but after the Crimean War, which ended in 1856! Despite the potential for an abundance of food and water, far more hygienic sanitation and living conditions and huge leaps in medical science, we as a society are subject to a decline in fitness and health. This is largely due to our sedentary lifestyle.

During the course of this chapter we will examine the reasons for promoting active leisure, the pressures that have driven the campaign for active leisure, the dangers of not following an active lifestyle and the requirements needed by individuals in order that they can become and remain active.

REQUIREMENTS FOR PARTICIPATION

Fitness, ability, resources and time are considered as basic requisites necessary to partake in sport or physical activity.

FITNESS

Fitness, or rather a lack of it, is often used as a reason why people do not regularly partake in physical activity. When this is the case the term fitness has often been used incorrectly as a synonym for health. (See Chapter 2 Healthy lifestyle for further information and definitions.) Fitness in itself can be obtained, maintained or improved assuming that basic health is present. However, a lack of fitness will limit the effectiveness of the performer within the sporting context.

KEY TERM

health-related fitness
a basic level of physical fitness components which facilitate a good level of health

ABILITY

This refers, in large, to the experiences that an individual has had.

■ Do you feel confident to play the game?

■ Do you have sufficient knowledge of the rules and laws of the activity?

- Do you know the skills of the activity and are you able to execute them to a level that would enable you to participate effectively?
- Do you have the confidence to place your ability on the line in a sporting performance?

RESOURCES

These are essential in order to take part in physical activity and sport. They can be categorised into three main areas: the physical equipment necessary to take part, sufficient people to take part with or against and the money to pay for hire or purchase of facilities and/or equipment.

Clearly the activity and level at which you wish to participate will affect your reliance upon these resources. At one extreme some activities may require only minimal resources and consequently incur little cost, such as running for health and general physical benefits requires little in the way of resources; however, as the pursuit develops then so too does the demand on resources. For example running competitively requires training equipment, adequate nutrition, race venues/stadia, opponents/ organised competition and so on.

For sporting activity to take place on a large scale society must possess both the economic will and the political and cultural desire. Clearly a developing culture may not possess the financial ability to support activities that are more reliant on technology and investment but it may have the cultural desire and political need for sporting success. In such a country activities that are deemed as requiring the fewest resources would be encouraged, for example distance running in Kenya.

▶ *The cultural tradition of long distance running in countries such as Kenya is encouraged*

TASK

Compare and contrast the resources necessary to take part in these two different types of activities.

TIME

Time, or lack of it, is often described as the western disease. Increased leisure time from work has been affected by an almost apparently linear increase in social demands. When this is coupled to the wider variety of recreational activities available and the tendency to be sedentary at work, the result is a growing physical apathy, certainly among some groups in society.

CASE STUDY SPORT SURVEY

Men in managerial and professional, and skilled non-manual households reported higher participation in sports and exercise (45–49 per cent) than those in the remaining three categories of skilled manual, partly skilled and unskilled households (30–35 per cent).

In both men and women and in all age groups, low educational attainment is associated with higher levels of inactivity.

- From what has been covered so far, identify reasons why the facts in the case study might be accurate.

CONCEPTS OF RECREATION AND ACTIVE LEISURE

Leisure is defined as '*a period of time spent out of work and essential domestic activity.*

It is also the period of discretionary time before or after compulsory activities such as eating and sleeping, going to work or running a business, attending school and doing homework, household chores, and day-to-day stress.

The distinction between leisure and compulsory activities is loosely applied, i.e. people sometimes do work-oriented tasks for pleasure as well as for long-term utility….

For an experience to qualify as leisure, it must meet three criteria:
1) *the experience is a state of mind*
2) *it must be entered into voluntarily*
3) *it must be intrinsically motivating of its own merit.*'

(Neulinger, 1981)

Recreation can be defined as '*the use of time in a manner designed for therapeutic refreshment of one's body or mind. While leisure is more likely a form of entertainment or rest, recreation is active for the participant but in a refreshing and diverting manner.*

As people in the world's wealthier regions lead increasingly sedentary lifestyles, the need for recreation has increased.

The rise of so called active vacations exemplifies this.'

(Encyclopedia, 2007)

Although there has always been some form of leisure throughout history, people do now have more leisure time and can choose from a far greater list of activities than in the past. This in itself can, and possibly has, contributed to a decrease in the amount of active recreation and leisure pursuits.

Dramatic changes in work (the move away from manual to non-manual types of jobs, the use of machinery to perform the physically arduous tasks), in transport (the growth of car ownership and usage), and in spending patterns have all contributed to a naturally more sedentary population. This is highlighted further when we consider that there has been a decline of over 20 per cent in miles walked and over 10 per cent in miles cycled since the mid-1980s (National Travel Survey, 2001).

'*Consequently we need a culture shift if we are to increase physical activity levels in England. This will only be achieved if people are aware of, understand and want the benefits of being active. Opportunities will be created by changing the physical and cultural landscape – and building an environment that supports people in more active lifestyles.*'

Department for Culture, Media and Sport, 2002.

APPLY IT!

Research the most popular recreation activities performed by twelve of your classmates. Do they support the trends identified? If not, was your sample representative of society as a whole?

TASK

What's in a name? Try and find a local leisure centre and a local recreation centre. Investigate any differences that might exist and then seek an interview with the manager of each centre.

RECREATIONAL SPORT (MASS PARTICIPATION/GRASS ROOTS)

The need to increase the amount of physical activity and also the clamour to increase a nation's sporting success frequently results in a renewed call for 'mass participation and/or sport for all'. Here we are looking at encouraging people to willingly take part in activities at a grass roots level in order to promote their physical well-being.

Grass roots sport refers to sport played at the lowest organised levels. 'Masses' of people are encouraged to take part in activities of their choice where physical, social and mental benefits are deemed to be possible. A variety of activities are promoted by governments and health bodies (pushing the need for healthy pursuits) as well as sporting governing bodies, clubs and organisations themselves keen to see an increase in membership to increase financial income or discover the next elite performer!

Few would argue that the opportunity to take part in sport or physical activities should be available to everyone. However, obstacles do exist and for many these have proved insurmountable, hence the trend for apathy and sedentary activities. Obstacles such as a perceived lack of fitness, experience, time, money, and so on are targeted by programmes that promote mass participation which seek to break down these constraints and to encourage as many people as possible to take up sport.

TASK

'Sport for all'-type promotions or programmes are not exclusive to the UK. France, Australia, New Zealand, the USA and South Africa have all had similar drives.

Research the names of these initiatives in each of the countries mentioned and find out the background for them.

The growth behind the 'Sport for all campaign' was established as far back as 1972 but was given a fresh kick start in 1994. Initially it was designed to increase the opportunities for sport and recreation through developing more facilities, and by informing and educating the public. As the reasons for growing apathy began to be fully appreciated, the campaign began to target groups of the community that remain under-represented in sport. Campaigns such as '50+ and All to Play For' (aimed at the over-fifties) and 'What's your Sport?' (aimed at women) were developed.

Fig. 1.1 Choosing Activity: a physical activity action plan *(2005) is a government publication in the spirit of 'sport for all'*

The reshaping and rebranding of the Sports Council in 1994 saw a renewed emphasis on the topic of 'sport for all'. Now under the title of Sport England and working with Sport Scotland, Sport Wales (Cymru) and Sport Northern Ireland to form UK Sport, Sport England receives over £250 million a year which is used to run the regional councils, fund campaigns and capital projects, and provide information services. Most of it is redistributed to sports governing bodies, such as the Lawn Tennis Association (LTA), English Football Association (EFA) and the Rugby Football Union (RFU) and many other institutions as grants to be used for increasing sports participation, building new facilities and setting up recreation programmes.

HOTLINKS

Visit the website for UK Sport (at **www.uksport.gov.uk**) and try to discover what initiatives have been implemented to attempt to lead sport in the UK to world class success.

CASE STUDY   EXCESS FAT?

Research undertaken by the Department of Health (2005) stated that, 'Physical inactivity, along with unhealthy diets, has contributed to the rapid increases in obesity in both adults and children with 22 per cent of men and 23 per cent of women in England now obese… Without intervention the figures on obesity in the UK will rise to 33 per cent of men and 28 per cent of women by 2010.'

■ Why do think this is?

CONTEMPORARY CONCERNS

What is often seen as a positive societal development may also contribute, inadvertently, to several negative issues. Society has undergone, and continues to undergo, massive changes, from decade to decade and century to century. With an ever changing and developing society come issues and concerns. Within this context contemporary concerns relate and refer to issues that may result from inactivity or indeed societal pressures and developments that might actually assist in the perpetuation of further inactivity.

OBESITY

This refers to the degree of body fat over and above the accepted gender norm. For example, the body fat level of a healthy male is considered to be 13–17 per cent while for healthy females it is 21–25 per cent.

If your body fat level is deemed to be in excess of these figures then you are classed as being 'over fat'. If that 'over fat level' reaches 25 per cent or greater than your healthy gender norm then you would be classified as being clinically obese.

We often think of obesity as being an ageing problem. However, 16.8 per cent of boys, and 16.9 per cent of girls aged 2–10 in England were classified obese in 2005, an increase from 10.9 per cent and 12.0 per cent for boys and girls respectively in 1995 (Department of Health, 2005).

Obesity is also linked with many other problems and diseases including coronary diseases, diabetes, high blood pressure and certain forms of cancer.

CORONARY HEART DISEASE

Coronary heart disease (CHD), also known as coronary artery disease, is the result of the accumulation of fatty deposits forming plaques within the walls of the arteries that supply the myocardium, the muscles of the heart. Consequently these blood vessels begin to clog and passage through them becomes restricted. As a result the cardiac muscle begins to be starved of nutrients and oxygen.

Unfortunately early symptoms of CHD are hard to detect and for many people the first clear symptom is when the disease is at an advanced stage and may appear in the form of a sudden heart attack. There are a number of factors that are recognised as increasing your risk of CHD as illustrated in Figure 1.2.

REMEMBER

- CHD is the most common cause of sudden death and is also the most common reason for death of men and women over 20 years of age.
- According to the *Guinness Book of Records* (2007), Northern Ireland is the country with the most occurrences of CHD.
- CHD has hereditary links with the link being even stronger if a parent suffered with the disease before the age of 50.

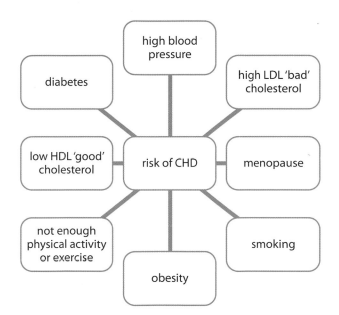

Fig. 1.2 The risk factors associated with CHD

Prevention is preferable to cure for CHD with medical guidelines suggesting the following:

- avoid or reduce stress as best as you can
- do not smoke
- eat well-balanced meals that are low in fat and cholesterol and include several daily servings of fruits and vegetables
- get regular exercise: if your weight is considered normal, get at least 30 minutes of exercise every day; if you are overweight or obese, experts say you should get 60 to 90 minutes of exercise every day
- keep your blood pressure, blood sugar, and cholesterol under control.

As the disease results in a narrowing of the arteries many sufferers have taken aspirin, which thins the blood, on a daily basis.

DIABETES

Diabetes is a disease that is characterised by the inability of the body to make sufficient insulin or alternatively the resistance of the body to insulin. Consequently, the body is unable to regulate blood sugar levels efficiently in order to prevent hyperglycemia (too much glucose in the blood). There are two principal types of diabetes mellitus:

- type I is insulin dependent and usually appears in young people between 10–16 years old
- type II is non-insulin dependent and usually appears gradually, mainly in the over 40s.

All types of diabetes have been treatable since insulin became medically available in 1921, although dietary and other lifestyle adjustments are part of the management of the disease.

The characteristic symptoms are excessive urination, excessive and continued thirst, increased fluid intake, and blurred vision.

The World Health Organization (2002) recognises that '*three main forms of diabetes exist which have similar signs, symptoms, and consequences, but different causes and population distributions.*'

Diabetes can cause many complications and, if ignored or not treated effectively, diabetes can lead to serious long-term complications such as:

- cardiovascular disease
- chronic renal failure
- retinal damage (which can lead to blindness)
- nerve damage (of several kinds)
- microvascular damage, which may cause impotence and poor healing. Poor healing of wounds, particularly of the feet, can lead to gangrene, and may result in amputation.

Adequate treatment of diabetes, as well as increased emphasis on blood pressure control and lifestyle factors (such as not smoking and keeping a healthy body weight), may improve the risk profile of most of the complications listed above.

REMEMBER

- A high risk profile for diabetes is an inactive, overweight individual whose diet is based around saturated fats and simple sugars and consequently who has high cholesterol and also high blood pressure.

CASE STUDY
SUGAR OR NO SUGAR?

In the developed world, diabetes is the most significant cause of adult blindness in the non-elderly and the leading cause of non-traumatic amputation in adults.

Sir Steven Redgrave is Britain's most successful ever Olympian. He has won a gold medal in rowing at five consecutive Olympic Games. That covers a period of 20 years! However, he won the first four medals as a non-diabetic and the last as a diabetic!

■ Do you have an explanation for this?

HIGH BLOOD PRESSURE

High **blood pressure** is often referred to and linked with coronary heart disease. Every time the heart beats, blood is ejected into the arteries under quite strong pressure. Your blood pressure is highest when your heart beats, pumping the blood. This is called systolic pressure. When your heart is at rest, between beats, your blood pressure falls. This is the diastolic pressure.

Your blood pressure reading uses these two numbers, the systolic and diastolic pressures. Usually they are written one above or before the other. A reading of:

■ 120/80 or lower is normal blood pressure

■ 140/90 or higher is high blood pressure.

Note that between 120 and 139 for the top number, or between 80 and 89 for the bottom number, is indicative of prehypertension.

■ Optimal blood pressure is less than 120 mm Hg systolic and 80 mm Hg diastolic.

■ High blood pressure, or hypertension, is a condition in which blood pressure levels are above the normal range.

■ Blood pressure is considered high if it is 140 mm Hg and/or 90 mm Hg or higher.

High blood pressure usually has no symptoms, but it can cause serious problems such as increasing the risk for heart attack, heart failure, angina, stroke, kidney failure and peripheral artery disease (PAD). The risk of heart failure also increases due to the increased workload that high blood pressure places on the heart.

KEY TERM

blood pressure
the force exerted by your blood within the arteries

HIGH CHOLESTEROL

Often receiving a bad press, cholesterol is frequently blamed for a multitude of illnesses. The truth is that cholesterol is essential for bodily function and is not dangerous. But too much of the wrong sort of cholesterol is very dangerous. There are several factors that may contribute to high blood cholesterol (see Figure 1.3):

■ diet – one that is high in saturated fat combined with lack of exercise may increase LDL (bad) cholesterol and decrease HDL (good) cholesterol (see page 34)

■ family history – people are at a higher risk of high cholesterol if they have a direct male relative aged under 55 years or a female relative aged under 65 years affected by heart disease

■ weight – being overweight may increase LDL (bad) cholesterol and decrease **HDL** (good) cholesterol

■ age and sex – cholesterol generally rises slightly with increasing age, and men are more likely to be affected than women

■ alcohol – drinking more than the recommended amount.

CASE STUDY
HIGH OR LOW?

Contrary to common opinion only a small amount of cholesterol comes directly from your diet – the majority is produced by your liver. However, if your diet is high in saturated fats and cholesterol this can cause your liver to produce more LDL (bad) cholesterol. The influence of diet on cholesterol levels varies from person to person.

■ What are the current figures for the maximum cholesterol levels?

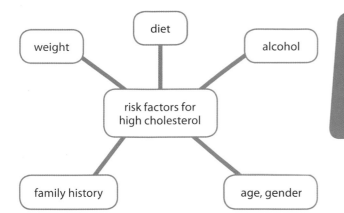

Fig. 1.3 *Factors that increase the risk of high cholesterol*

> **REMEMBER**
>
> ■ Cardiovascular disease, including heart disease, stroke and cancer, are the major causes of death in England, together accounting for almost 60 per cent of premature deaths (British Heart Foundation, 2007).

> **KEY TERMS**
>
> **LDL (low density lipoprotein)**
> a lipoprotein which has less protein in relation to fat (bad cholesterol)
>
> **HDL (high density lipoprotein)**
> a lipoprotein which has more protein in relation to fat (good cholesterol)

> **TASK**
>
> *Attempt to discover the total amount of fat that you consume in a normal day and then compare the level that you consume with the recommended daily average.*

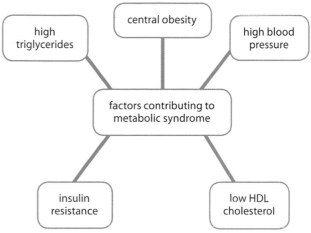

Fig. 1.4 *Metabolic risk factors that contribute to metabolic syndrome*

> **REMEMBER**
>
> ■ Metabolic syndrome has become increasingly common in the US. It's estimated that over 50 million Americans have it.

METABOLIC SYNDROME

Metabolic syndrome is a combination of medical disorders that increase the risk of cardiovascular disease and diabetes. It is characterised by the presence of a group of metabolic risk factors. They include:

- abdominal obesity (excessive fat tissue in and around the abdomen)
- atherogenic dyslipidemia (blood fat disorders – high triglycerides, low HDL cholesterol and high LDL cholesterol – that foster plaque build-ups in artery walls)
- elevated blood pressure
- insulin resistance or glucose intolerance (the body can't properly use insulin or blood sugar).

People with metabolic syndrome are at increased risk of coronary heart disease and other diseases related to plaque building up in artery walls (e.g. stroke and vascular disease) and type II diabetes. The dominant underlying risk factors for this syndrome appear to be abdominal obesity and insulin resistance. Insulin resistance is a generalised metabolic disorder in which the body can't use insulin efficiently. This is why metabolic syndrome is also called the insulin resistance syndrome. Other conditions associated with the syndrome include a lack of physical activity, ageing, hormonal imbalance and genetic predisposition.

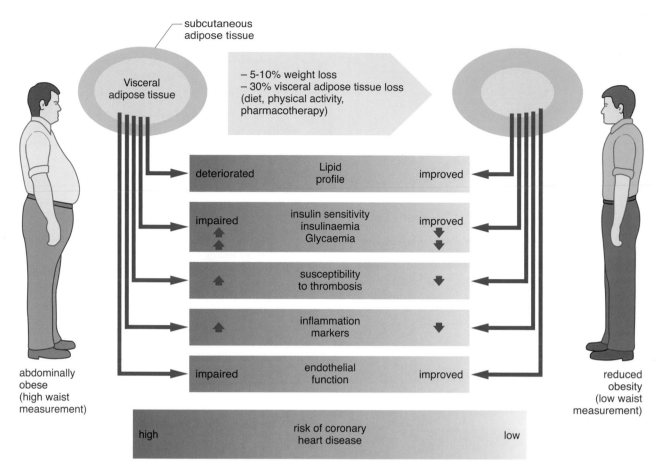

Fig. 1.5 *Reducing the risk of cardiovascular disease helps in the treatment of metabolic syndrome*

The main target in the treatment of metabolic syndrome is to reduce the risk for cardiovascular disease and type II diabetes, i.e. reduce LDL cholesterol, blood pressure and glucose levels to the recommended levels.

SEDENTARY LIFESTYLES

'*Following a sedentary lifestyle is more dangerous for your health than smoking, says a new study reported in the* South China Morning Post, *and carried out by the University of Hong Kong and the Department of Health. In the study, researchers looked at the level of physical activity in people who died and were able to correlate their level of physical activity with their risk of dying.'*

Target News.com

However, when the list of contemporary concerns is examined it is clear that the common theme of regular exercise could combat all of them. Exercise in itself will not eradicate the **hypokinetic disorders** but it can go a long way towards lessening their effect. With this in mind the quote is not surprising; a lack of exercise – coupled to poor diet, predisposition to hereditary illnesses and a hectic lifestyle – is often synonymous with poor health.

KEY TERM
hypokinetic disorder
a disorder that is totally or partly attributed to a lack of physical activity

KEY TERM
sedentary lifestyle
a lifestyle that is predominantly lacking in physical activity

CASE STUDY EXERCISE IS GOOD FOR YOU

Regular physical activity reduces the risk of depression and has positive benefits for mental health including reduced anxiety, and enhanced mood and self-esteem.

Increasing physical activity levels will contribute to the prevention and management of over 20 conditions and diseases including coronary heart disease, diabetes and cancer, positive mental health and weight management.

Inactive and unfit people have almost double the risk of dying from coronary heart disease. Physical activity is also an independent protective factor against coronary heart disease.

Increasing activity levels also has beneficial effects on musculoskeletal health, reducing the risk of osteoporosis, back pain and osteoarthritis.

■ Interview ten of your peers to ascertain their activity levels and their perceived state of health. Is there a correlation between social attitude, mental and physical health and activity levels?

ACTIVITY PATTERNS

■ Poor nutrition and lack of physical activity are responsible for an estimated 300,000 to 600,000 preventable deaths each year in the US alone.

■ This figure rises to over 2 million worldwide, a fact that becomes even more startling when we consider that a sedentary lifestyle is a Western/developed world phenomenon!

■ An estimated one-third of all cancers are attributable to poor nutrition, physical inactivity, and being overweight.

TAKE IT FURTHER

Many primary care professionals are already involved in schemes to refer patients to facilities such as leisure centres or gyms for supervised exercise programmes.

Can you list all of the potential benefits to the well-being of an individual as a result of taking part in regular physical activity?

AGEING POPULATION

'The UK's population is ageing. Although the population grew by 8 per cent in the last thirty-five years, from 55.9 million in 1971 to 60.6 million in mid-2006, this change has not occurred evenly across all age groups.

The population aged over 65 grew by 31 per cent, from 7.4 to 9.7 million, whilst the population aged under 16 declined by 19 per cent, from 14.2 to 11.5 million.

The largest percentage growth in population in the year to mid-2006 was at ages 85 and over (5.9 per cent). The number of people aged 85 and over grew by 69,000 in the year to 2006, reaching a record 1.2 million. This large increase reflects improving survival and the post World War One baby boomers now reaching this age group.'

(Office for National Statistics, 2005)

REMEMBER

- 16% of the UK population are aged 65 or over.

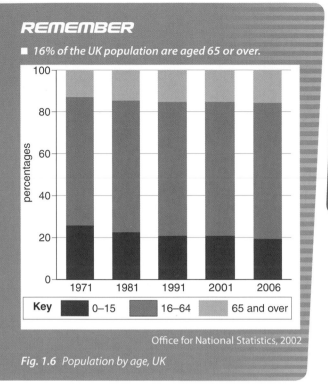

Office for National Statistics, 2002

Fig. 1.6 Population by age, UK

TASK

- Research why the groups listed may have less opportunity to participate in sport.

- Research strategies that have been used in order to try to counter the obstacles of opportunity and thus encourage greater participation of these groups.

- Have the strategies been successful?

- What evidence is there?

ACCESS

In terms of sport and physical activity access is a term that covers both opportunity and provision.

Many people do not have equal access to sport, often as a result of discrimination due to cultural variables. As a result a number of target groups have been identified, all of whom have, for a variety of reasons, found it difficult to access sport and recreation.

OPPORTUNITY

Cultural factors may provide a barrier to the potential opportunity of a number of groups in society due to gender, class, race, age and ability (see Figure 1.7).

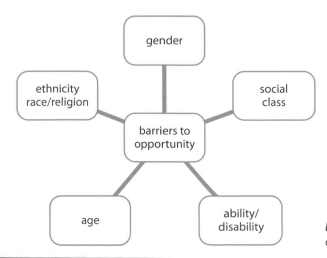

Fig. 1.7 Cultural groups affected by possible barriers to opportunity

PROVISION

Are the facilities that allow you to participate available to you? Living in a poorer or inner-city area might in the past have discriminated against the population on geographical grounds. However, recent regeneration and funding in these areas has, in some cases, reversed the trend. For many people, living in a rural area where transport is required in order to travel to the various institutions, many of which may be quite dispersed throughout the geographical region, may prove to be a hindrance in terms of provision.

Also some activities may require equipment, which can be expensive, and an inability to afford such equipment can directly restrict access through a lack of provision, or indirectly through a lack of self-esteem. The consequence of this is applied self-discrimination.

STRESS

We frequently and automatically assume that stress is bad and to be avoided. However, there are different types of stress and different ways of dealing with them. When particular types of stress are present or build up beyond our capacity to cope, then we might start to experience problems.

The body reacts to stress. It is with this in mind that we as athletic performers undertake physical activity. We undertake specific pre-event rituals because they 'stress' the body. As a result the body makes temporary changes to help it deal with the stress. These temporary changes are called responses and help us to perform better. The ritual is a warm-up.

Likewise, regular exercise in the form of training is a stress. The body reacts to the regular **catabolic** state that the exercise puts it in by growing bigger, getting stronger, getting fitter and so on. These are adaptations.

> ## KEY TERMS
>
> **catabolic**
> describing the breakdown phase, such as training
>
> **anabolic**
> describing the build up or recovery phase

Similarly, we may react to other types of stress at work or in life as a form of challenge that we must meet. It can be thought of as the body's way of rising to a challenge and preparing to meet a tough situation with focus, strength, stamina, and heightened alertness.

The events that provoke stress are called stressors, and as described, cover a variety of situations. The body responds to stressors by activating the nervous system and the production of certain hormones. The adrenal gland is stimulated to produce more of the hormones adrenalin and cortisol which are released into the bloodstream. These hormones have a number of effects on the body (see Figure 1.8).

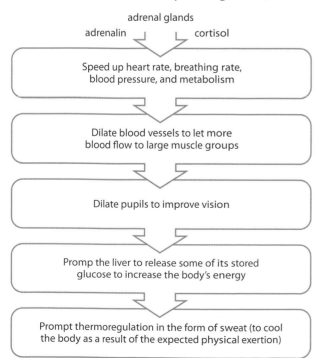

Fig.1.8 The stress response called the 'fight or flight' response

This chain of reactions is known as the stress response (also called the fight or flight response). Working properly it can enhance a person's ability to perform well under pressure. But the stress response can also cause problems when it over-reacts or fails to turn off and 'reset' itself properly.

GOOD STRESS AND BAD STRESS

The stress response is critical during emergency or potentially dangerous situations, when a person might literally have to fight or run. It can also be activated in a milder form at a time when the pressure is on but there is no real danger, such as taking a penalty or sitting down for a final exam. It is widely accepted that at these times a degree of stress can be beneficial.

However, stress doesn't always happen in response to things that are immediate or that are over quickly. It can build up over time with low level stressors. These low level stressors are often not recognised; they may not produce the physiological response mentioned earlier simply because they are at such a low level. However, long-term stressful situations can produce a lasting, low-level stress that can have a negative effect.

The nervous system begins to sense a build-up of stress and continued pressure. Consequently it may remain slightly activated and continue to pump out extra stress hormones over an extended period. This can weaken the body's immune system, and cause other related health problems such as lethargy, mood swings, sleep deprivation, depression, increased blood pressure and elevated heart rate. A build-up of 'bad stress' may show itself through any of a range of symptoms (see Fig. 1.9).

Being aware of the triggers and/or symptoms is crucial for those who suffer from the adverse effects of stress. Setting realistic goals, good diet, regular exercise and regular sleep patterns have all been identified as providing relief from a build-up of bad stress.

IN SUMMARY

The potential benefits of leading a healthy lifestyle are widely reported and will be covered later in more detail. As a result of huge advertising campaigns figures suggest that the proportion of people who choose to be active in their leisure time is showing an upward trend. However, we should be aware that participation in sports and exercise varies by age, sex, social grouping and ethnicity. (See also Chapter 7 Lifelong involvement).

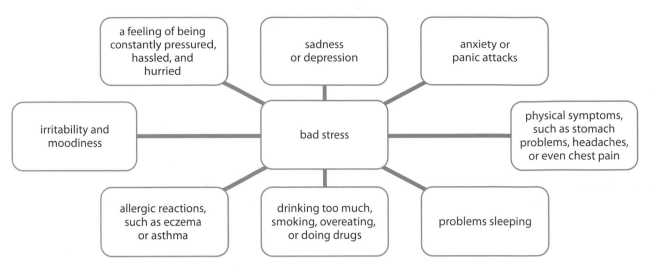

Fig. 1.9 The range of symptoms displayed through 'bad stress'

REMEMBER

■ The cost of inactivity and consequent poor health is not lost on government as indicated by a report by the Chief Medical Officer:

'Besides the human costs of inactivity in terms of mortality, morbidity and quality of life, the report highlighted an estimate for the cost of inactivity in England to be £8.2 billion annually. This excludes the contribution of physical inactivity to overweight and obesity, whose overall cost might run to £6.6–£7.4 billion per year according to recent estimates.'

(Department of Health, 2005)

So we accept that physical activity is beneficial to us individually and collectively, as a society. It is important to understand what is meant by 'physical activity'. Literally it can be defined as anything that requires movement of the body; however, within the context of health and lifestyle we must be more specific.

On its 'Healthy Living' website the UK government states that '*being physically active involves moving your body and using energy (expressed in kilocalories, Kcals) at an intensity that makes you warm and breathe a bit deeper than usual (such as brisk walking). Anyone can do this and achieve a healthier lifestyle!*'

The US government describes physical activity as meaning 'movement of the body that uses energy. Walking, gardening, briskly pushing a baby stroller, climbing the stairs, playing soccer, or dancing the night away are all good examples of being active.'

Both governments categorise physical activity as moderate or vigorous as described in Table 1.1.

This is qualified with guidelines as to the amount of activity that is required in order to improve or maintain health (see Table 1.2).

Moderate physical activities include:	Vigorous physical activities include:
■ Walking briskly (about 3½ miles per hour)	■ Running/jogging (5 miles per hour)
■ Hiking	■ Cycling (more than 10 miles per hour)
■ Gardening work	■ Swimming (freestyle laps)
■ Dancing	■ Aerobics
■ Golf (walking and carrying clubs)	■ Walking very fast (4½ miles per hour)
■ Cycling (less than 10 miles per hour)	■ Heavy yard work, such as chopping wood
■ Weight training (general light workout)	■ Weight lifting (vigorous effort)
	■ Basketball (competitive)

Table 1.1 Moderate and vigorous activity levels used by UK and US governments

Category	Activity level	Frequency
Children and young people should	achieve a total of at least 60 minutes of at least moderate-intensity physical activity	twice a week.
Adults should (for general health benefits)	achieve a total of at least 30 minutes a day of at least moderate-intensity physical activity	five or more days of the week.
Adults should (for beneficial effects for individual diseases and conditions)	achieve 45–60 minutes of moderate-intensity physical activity a day (to prevent obesity)	five or more days of the week.

Source: Chief Medical Officer's recommendations to the government, 2005.

Table 1.2 *Guidelines for the levels of physical activity recommended by US and UK governments*

CASE STUDY
NEVER TOO OLD

The proportion of people engaging in physical activity declines with age and especially after the age of 35. In particular, participation in walking has been shown to decline from 45 per cent among men aged 16–24 to 8 per cent among men aged 75 and over. Among women, walking remained relatively stable among those aged 16–54 (28–32 per cent) but declined rapidly to 5 per cent for those aged 75 and over (Department of Health, 2005).

When all sources of activity are considered, only 37 per cent of men and 24 per cent of women currently meet the Chief Medical Officer's minimum recommendations for activity in adults and are sufficiently active to benefit their health.

■ Comment on these percentages.

TAKE IT FURTHER

People have potentially more leisure time than ever before, there are more programmes promoting active recreation, there are programmes and initiatives aimed at involving specific groups in active recreational activities, but still our society is increasingly sedentary.

Prepare a 15-minute presentation stating why you believe that activity levels are still declining.

▶ *Exercise and physical activity can give you a feeling of health and well-being*

Refresh your memory

Revision checklist

▷ Know the four basic requirements for physical activity

▷ Be able to define the concepts of leisure and recreation

▷ Know the current trends in terms of active leisure and recreation and factors that affect them

▷ Know the initiatives designed by the various governing and sporting bodies to increase grass roots mass participation

▷ Know the main contemporary concerns as being:

  o obesity

  o coronary heart disease

  o high blood pressure

  o high cholesterol

  o stress

  o diabetes

  o metabolic syndrome

  o sedentary lifestyle

  o ageing population

  o access

  o opportunity

  o provision

For each one you should be able to provide a definition and state the effect that it has on the individual or society

▷ Know and understand the role of physical activity in offsetting these contemporary concerns

Get the result!

Sample question and answer

Exam question

a. A number of contemporary concerns are labelled as hypokinetic disorders. Explain what a hypokinetic disorder is and describe **three** such contemporary disorders. **(4 marks)**

b. Explain how exercise can help to act as a cure for each disorder identified in your answer to part a. **(3 marks)**

Student answer – candidate A

Obesity, coronary heart disease and high blood pressure are all classed as being hypokinetic disorders. They all have several things in common, e.g. exercise can help to limit the effect that they might have. Regular aerobic exercise if performed at a low intensity will use fat as a fuel. This will mean that a person who is not regularly exercising is likely to have a higher body fat level while someone who is exercising for at least 30 minutes three times a week would be more likely to have a lower body fat level. The person who is not exercising will often be more open to suffering from stress which is also a hypokinetic disorder.

Examiner says:

Here are two typical answers to part **a** and **b** of the question.

Examiner says:

This is a particularly poor answer and would fail to score any marks at all.

The candidate has waffled/skirted around the subject using generic and vague terms and although much of what they have written is accurate it is not answering the question.

Firstly they have not tackled the first part of the question which was to … *Explain what a hypokinetic disorder is…* Secondly, they have not split the answer into part **a** and part **b**.

The start of the answer looks promising with the correct identification of three hypokinetic disorders. However, it is essential to know how many marks are available and how they are allocated before you attempt to answer a question.

If this question had been for 7 marks then there would have been:

- 1 mark for explaining hypokinetic disorders
- 3 marks for identifying three such disorders
- 1 mark for the description of each disorder.

This candidate would have scored 3 marks as three disorders were identified, which would be a D grade answer; however, it still would lack clarity and structure.

However, as the question was out of 4 marks then the allocation would be:

- 1 mark for explaining hypokinetic disorders
- 1 mark for each identified and explained disorder.

This candidate did not explain any of the three disorders; instead they began a generic description of disorders and the role that exercise might play. This is not part of question a but part of question b, which may have confused the candidate. Finally, in an attempt to gain another mark in a 4-mark question the candidate goes on unnecessarily to mention a fourth disorder. This candidate would have scored 0 marks.

Student answer – candidate B

Examiner says:

On the whole this is a good answer. It is well structured and easy for the examiner to follow. The candidate clearly understands where the 4 marks are to be allocated and has set their answer out accordingly. The first sentence clearly collects the mark for the explanation of a hypokinetic disorder.

a) A hypokinetic disorder is when you suffer from a disease that might be brought about as a result of a lack of exercise or might be improved if you were to start to exercise.

Obesity is when you are excessively overweight.

Coronary heart disease is when the arteries that feed the heart have been damaged.

Examiner says:

Unfortunately the second part of the answer is too vague and also uses incorrect terminology: weight is used when it should be fat.

The third sentence is very clear and succinct so no time has been wasted here: 2 marks out of 3 so far.

Blood pressure is measured when your heart contracts and relaxes. The level is the pressure that the blood exerts when in the arteries. If your readings are higher than 140/90 then your blood pressure is classed as being too high.

Examiner says:

The final sentence waffles and the candidate does not actually state that high blood pressure is the disorder, indeed, at first it appears that blood pressure is the disorder being described. However, the final part of the last sentence does enough to allow the examiner to award a 'benefit of the doubt' mark.

This candidate would have scored 3 out of the 4 marks allocated.

model answer

a) A hypokinetic disorder is a disorder that is totally or partly attributed to a lack of physical activity. **(1 mark)**

Obesity is when a person's body fat levels are 25 per cent greater than their suggested gender norms. **(1 mark)**

Coronary heart disease is the end result of the accumulation of plaques and fatty deposits within the walls of the arteries that supply the myocardium. **(1 mark)**

Blood pressure is a measure of the force exerted by your blood within the arteries. High blood pressure is when the systolic and diastolic readings are higher than 140/90. **(1 mark)**

CHAPTER 2 HEALTHY LIFESTYLE

LEARNING OUTCOMES

By working through this chapter, you should:

■ know the definitions of and differences between health and fitness and the different roles that exercise will play in achieving either

■ know what the contemporary concerns are and understand the positive effects that exercise can have on them

■ know the seven food groups and the main role of each of the seven

■ know the necessity for optimum water balance

■ compare trends on health in the UK with at least one other country

■ know the effects that ageing can have on athletic performance and how exercise can offset the ageing process

This second chapter will focus on the *healthy lifestyle* to give you an understanding of the concepts involved in *health*, *fitness* and *exercise* so that many contemporary and hypokinetic disorders can be avoided. It will include an examination of what constitutes both a healthy and necessary diet, through correct and sensible *nutrition and weight management* for an active individual. It will also examine the effects on performance and health of mismanaging diet and the need for individuals to *balance their lifestyles*. The *effects of ageing* upon health and fitness both through physical maturation and thereafter, when a decline in performance is taken for granted, will be examined. Here we will look at how sensible exercise can, in many ways, offset the ageing process. There will also be the opportunity to *compare trends in health* within the UK with other societies such as the US, Japan or Finland.

HEALTH, FITNESS AND EXERCISE

THE DIFFERENCES AND SIMILARITIES BETWEEN HEALTH AND FITNESS

The terms health and fitness are often inaccurately used as pseudonyms for one another. They are, within many contexts, related and quite often appear to be dependent upon each other. Indeed, their definitions may even seem to overlap and in many

cases may seem to have an identical sense. However, there are very subtle differences between the two concepts. If you are about to embark upon an active lifestyle then it is important for you to know whether you are pursuing health or fitness benefits.

Definitions of 'health' may differ slightly depending on your source of information; however, the sense can be summarised as follows:

'*A complete state of physical and mental well-being and not merely the absence of disease or infirmity.*'

The term 'fitness' can be equally problematic to define with some sources describing it as an essential element in health! However, in its purest and simplest form it is defined as:

'*The ability to meet the demands of the environment without undue fatigue.*'

Consequently, the similarities in the two terms are that they meet the demands of one's environment.

In the case of health the environment is your personal lifestyle. Are you able to function efficiently and effectively within your environment? For example, you might have a variety of positive physical attributes yet if your job is within the Stock Exchange and creates stress that you are unable to deal with then you are not meeting the demands of your environment. Equally if you have huge mental capacity but your job involves manual labour that reduces you to a crippled wreck then, once again, you are not meeting the demands of your environment.

The environment in which we associate fitness is sport. As each sport, and even the positions and roles within the same sport, can differ so greatly then your environment becomes very specific. For a marathon runner your environment is usually an undulating 42,000 metre race (just over 26 miles!). Being fit for this sport would mean that you could race the distance and not simply survive it. The environment of a boxer requires the ability to sustain relatively high intensity activity for 3 minutes with a regular 1 minute interval. You may possess all of the boxing skills imaginable, such as quick reflexes, power and so on, yet if after the fourth of twelve rounds you are so fatigued that you are unable to utilise your skills then you were not fit for your environment.

US boxer Floyd Maryweather weighs in before a bout in Las Vegas, 2007

Both images are of very fit athletes at the peak of physical fitness. Both have trained extremely hard taking into account the demands that their own sport would place on them. Yet both look very different.

The reference to '…without undue fatigue' refers to the ability to perform within the sport to your ability or skill level for the entire duration of the event. If your skill level drops off as a result of fatigue then you would not be classed as fit for the sport at the intensity at which you have competed.

The term '**health-related fitness**' has often been used. This refers to the physical components of fitness that are considered essential to provide the individual with health and the 'complete state of physical well-being,' such as flexibility, aerobic or cardiovascular fitness and basic **anaerobic** fitness.

UK marathon runner Paula Radcliffe taking part in the New York City Marathon, 2007

equipped. Equally, if the environment was the marathon course then the marathon runner would be the better equipped. To ask who has the greater aerobic fitness would be a valid question, as would the question of who possesses the greatest anaerobic capacity. It is this type of question that has identified cross-country skiers with having the greatest levels of VO_2 max of any athlete. However, it would be wrong to use the information to state that cross-country skiers are the fittest athletes.

KEY TERMS
aerobic
with oxygen
anaerobic
without oxygen

KEY TERM
VO_2 maximum (or VO_2 max)
the maximum amount of oxygen that can be taken in, and used, per kg of bodyweight

Questions that require a comparison of fitness levels between contrasting sports are frequently asked. To ask who is the fitter athlete, the marathon runner or the 100 metre sprinter, however, is invalid. If the environment is the 100 metre track then undoubtedly the sprinter would be the best

Within the world of sports, fitness is achieved as a result of maximising one or more fitness components as determined by the nature of the sport. No fitness component is of a higher standing or importance than another in general terms, only in sporting specific environments. (See page 72 for a more detailed analysis of the components of fitness.)

TASK

Do the two images create the same impression? Or does one appear to represent running for health and the other running for sport? If the latter is the case, does that also suggest something about our social perceptions and gender expectations?

In summary, health is life-related while fitness is sport-related. Both are specific with regards to how well you meet your environment.

EXERCISE

Exercise is defined as 'a physical activity that produces a positive physiological adaptation.' As such, it is assumed that the 'exercise' is performed repeatedly and with sufficient intensity to stimulate the necessary responses and eventual adaptations.

In Chapter 1 we examined many of the contemporary concerns, most of which are classed as hypokinetic disorders (diseases or disorders either brought about as a result of a lack of regular physical activity or those that can be offset as a result of regular physical activity). The presence of any one of these disorders or diseases classifies the sufferer as being in poor health. So exercise is deemed to be essential to achieve and maintain a good level of health.

Without exercise fitness could not be achieved, but as we've already seen, there is a variety of different components of fitness which makes the type of exercises crucial to the outcome or benefits achieved (see pages 76–89 on training for a more detailed explanation).

ONE WITHOUT THE OTHER?

Is it possible to have health without fitness or fitness without health? The simple answer is yes, in both cases. For example:

- Basic levels of good quality and regular exercise, a good balanced diet which considers calorific income and expenditure, regular quality sleep, avoidance of social drugs such as cigarettes and alcohol could, and probably would, lead to a healthy individual. However, that would not qualify you as being physically prepared to run a marathon, climb a mountain, cycle a 100 mile criterium or even play 90 minutes of football. You would be healthy without being fit.

- The majority of athletes in their prime should, with some justification, be able to consider themselves as being healthy. However, consider:

  o the top-class sprinter who smokes regularly

  o the sumo wrestler who is grossly over fat to the point of being clinically obese

  o the football player who has to have regular cortisone injections into his knee to enable him to play

  o the athlete who takes **rhEPO** or Blood Dopes in order to work for longer o   the rugby player who takes anabolic steroids in order to recover more quickly

o   the boxer who suffers from concussion

o   the gymnast who may struggle to walk upright when much older.

> ## KEY TERM
>
> **rhEPO**
> the hormone (erythroprotein) that stimulates red blood cell production

Consequently, it could be argued that some exercise is of benefit, more is of greater benefit but, as with all things, too much of it might become disadvantageous.

THE POSITIVE BENEFITS TO ACHIEVING HEALTH AND/OR FITNESS

As stated on pages 14–15, exercise has been prescribed by physicians and health trusts within the UK as an effective tool to fight many of the identified hypokinetic disorders. Regular exercise has been, and continues to be, used as one of the main weapons to fight deteriorating health. When someone has achieved what is considered to be a good standard of health then it might be clearly visible for others to see through a change in body mass through loss of fat.

The physiological benefits of losing excess body fat levels have already been discussed and will be

covered again later within this section. However, the result of fat loss and consequent improved health benefits achieved not only have physiological benefits but the psychological benefits can be equally impressive (see Figure 2.1).

ENERGY EXPENDITURE AND FAT LOSS

Exercise within the context of fitness is usually targeting:

- improved fitness components (i.e. increased strength, speed, etc.)
- weight loss (can be considered an improved fitness component, as excess weight in the form of fat adversely affects your VO_2 max).

Exercise within the context of health usually targets one or more, or perhaps all, of the following:

- weight management – either fat loss, body mass increase or body weight maintenance
- improved cardiovascular and/or cardiorespiratory efficiency and functioning
- improved range of movement (ROM).

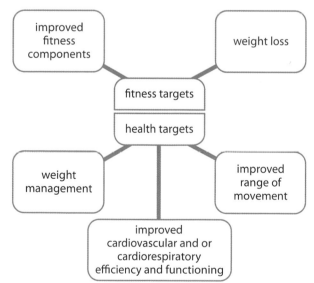

Fig. 2.2 Comparison of health and fitness targets during fat loss

In this section we will look at energy expenditure. (The calorific value of foods and calorific expenditure while active are covered in greater detail below.)

There are numerous gimmicks and fads, all of which add up to a huge commercial industry claiming to have discovered the secret to weight loss or muscle mass gains.

Fig. 2.1 Fat loss can have psychological benefits as well as physiological benefits

Diet	Activity	Outcome
If energy in equals	energy out	then body weight is maintained over time.
If energy in is greater than	energy out	the body will store this excess energy as body fat.
If energy in is less than	energy out	the body will use stored fat as energy and fat loss will occur.

Table 2.1 The three energy expenditure statements

Despite these claims the facts are outlined in Table 2.1.

RATE OF FAT LOSS

The rate of fat loss should be steady and slow, and 1–2 pounds of fat loss per week is considered a good rate. A slow rate such as this is sustainable over a long period because the body is able to adapt to any changes. As a result these losses tend to be more permanent.

APPLY IT!

Vigorous cycling will burn between 500 and 700 calories per hour. There are 3200 calories in one pound of fat (or 7040 calories to 1 kg of fat).

Assuming an average of 600 calories is the norm when cycling, calculate the appropriate amount of time in days or weeks that it should take a 14 stone man to get down to 12 stones in weight (a loss of 12.72 kg). Explain your result.

TAKE IT FURTHER

If your weighing scales say that you have lost '6 pounds of weight this week' have you really done 36 hours of cycling or the equivalent?

If calorific restriction is used in an attempt to reduce body mass then initially weight will be lost, but the rate of weight loss will eventually slow down and then stop altogether until the calorific content is reduced further. However, while this is happening you will probably be encouraged to continue because the weighing scales indicate that you are losing weight. In short, it seems to be working, so let's continue. While the number of calories are being reduced the following things are happening in your body:

- The body loses fluids which are essential for efficient functioning, resulting in lethargy and demotivation.
- The body will automatically assume that it is enduring a famine and will:
  - become more efficient at surviving on less fuel. It will use less calories than before to carry out the same activity
  - hold on to what it considers to be the most essential elements, such as fat, and lose the non-essential elements such as lean muscle mass!
  - ensure that muscle burns fewer fat calories even at rest in order to conserve the supply of fat stores
  - lower the **basal metabolic rate (BMR)**.

KEY TERM
basal metabolic rate (BMR)
the rate at which calories are burned

REMEMBER
- A large cheese burger, fries and a strawberry milk shake contains 1330 calories. And that's without the dressing!

If caloric restriction is too severe:	If body weight loss is too rapid, some fat is lost, but:
Loss of significant amounts of lean tissue is likely (muscle and bone nutrients). Overall nutrient intake is less likely to be balanced. It might initiate a habit of binge eating.	Large amounts of fluid are lost. Some lean tissue is lost.

Table 2.2 Dangers of restricting calorific intake alone

IN SUMMARY

Simply cutting back on the amount you eat will not be enough to help you if your goal is fat loss. You will hold on to the fat, lose muscle tissue first and slow your metabolism down. It will be easier for you to gain fat at a faster rate if you ever resume your previous eating habits.

BASAL METABOLIC RATE

Your basal metabolic rate (BMR) is the speed at which your body converts and uses calories to fuel the activities that you undertake. One of the keys to successful fat loss is to maintain a high BMR. People with a high BMR are usually thin, while people with a low BMR are usually carrying excess weight in the form of fat.

Exercise is seen as offering significant positive benefits to many of the contemporary concerns identified earlier.

Factors that will raise your BMR	Factors that will lower your BMR	Reason for increase
Eating frequent meals		The act of digestion requires energy to break down the food and convert it into usable nutrients. The key is lots of small meals throughout the day
Exercise		This will increase the need for energy during the activity, and depending upon the intensity, duration, time of day and type of exercise undertaken may also lead to an elevated BMR for several hours after exercise
Muscle mass		Muscle is a fat hungry tissue and requires more energy than other tissues even at rest
Age (up to peak physical maturation, mid 20s)		Increase in lean muscle mass HIgh levels of natural growth hormone and anabolic steroids
	Age (after peak physical maturation, early 30s onwards)	Decrease in muscle mass More likely to be sedentary Less growth hormone and anabolic steroids produced
Height		Tall, thin people have a higher BMR
Getting pregnant		The growth of the unborn baby and the changes taking place all require significant quantities of energy
Environment		Extremes of both hot and cold temperatures require the body to work hard in order to maintain a balanced body temperature
	Fasting/Starvation	The body hoards what it has
Hormones	Hormones	Thyroxin produced by the thyroid can raise or lower BMR by 50%
Smoking/Caffeine		Raises energy expenditure
	Sleep	The body is at its least active and so requires less energy

Table 2.3 *Comparison of high and low BMR*

CORONARY HEART DISEASE (CHD)

Surplus fats, particularly those from LDL cholesterols found in saturated fats, are transported in the blood stream in order to be stored as subcutaneous fat. During this process deposits of these fats will occur in the blood vessels themselves as the fat sticks to the walls of the arteries. This can have two immediate problems for the body:

- Firstly, the fat deposits, in the form of plaques, will begin to reduce the available diameter, or lumen, of the blood vessel.
- Secondly, the attachment of these fatty plaques will reduce the elasticity of the blood vessel, in this case the artery.

The consequences of these developments are:

- Reduced space within the blood vessel means that:
  o heart rate increases – the heart has to work harder in order to push the same amount of blood through a smaller area
  o there will be an increase in blood pressure within the artery.
- Reduced elasticity within the artery means that the artery is not able to respond to increases in blood surge, or flow, through the vessel by stretching in order to maintain a constant blood pressure.

As a result there is danger that:

- the artery will rupture
- there will be a blockage within the artery, thus starving either the brain (leading to a stroke) or the heart (leading to a heart attack).

EXERCISE CAN HELP

If the intensity of the activity being performed is low then fats will make up a significant portion of the energy used, thus restricting the storing and build-up of fatty deposits. If the intensity of the activity is high then surges of blood will help to flush the arteries. In addition, fat stores will be used after the activity to help fuel the recovery and also to help refuel the glycogen stores in the muscle. Exercise can also contribute to beneficial heart rate, blood pressure and cholesterol levels (see Figure 2.3).

OBESITY

Obesity is defined as the state when body fat levels are 25 per cent greater than the gender norm. There are many contributory causes to obesity. However, it is clear that a calorie surplus is created when the calorific intake exceeds the calorific expenditure. If calorific intake alone is reduced this would invariably result in a reduced calorific burn and reduced basal metabolic rate (BMR). The body would become more efficient and require fewer calories to perform basic functions. A combination of healthy eating and an increase in physical activity would offer greater success.

OSTEOPOROSIS

Osteoporosis is a disease in which bones become more and more fragile. If left untreated, the bones will continue to weaken until a bone breaks. Any bone can be affected but typically fractures occur in the hip, spine and wrist areas.

Bones that break as a result of osteoporosis can cause prolonged or permanent disability or even death. Spinal or vertebral fractures also have serious consequences, including loss of height, severe back pain and deformity.

Bone is living tissue that responds to exercise. The strength and density of a bone will increase the more it is used. Equally if you are inactive then density and strength will deteriorate. That is why elderly people, who perhaps do less physical activity, are more prone to suffer from osteoporosis.

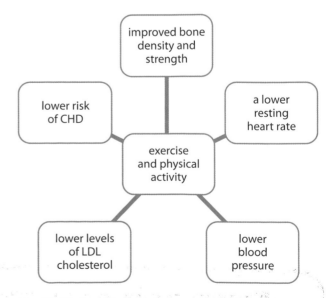

Fig. 2.3 *The benefits of exercise*

REMEMBER

- Obesity is a clinical condition and as such anyone who is obese should seek medical guidance before embarking on any sort of exercise programme.
- An average-sized bowl of sweetened cereal contains two tablespoons of sugar.
- The difference in weight between a lorry carrying Diet Coke and one carrying regular Coke is exactly 1 ton!

TASK

Consider your own diet. Record accurately everything that you eat and drink over a 48-hour period. How healthy is your diet in terms of the quality of consumed calories? Could you make any small changes that would have big effects?

The best types of exercise for improving skeletal strength are those where the bones are placed under stress directly. **Weight bearing** (jogging, walking, stair climbing, dancing or any activity where you support your body weight) activities place stress on the bones and the direction of the stress promotes new and stronger stress lines. For example, running places stress through the length of the femur, so it becomes stronger in that direction.

Resistance exercises (such as weight lifting) are activities that use muscular strength to improve muscle mass and strengthen bone. Using free weights and weight machines found at gyms and health clubs will strengthen your bones.

TASK

If you X-ray the arms of a tennis player, you would see that the bones in the playing arm are bigger and denser than the bones in the non-playing arm.

Analyse your own lifestyle, including your diet and physical activity history. How strong would you anticipate your skeletal system to be? And what could you do to increase the strength and density of your bones?

TYPE II DIABETES

Insulin is necessary for the body to be able to use sugar. Type II diabetes is the most common form of diabetes and is due to the inability of the body to produce sufficient insulin or to the cells of the body ignoring the insulin that is produced.

Sugar is the basic fuel for the cells and insulin stimulates the cells to remove sugar from the blood for use as energy or storage of energy (in the form of fat). When sugar (or glucose) builds up in the blood it can cause problems. Your cells may be starved of energy but also prolonged high blood glucose levels can damage your eyes, kidneys, nerves or heart.

While anyone can develop type II diabetes some groups have a higher risk than others. Type II diabetes is more common in groups within society who are prone to putting on excess weight. This can include ethnic groups (due to diet or hereditary body compositions), social groups (as a result of diet or lifestyle) or age-defined groups (such as the older population).

CASE STUDY
EDUCATION OR MEDICATION?

The results of the Diabetes Prevention Programme (DPP) showed that 'moderate diet changes and physical activity can delay and prevent type II diabetes'. Two approaches to preventing diabetes were tested by the DPP: 'lifestyle change' and 'medication'.

Lifestyle change included a programme of healthy eating and exercise. People in the lifestyle change group exercised about 30 minutes a day 5 days a week, usually by walking, and lowered their intake of fat and calories. Those following the programme of medication made no lifestyle changes. They took prescribed medication in the form of Metformin, which is an established drug used to treat diabetes. The results showed that:

- People in the lifestyle change group reduced their risk of getting type II diabetes by 58 per cent.
- In the first year of the study, people lost an average of 15 pounds.
- Lifestyle change was even more effective in those aged 60 and older. They reduced their risk by 71 per cent.
- People receiving Metformin reduced their risk by 31 per cent.
- Those who took Metformin received information on exercise and diet.

- Which is best, education or medication?

UXBRIDGE COLLEGE
LEARNING CENTRE

NUTRITION AND WEIGHT MANAGEMENT

FOOD GROUPS AND A BALANCED DIET

The term diet is frequently used when someone is describing a weight, or more often a fat, loss eating pattern. In an attempt to lose excess body fat levels they have reduced the quantity of food that they eat and may even have restricted the eating of foods perceived to be 'high in fats'. As discussed, the consequences of following such an eating pattern alone would be some initial weight loss, of which some would be body fat, but most would be lean tissue, together with a lowering of the metabolic rate.

However, the term diet refers to what you eat and drink, in short what you consume. We are all on a diet because we all eat and drink to survive. The former is more accurately described as a calorific restriction diet.

All of the foods that we consume can be divided into seven categories, or groups. These are carbohydrates, fats, proteins, vitamins, minerals, fibre and water. These can further be categorised into energy providers and non-energy providers (see Table 2.4).

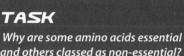

TASK
Why are some amino acids essential and others classed as non-essential?

	Food group	Main bodily function	Good source of the food group
Energy providers	Carbohydrates	High-intensity fuel source. Aids the utilisation of fats as an energy source. There are two types of carbohydrate: simple and complex	Foods containing sugars and starch. Fruit, pasta, wheats, cereals, chocolate
	Fats	Low-intensity energy. Insulation. There are soluble and insoluble fats	Fish, animal and dairy products
	Proteins	Required for growth and repair. Acts as 'last resort' energy source. Proteins are made from amino acids of which there are two types: essential and non-essential	Meats, soya, dairy products
Non-energy providers	Vitamins	Required to facilitate physiological functions. There are fat soluble and water soluble vitamins	Animal and dairy products. Fruits, vegetables and grains
	Minerals	Aid vitamin absorption. Provide the structure for bones and teeth, and are essential in many bodily functions. Major minerals include calcium, magnesium, potassium, iron and sodium. Trace minerals include zinc and fluorine	Vegetables, fruits, fish, nuts
	Fibre	Essential for healthy bowel function. There are no calories, vitamins or minerals in fibre and it is not digested. There are two types of fibre: soluble and insoluble	Plant foods, fruit, vegetables, beans and oats
	Water	Major component of the body. Involved in almost every bodily function. Primarily seen in its role of thermoregulation and transport	Fruits and water as a drink

Table 2.4 Classification of food groups into energy providers and non-energy providers

TASK

- Research the recommended daily allowance (RDA) of each of the seven food groups for a person of your age, height and gender. Now compare the RDA with your own diet.

- Plan an effective diet for two people both of whom wish to lose excess body fat. They verge on being classified as obese. One wants to use diet alone while the other wants to exercise too, with the aim of walking to begin with, building up to jogging up to three times a week. How will the two diets differ?

TASK

- Research fat soluble and water soluble vitamins. Think about which ones are stored in the body and which are excreted. What are the implications when cooking vegetables?

TAKING ENERGY IN

We consume energy and food through eating which is something that we perhaps take for granted and do not think too much, or enough, about. Mostly we eat what we like, when we like. However, what is it that tells us what to eat and when?

When examined eating is found to be a relatively complex behaviour that is controlled by physiological, psychosocial and metabolic factors.

Hunger is a **physiological factor** or response. Our stomach is designed to digest food every four to five hours. This is because of its size and ability to empty itself when full. Once emptied a message of hunger will be initiated and sent to the brain. Hunger is initiated by one or several of the following:

- gastric constriction
- an absence of nutrients in the small intestine
- lower concentrations of gastro-intestinal hormones.

Although designed to digest food every four to five hours, few of us eat in this way, often eating larger but more infrequent meals. As all aspects of the body adapt to a new environment then so too does the digestive system. The capacity of the stomach will adapt to what it is exposed to. Larger meals and binge eating will increase its size while starvation will reduce its size. So when initially trying to reduce the amount of food eaten there will be a sense of hunger. However, this will gradually disappear as the stomach begins to shrink.

Appetite is a learned or **psychological response** and is a result of the sight, smell or thought of food. Appetite can be brought on by a variety of factors such as:

- boredom
- anxiety
- grieving or celebrating
- the time of day
- the availability and variety of foods
- stress, either positively or negatively, causing appetite or hunger suppression.

TAKE IT FURTHER

- Which part of plants does fibre come from?
- Why is it not digested in humans?

KEY TERMS

physiological factor or response
a factor or response that is dependent on the functions or workings of the human body

psychological factor or response
a factor or response that arises in the mind and is related to the mental and emotional state of the individual

INDIVIDUAL MINERALS

Calcium	Needed for bone and tooth formation, heart function and blood coagulation, muscle contraction	Dark vegetables, sesame seeds, oats, almonds, sunflower seeds, sardines/salmon
Phosphorus	Works together with calcium and must be balanced to be effective. Needed for building bones and teeth	Whole-grains, seeds, nuts, legumes, dried fruit, corn
Magnesium	Needed for healthy muscle tone and healthy bones and heart. A natural tranquilliser	Nuts, soybeans, green vegetables, figs, apples, lemons, peaches, almonds, salmon
Potassium	Important in keeping acid–alkaline balance in the blood. Essential for muscle contraction and normal heart beat	Green vegetables, oranges, whole grains, sunflower seeds, bananas, fresh salmon
Sodium	Regulates fluid and acid–base balance; sodium is necessary for hydrochloric acid production in the stomach	Celery, lettuce, watermelon, sea salt
Chlorine	Essential for the production of hydrochloric acid in the stomach. Helps the liver in its detoxifying activity	Seaweed, watercress, avocado, chard, tomatoes, cabbage, celery, cucumber, oats
Sulfur	'The Beauty Mineral'. Vital for healthy skin, hair and nails. Aids in reducing oxidation	Radish, turnip, onions, celery, horseradish, watercress, soybeans, fish
Iron	Builds resistance to stress and disease. Essential for the formation of haemoglobin	Apricots, peaches, bananas, prunes, raisins, whole-grain cereals, turnip greens, spinach, dry beans, lentils
Zinc	Component of enzymes and insulin; aids in wound healing, growth, tissue repair, and sexual development	Wheat bran, pumpkin seeds, sunflower seeds, brewer's yeast, onions, oysters, green vegetables
Iodine	Essential in the formation of thyroxin – the thyroid hormone which regulates much of physical and mental activity	Seaweed, turnip greens, garlic, watercress, pineapple, pears, citrus, seafood and fish liver oils
Copper	Iron cannot be absorbed without copper. Involved in protein metabolism, in healing processes and in keeping hair's natural colour	Same as iron. Also almonds, peas, beans, green leafy vegetables, whole-grain products, prunes, raisins
Manganese	Importantly involved in the metabolism of carbohydrates, fats and proteins. Helps to nourish the brain and nerves	Spinach, beets, blueberries, oranges, grapefruit, apricots, kelp, green leafy vegetables
Fluorine	Essential for bone and tooth building. Protects against infections. Excess (as in fluoridated water) causes mottled teeth and can be toxic	Oats, sunflower seeds, carrots, garlic, almonds, sea water and natural hard water

Table 2.5 The minerals essential to the human diet

Vitamin	Role	Source
A	Needed to maintain skin, mucous membranes, bones, teeth, and hair, vision, and reproduction	Green vegetables, melon, squash, yams, tomatoes, fish-liver oils
D	Helps body absorb calcium and phosphorus, needed for bone growth and maintenance	Fish-liver oils, sprouted seeds, mushrooms, sunflower seeds
E	Helps form red blood cells; prevents oxidation damage	Seeds, nuts and grains, green vegetables, olive oil
K	Needed for blood clotting, normal liver function	Kelp, alfalfa, soybean oil, naturally present in healthy intestines
B1	Needed for nervous system function; helps release energy from carbohydrates	Brewer's yeast, wheat germ/bran, whole-grain cereals, seeds and nuts, beans, green vegetables
B2	Helps release energy from foods. Essential for healthy eyes, skin, nails and hair	Whole grains, brewer's yeast, wheat germ, almonds, sunflower seeds
B3	Needed for nervous and digestive system functions, essential for protein and carbohydrate metabolism	Brewer's yeast, wheat germ, rice bran, nuts, sunflower seeds, brown rice, green vegetables
B6	Needed for metabolism, helps form red blood cells. Important for normal reproductive processes and healthy pregnancies	Brewer's yeast, bananas, avocado, wheat germ/bran, soybeans
B12	Helps form red blood cells. Prevents anaemia. Promotes growth in children	Brewer's yeast, sunflower seeds, bananas, peanuts
C	Necessary for healthy teeth, gums and bones. Essential for proper functioning of adrenal and thyroid glands	All fresh fruits and vegetables

Table 2.6 The vitamins essential to the human diet

HYDRATION

Water, oxygen and heat are possibly the three most important elements required by the body to ensure its survival.

- Water is essential for the body to function. Every physiological process within the body requires water and the body is made up of almost two-thirds water.

- Oxygen is required to produce energy for the physiological processes.

- The correct heat is essential for the physiological processes to take place. Too much or not enough heat will result in death. The importance of not overheating can be understood when the body gives away water (identified as one of the most important aspects of human survival) to avoid overheating.

WATER AND HYDRATION

The term hydration is used to describe a physiological state of optimum water balance. With water performing so many different roles within the body and accompanied by the fact that the body is constantly losing water through perspiration and urination, it is probably safe to state that most of us live in a state of dehydration.

Dehydration refers to a state where the body does not have optimal water balance and so is not functioning as efficiently as it can. Dehydration is

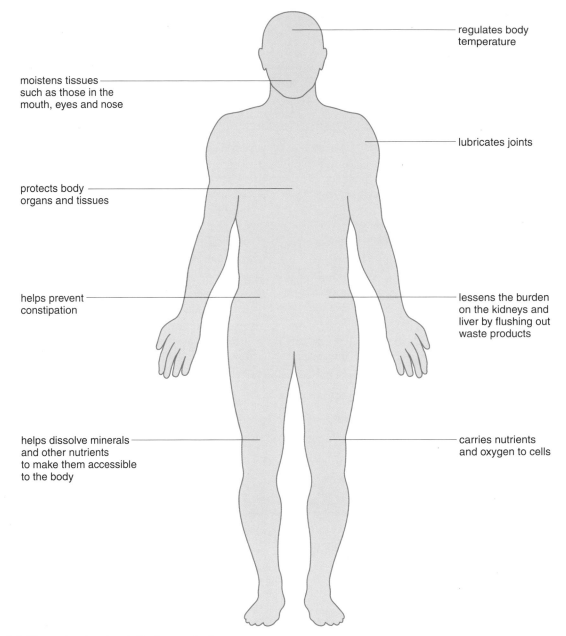

regulates body temperature

moistens tissues such as those in the mouth, eyes and nose

lubricates joints

protects body organs and tissues

helps prevent constipation

lessens the burden on the kidneys and liver by flushing out waste products

helps dissolve minerals and other nutrients to make them accessible to the body

carries nutrients and oxygen to cells

Fig. 2.4 *The part water plays in the human body*

usually expressed as the loss of a certain percentage of body weight. Scientists define dehydration as fluid losses greater than only 1 per cent of body weight.

THE ROLE OF WATER

Water has many functions within the body, e.g.:

- in saliva and gastrointestinal secretions it helps to digest food
- in blood, it helps transport nutrients and oxygen to all the cells of the body
- in body fluids, it helps lubricate joints and cushions organs and tissues

- in urine, it carries waste products out of the body
- in sweat, it removes body heat generated during exercise.

LOSING WATER

The most obvious loss of water is through daily urine output.

We also lose water through our skin and through our lungs in respiration; the more we exercise the more we respire.

When the body is hot we sweat; the more we exercise the more heat we generate and so the more water we lose.

Water is lost first from the blood which is 90 per cent water, so blood **viscosity** increases and this leads to an increased heart rate, increased blood pressure and a loss of cardiovascular efficiency.

DEHYDRATION

The first sign of dehydration is thirst. By the time you experience thirst you are already dehydrated. If you experience thirst while performing then it will not be possible to achieve full hydration again until after the exercise or performance has stopped.

Headache and fatigue are also signs of dehydration.

If you continue to lose water then the severity of the dehydration will increase. Severe dehydration is accompanied by nausea, chills, increased heart rate, inability to sweat, and light-headedness. This is a very serious state and medical attention should be sought urgently.

If water deprivation continues, some cells will start to donate their water to essential organs. Gradually these organs themselves will shut down.

Dehydration can become fatal when 9–12 per cent of your body weight is lost because of water loss.

MAINTAINING HYDRATION

The amount of water you require is dependent on many factors. The generally accepted norm is that a sedentary adult living in a temperate climate would require eight average-sized glasses per day. Exercise and climate are also huge factors in determining how much water you will require per day. You need about 1 ml of water for every calorie you burn.

CASE STUDY H₂O

If you burn 3000–4000 calories per day, you would need 3–4 litres of water. A Tour de France cyclist might burn as many as 11,000 calories in a day, and sometimes in temperatures in excess of 38 degrees Celsius. That's a need in excess of 11 litres of water above the normal requirements!

Drinking water is clearly an excellent way to maintain hydration. However, you need to be aware that if you have lost water through sweating then you will have lost **electrolytes** also. Simply drinking water in this case would not help to rehydrate you as the loss of electrolytes would prevent the body from regulating the water content. You would either continue to dehydrate further or the body would hold on to too much water and organs would effectively drown.

Eating fresh fruits can help to restore some of these electrolytes; alternatively specific electrolyte drinks can be purchased. Drinks that contain caffeine and alcohol are **diuretics** which encourage the body to reduce its water levels and so these should be avoided.

KEY TERMS

electrolyte
a mineral soluble in body fluids and associated with cell membrane electrical potential. The main ones are sodium, potassium and chlorine

diuretic
a substance that has the effect of increasing urination

thermoregulation
the process of keeping the internal environment of the body at an acceptable temperature

viscosity (of blood)
the fluid thickness or stickiness of blood

In summary

- Losses of electrolytes can interfere with transport systems in the body, upset fluid balance and affect **thermoregulation**.
- Imbalance of electrolytes can and will affect heart and muscle function.
- Sweating is the main weapon used to regulate temperature.
- Rates vary with the individual, environmental temperature, humidity and clothing.
- Excessive water loss (2 per cent of body mass) can lead to heat exhaustion or heat stroke.
- Since the thirst sensation lags behind water replacement needs, drink water before, during and after exercise.

FOOD PYRAMID

As we have seen, the food that we eat can be sorted into seven scientific categories. However, categories might not be helpful for people to understand what they might require in order to achieve a healthy, balanced diet. Consequently the US government through the various health agencies has devised a food pyramid to show similar types of food and the quantities of them required (see Figure 2.5).

This idea has been adopted by many other countries and societal groups within countries. Each group has adapted the idea to suit their particular needs, i.e. a pyramid for under 11s, over 70s and so on.

Fig. 2.5 *Food pyramid to show different types of food*

CHOLESTEROL

Cholesterol is a fat which is naturally present in cell walls or membranes throughout the body, including the brain, nerves, muscles, skin, liver, intestines and heart. It is used by the body to help produce many essential hormones, some vitamins and also the acids that help the body to digest fat.

Cholesterol is transported around the body in the blood attached to a protein. This combination of fat and protein is called a lipoprotein. Lipoproteins can be high density (HDL), low density (LDL) or very low density (VLDL), depending on how much protein

there is in relation to fat. Low-density lipoprotein (LDL) is classed as 'bad cholesterol' while high-density lipoprotein (HDL) is less harmful. Women tend to have higher levels of HDL cholesterol than men. Having too much LDL in your bloodstream will lead to the excess being deposited in arteries, including the coronary (heart) arteries, where it contributes to the narrowing and blockages that cause the signs and symptoms of heart disease.

Exercise will either use fats as a direct energy source if the intensity is sufficiently low, or alternatively fat

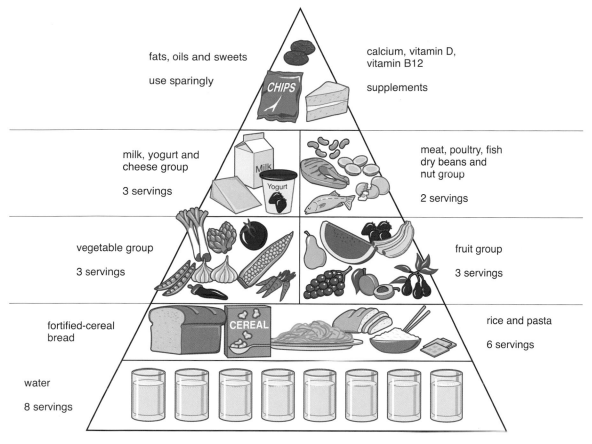

Fig. 2.6 *This food pyramid has been designed as a healthy guide for over 70s*

deposits will be used after exercise both to replenish muscle **glycogen** and **phosphagen** stores and also to fuel the recovery process and post-exercise elevated metabolic rate. Exercise will also ensure that the arteries are flushed regularly, helping to prevent **plaque** deposits attaching and building up on the artery walls.

KEY TERMS

glycogen
a substance (polysaccharide) deposited in body tissues as a store of carbohydrates

phosphagens
energy storage compounds, found mainly in muscle tissue as a reserve of high-energy phosphate bonds

plaque
a raised region of tissue resulting from deposits of 'bad' cholesterol

---

DIETARY REQUIREMENTS FOR EXERCISE

We have discussed the dietary needs in order to maintain general health. Any activity or change to the norm will require that your diet is modified to take the changes into account. For example:

- If the activity requires lots of energy then an increase in carbohydrates will be needed to meet the demand.

- If the muscles are worked excessively then a high protein diet will be needed to aid growth and repair.

- If the activity is of a long duration then extra B vitamins will be required to help respiration and the production of more red blood cells.

- If the activity is of a long duration and/or is in a hot or even a cold climate then extra liquids – water and electrolytes – will be needed.

The body has glycogen stores in muscle tissue that can fuel approximately 90 minutes of activity. If an activity is of a longer duration then supplementation during the activity will be required. The body will need to eat foods and produce energy but the food must be quick and easy to eat and digest. Foods high in simple carbohydrates or energy bars or gels are best suited to this.

CURRENT TRENDS IN HEALTH

The Japanese government has launched a three-wave attack at achieving better health levels in their country. The concern for the government was that an ageing and perhaps unhealthy population would put a huge burden on a smaller working population. As a result the country has reversed a trend of continued population growth and now, through declining birth rates, has a falling population. Below are reports and case studies which look at the current trends and policies on health improvement in Japan.

HOTLINKS

The Japanese Department of Health reviews current trends in health and reports their findings at **www.jpha.com**.
Visit **www.niph.go.jp/English/index.html** to research the activities and role of the National Institute of Public Health in Japan.

The first wave of attack was one of health promotion where diseases that were previously considered 'ageing-related diseases' were renamed 'lifestyle-related diseases'. Research has shown that intervention in personal lifestyle was more effective than medical attention. National campaigns to appeal to and educate the general public were launched.

The second of these three waves was called 'Active 80 Health Plan'. It was established to cater for the prolonged life span, of 80 years or more, of the population. Emphasis was placed on physical activities and a drive to promote physical fitness.

A new qualification of 'Health Trainer' was initiated in 1988. As a health trainer an individual would possess knowledge of both medical and physical

science to make a prescription for recommended physical activities tailored to individual conditions and medical needs. Also, fitness clubs satisfying certain requirements such as having a certain number of qualified health trainers were given special designation by the government.

Such promotion, coupled with economic booms at that time, spurred mushrooming of fitness clubs and stimulated the growth of the health and fitness industry.

The third wave was launched in 2000 and called 'Healthy Japan 21 (2000–2010).' It is currently being actively promoted. The period considered is between the year 2000 and 2010 with a defined set of goals. In this campaign, emphasis is placed on the prolongation of a 'healthy lifespan' aiming towards a lifespan without disability. This emphasis reflects resentment over a considerable number of elderly with disabilities in the face of the world's longest lifespan.

The HJ21 campaign set out explicit goals against which its achievement is appraised. There are 70 goals in nine areas of health to be achieved by 2010 with an interim appraisal in 2005. The interim appraisal was disclosed in September 2005 with some disappointing results. Not many goals showed any improvement above the baseline set at the start of the campaign and some goals showed a downturn in achievement! Overall, the outcome of the campaign was far from being satisfactory:

- **nutrition/diet**
  A prevalence in obesity has increased, particularly in men in their 30s and 60s. Salt intake and rate of energy intake from fat has declined, but the proposed goal of eating more than 350 grams per day of vegetables has not been achieved.

- **physical activities**
  The goal of 9200 steps for men and 8300 steps for women per day was set but feedback shows that the average is less.

- **mental health**
  The emphasis here was to reduce hospitalisation of mental health patients and provide for them in the community. The progress has been slow.

- **tobacco**
  The rate for smoking tobacco in men has declined but the rate for women has not declined.

▶ *The Japanese nation set health targets based on physical activities to reach by 2010*

- **alcohol**
  The number of people suffering from excess alcohol consumption has increased. This is based on the increased number of patients being treated for alcohol-related conditions, such as liver diseases.

- **dental health**
  Overall the dental health of all the population improved, but especially among the elderly.

- **diabetes**
  The number of possible diabetics is estimated to be 16.2 million and shows no sign of decline. The rate of continued treatment for diabetes did not show any improvement.

- **cardiovascular disease**
  Some risk factors, such as hypertension and diabetes, did not improve at all.

- **cancer**
  The cancer screening rate did not increase and there is still an imbalance in occurrences throughout the country.

Since the interim review of 2005 the Japanese government has set the following targets, which are to be met by 2015:

- Prevention of lifestyle-related diseases
  - increase 5 year survival of all cancers by 20 per cent
  - decrease cardiovascular disease mortality by 25 per cent
  - decrease cerebrovascular disease mortality by 25 per cent
  - decrease incidence of diabetes by 20 per cent
- Reduction of disability
  - prevent worsening of the disabled elderly in borderline and level 1 to level 2 by 10 per cent
  - prevent becoming disabled (borderline and level 1) by 20 per cent

TASK

What contrasts and comparisons in current trends in health can be made between the UK and Japan? Discuss the relevance of each wave of activity in Japan.

Here are two more case studies which show interesting and different views on Japanese health.

CASE STUDY HEALTHY OKINAWA

Okinawa, one of the Japanese islands, is well-known for its healthy, long-living population. The facts show that:

☐ There are fewer deaths from chronic diseases such as cancer than anywhere else in the developed world

☐ the life expectancy of the population is the highest in the world

☐ the percentage of people over 100 years old is the highest in the world.

How do they do it?

Thanks to the strict record-keeping and census policy of nineteenth-century Japan, researchers have been able to search for an answer to this question. As a result, the scientific community has been able to explain why it is that Okinawans have such long healthy lives. Their results and conclusions are summarised here:

Genetics: Studies show that the genetic make-up of Okinawans helps them resist diseases. Relatives of long-lived Okinawans also tend to live long lives. However, Okinawans do not live as long when they move away from the island (and change their lifestyle habits). This shows that it is not only genetics that influence a longer life, but environment and lifestyle too.

Diet: The Okinawans have a tradition of eating until only nearly full. So, they eat fewer calories than the average person and this results in the formation of fewer free radicals during the metabolic process. This has a positive effect on cardiovascular health and reduces the risk of cancers and heart disease.

Heart disease: The centenarians studied had low cholesterol and no evidence of plaque deposits in their arteries. Medical researchers attribute this to: a good diet of mainly fish, fresh fruit and vegetables; high levels of outdoor physical activity; low alcohol intake; low rates of smoking; and a positive outlook resulting in low stress levels.

Cancer: The Okinawans seem to have less risk of certain cancers. They have 50 per cent less risk of colon and ovarian cancers and 80 per cent less risk of prostate and breast cancers. Again, the medical researchers directly relate this to a healthy diet (low calorie intake, less animal fats, and lots of fibre from fresh fruits and vegetables) and regular physical activity.

Bone disease: The Okinawans also have less risk of fractures than the rest of the Japanese population. The researchers discovered that the rate of reduction of bone density for the Okinawans is slower than the average

ISLANDS OF JAPAN

Tokyo

Naha ● OKINAWA

rate. The islanders' outdoor way of life promotes high levels of vitamin D absorption from sunlight, and thus high levels of calcium absorption by the bones. This, together with an active lifestyle, reduces their risk of bone disease.

Ageing: Studies reveal that Okinawans not only live longer, but they age healthily. The centenarians studied had good diets and continued their high levels of physical activity well into later life. Both of these factors are known to contribute to low rates of heart disease, bone disease and cancer.

Stress: Further studies showed that the optimism of the Okinawans maintained them through all stages and stresses of life. The researchers believe it is this positivity, together with the Japanese sense of spirituality and purpose, that explains their natural ability to cope and their low risk of dementia.

Lifestyle: Researchers conclude, from the example shown by the Okinawan islanders, that living a healthy lifestyle will help us to live long, disease-free lives. Their answer to the quest for longevity is to embark on lifestyle changes that can add healthy years to your life and make you feel good now and into a centenarian generation.

■ Summarise reasons why the Okinawans might be so healthy. When you have produced a list of potential reasons, identify what can be done in the UK to mirror the health success of this group of islanders.

CASE STUDY   DISABILITY-ADJUSTED LIFE YEARS

The World Health Organization (WHO) scientists have developed a new way of calculating the number of years that a person can be expected to live in full health.

It is known as the DALY (Disability-Adjusted Life Years) system, and gives a much more realistic picture of the health of a country than simply studying death rates. To calculate the DALY of a population, the years of ill-health are weighted according to severity and subtracted from the expected overall life expectancy to give the equivalent years of healthy life.

The system has been used to rank the world's top 100 countries and has uncovered some interesting findings. Japan is the most healthy country with an average healthy life expectancy of 74.5 years. Australia is second and France third on the list, while the US ranks only number 24. The UK is 14th, with an average of 71.7 years.

We know that, on average, women live longer than men but the DALY results showed a notable gender gap in many countries. For instance, in Russia women can expect 66.4 years of full health, compared to just 56.1 years for men. For UK women the average is 73.7 years, for men it is 69.7 years.

Also the DALY results showed that people in the healthiest regions lose 9% of their lives to disability, compared to 14% in the worst-off countries.

The director of WHO's Global Programme on Evidence for Health Policy, said: 'The position of the United States is one of the major surprises of the new rating

▶ *Japan has the highest life expectancy of any country*

system. Basically, you die earlier and spend more time disabled if you're an American rather than a member of most other advanced countries.'

It may be that the US rates so low due to the very poor standard of health among people who live in the many inner cities of the US. Rates of coronary heart disease are also high.

All of the countries with the lowest ratings were in Africa, where the HIV-AIDS epidemic is widespread.

■ Compare life expectancy in the US with that found in Japan.

TASK

Using the Internet select either the US or Finland to research the issues and policies on health that are being discussed or promoted.

BALANCED LIFESTYLE

ENERGY BALANCE

An athlete who wants to maintain performance needs to ensure that they have sufficient energy to perform and recover. For elite athletes this means getting the calorific quantity and make-up exactly right. Too much of any one thing will mean an energy surplus which in turn will lead to excess body weight and drop-off in performance. Too little of anything will mean either a lack of available energy and so a reduced performance or a slower recovery which will

inhibit future performances. First of all, the athlete needs to know the total calorific content that is required. To do this you need to consider the energy spent on **basal metabolism** and the energy spent on the **physical activity**.

BASAL METABOLISM OR BASAL METABOLIC RATE (BMR)

This is the rate at which the body uses energy for maintenance activities. It includes maintaining body temperature, the activity of the lungs, heart, kidneys and other organs.

Estimating basal energy needs:

Men = 1 calorie / kg of body weight / hour

Women = 0.9 calorie / kg of body weight / hour

For example: a man weighing 84 kg would calculate his BMR as

1×84 kg $\times 24$ hrs = 2016 basal caloric needs

REMEMBER

■ The calculation of BMR is a 'rule of thumb' in the same way that maximum heart rate (MHR) = 220 – age (see page 59)

ENERGY REQUIRED FOR PHYSICAL ACTIVITY

Physical activity is defined as voluntary movement of the skeletal muscles and support systems. This places huge demands on the energy supplies of the body (see Table 2.7).

■ The muscles that are working require energy:
  o the more muscles that are used
  o the bigger the muscles being used
  o the intensity that the muscles are working at
  o the duration that they are working. All of these factors affect the energy usage.
■ The cardiovascular and respiratory systems require energy to supply the muscles with the energy.
■ Energy is required to remove the waste produced.
■ The more energy that is used the more heat is produced.
■ The body requires energy to regulate and maintain heat.

In an attempt to be a little more accurate with regards to predicting BMR an alternative equation was designed that factored in height and age. The Harris-Benedict equation is as follows:

For men: BMR = 66 + (13.7 × wt in kg) + (5 × ht in cm) − (6.8 × age in yr).

For women: BMR = 655 + (9.6 × wt in kg) + (1.8 × ht in cm) − (4.7 × age in yr).

For example, a man who is 84 kg in weight, 180 cm in height and 40 years of age would have the following BMR:

66 + (13.7 × 84) + (5 × 180) – (6.8 × 40)

= 66 + 1150.8 + 900 − 272

= 1844.8 calories

A more scientific means of calculating energy expenditure per minute is to calculate in metabolic equivalents (METS). Table 2.8 provides a means of computing estimated energy expenditure (per minute) using both body weight and the number of metabolic equivalents (METS) required to perform the activity.

One MET is equal to resting VO_2 max (volume of oxygen used) which is approximately 3.5 ml (oxygen) per kilogram (body weight) per minute.

Level of intensity	Type of activity	Activity factor (× BMR)
Very light	Seated/standing activities, painting, driving, typing, sewing, cooking	Men = 1.3 Women = 1.3
Light	Walking 2.5 to 3 mph, housework, childcare, golf, sailing, table tennis	Men = 1.6 Women = 1.5
Moderate	Walking 3.5 to 4 mph, weeding, cycling, skiing, tennis, dancing	Men = 1.7 Women = 1.6
Heavy	Walking with load uphill, digging, basketball, climbing, football, soccer	Men = 2.1 Women = 1.9
Exceptional	Athletic training, pro and amateur	Men = 2.4 Women = 2.2

Table 2.7 The activity factors of varying degrees of intensity of physical activity

Footnote: These energy factors should be considered with regards to a typical day before being applied. For example, a typical man has a BMR of 2016. If he was involved in light activities his calorific expenditure would be:

BMR × activity factor = calorific expenditure

BMR × 1.6 = 2016 × 1.6 = 3225.6 calories required per day

METS	Activity	Description
0.9	Inactivity, quiet	Sleeping
1	Inactivity, quiet	Sitting quietly, riding in a car, watching television, listening to music
2	Walking	Less than 2 mph, level ground, strolling, household walking, very slow
3	Walking	2.5 mph, level, firm surface. Canoeing, rowing, 2.0–3.9 mph, light effort, for pleasure
4	Cycling	Less than 10 mph, general leisure, to work or for pleasure. Horse riding, table tennis, volleyball, competitive
6	Cycling	10-11.9 mph, leisure, slow, light effort. Aerobics, low impact
6	Water activities	Water skiing, swimming, leisurely, not lap swimming
7	Dancing	Aerobic, high impact. Cross-country skiing, 2.5 mph, slow or light effort, ski walking
8	Cycling	12–13.9 mph, leisure, moderate effort. Circuit training, general. Walking upstairs, using or climbing up ladder. Running, 5 mph (12 minute mile pace)
9.0	Running	Running, 5.2 mph (11.5 minute mile pace)
10	Sports	Competitive soccer, rugby. Swimming laps, freestyle, fast, vigorous effort. Running, 6 mph (10 minute mile pace). Cycling 14–15.9 mph
11.0	Running	Running, 6.7 mph (9 minute mile pace)
12	Cycling	16–19 mph, racing/not drafting, very fast, racing general
13.5	Running	Running, 8 mph (7.5 minute mile pace)
14.0	Running	Running, 8.6 mph (7 minute mile pace)
15.0	Running	Running, 9 mph (6.5 minute mile pace)
16	Cycling	Greater than 20 mph, racing, not drafting. Running, 10 mph (6 minute mile pace)
18.0	Running	Running, 10.9 mph (5.5 minute mile pace)

Table 2.8 *Table of estimated energy expenditure*

For the benefit of calculating energy expenditure Table 2.8 gives a guide to the intensity of activity. For example running at 10 mph is shown to use 18 times more calories per minute than sitting quietly.

APPLY IT!

Select a sporting friend, ascertain their height, age and weight and then analyse their performance in a forthcoming competitive environment with a view to calculating their total calorific expenditure. You will need to record their physical activity, perceived intensity and duration of each to calculate your findings.

EFFECTS OF AGEING

PHYSICAL MATURATION

It is recognised that it is extremely important for children to take part in regular exercise, if for no other reason than to encourage it as a lifelong habit. However, the effect of over-training pre-pubescent children can also be extremely harmful to the health and well-being of the child. Repetitive training can cause injuries to bones and joints, as a result of incomplete bone growth in children. Other factors also related to their incomplete growth, such as smaller heart size and lung size together with their larger surface area compared to adults, means that children are not as mechanically efficient as adults, and cannot control their body temperature as efficiently.

Therefore, exercise for young children should be enjoyable and fun. However, it is important to stress the teaching of correct techniques at an early age. This will prevent the occurrence of injury as a result of poor technique, but will enable the child to refine his or her techniques to achieve possible elite sport performances in later life.

THE AGEING PROCESS

It has been a common assumption that, beyond a certain age, an athlete's fitness measures will gradually deteriorate, and performance levels will decrease. In some sports, such as swimming and gymnastics, athletes were thought to be past their prime once they had ceased to be teenagers.

In recent years, the performances of a number of athletes have suggested that this assumption may not be absolutely true.

- Martina Navratilova was appearing in a Wimbledon singles final at the age of 36.
- Merlene Ottey is another who has remained at an elite level beyond an age that is generally accepted as 'normal' for a world-class track athlete. She won an Olympic medal at the age of 36 years.
- Teddy Sheringham played professional football in the championship at 41 years of age.
- A number of boxers have made relatively successful 'come-backs' in their 40s.

REMEMBER

- However, it is true to say that in today's sporting climate elite performances may be the result of drug-enhanced performance.

▶ Martina Navratilova continued to play competitive tennis well into her fifties

Despite these exceptions, it is generally accepted that beyond 30 years of age, a degenerative process does occur, which tends to have a detrimental effect on the athlete's fitness measurements.

However, much of this degenerative process can be offset by maintaining activity levels, which, together with high motivation, may explain the performances of older elite athletes.

MUSCULAR STRENGTH

If muscular strength declines with age, what effect will it have upon performance?

Clearly the performer will not be able to generate the same degree of force, but a loss of skeletal muscle mass will also have other effects upon the body and subsequent performance.

Resting metabolic rate, regulation of blood glucose, maintenance of core temperature, and the protection of internal structures (bones, organs, nerves and blood vessels) are all dependent on skeletal muscle tissue.

Reasons why we might lose muscle tissue are not entirely understood but there is a variety of factors that will contribute to a loss of performance.

- As we age we might be less active. This might be through choice or as a result of a slower recovery rate. Either way less use of a muscle will lead to atrophy.

- There appears also to be a degeneration of the nerves supplying the muscles.

- Extra collagen fibres are laid down between the muscle fibres, which reduces the elasticity and flexibility of the muscle, with a resultant decrease in efficiency.

The effects of these on skeletal muscle mass would seem to have three main consequences:

1 The loss of motor neurons from motor units which leads to a loss of muscle fibres, especially **type II muscle fibres**

2 The reduction in muscle fibre size, which again appears to affect type II muscle fibres only

3 An increase in the amount of subcutaneous fat tissue within the muscle belly.

Studies have indicated that the effectiveness of **type I muscle fibres** is not affected by age. Also studies have discovered that regular resistance exercises can help to maintain muscular strength,

not through increased type II functioning but through improved type I fibre efficiency.

Reasons for this remain unclear; however, as people age they tend to carry out far less high intensity, interval training which in itself would account for less recruitment of type II muscle fibres.

So, perhaps we lose muscular efficiency because we think that as we age we will lose strength and so do fewer types of training that require strength. In other words, do our perceptions of the effects of ageing actually drive the effects of ageing? An interesting thought.

KEY TERMS

type I muscle fibre
slow twitch fibre suited to aerobic endurance activity

type II muscle fibre
fast twitch fibre suited to maximum intensity, short-duration anerobic activity

CARDIOVASCULAR AND CARDIORESPIRATORY ENDURANCE (LUNG FUNCTION)

Aerobic fitness generally increases, peaking at or before 30 years of age. From then there seems to be a decline in performance of up to 1 per cent per year which has been associated with ageing.

- The cardiorespiratory system also shows a significant decline in the capacity for aerobic activity after the age of 30 years.

- Maximal oxygen consumption decreases by as much as 15 per cent per decade after the age of 30.

- Maximal cardiac output is reduced by 20 per cent to 30 per cent in 60-year-old adults when compared to those of 30 years or younger.

Three main reasons that have been attributed to these decreases in cardiovascular and cardiorespiratory efficiency are:

1 A decline in maximal heart rate of up to 10 beats per minute per decade

2 Decreased left ventricular contractile performance resulting in a decreased stroke volume

3 A decline in total blood volume, plasma and red blood cells.

However, recent research has found that although the frequency of cardiac contractions decreases with age (decreased maximal heart rate) the natural enlargement of the heart through regular use actually compensates and in many cases the cardiac output was actually constant. It is therefore assumed that the loss of aerobic efficiency is a result of reduced muscular efficiency with regards to the usage of the oxygen.

A general stiffening of the blood vessels, together with cholesterol deposits being laid down in the walls of arteries, reduces the blood supply to many organs, and reduces the exercise capacities of the performer.

The potential causes for this have been identified as follows:

- a decline in the size and density of mitochondria of skeletal muscle
- an increase in blood pressure and systemic vascular resistance, as a result of a gradual stiffening and/or narrowing of the arteries
- reduced baroreceptor sensitivity, as a result of continued exposure
- increased presence of collagen-type substances in the myocardium and major blood vessels, decreasing the vessel elasticity and efficiency in dealing with oxygen.

LUNG FUNCTIONING

The pulmonary system demonstrates three major signs of advancing age:

- The alveoli increase in size with age; however, the degree and level of capillarisation decreases, resulting in a loss of area for diffusion.
- This results in reduced rate of gas exchange.
- A gradual loss of elasticity within the lungs brought about by increased collagen fibres results in a loss of elastic recoil of the lungs.
- This leads to an increase in physiologic dead space and again further reduces the volume for gas exchange.

RESTING METABOLIC RATE (RMR)

RMR is encouraged to decrease as we age. We tend to become more sedentary, either because we think we ought to or because of other societal pressures. This in itself will contribute to a lowering of RMR.

A secondary effect of being less physically active is a loss of lean tissue, muscle mass in this case.

Muscle is fat hungry and so losing muscle mass also encourages a lower RMR.

FLEXIBILITY

Wear and tear on connective tissue, such as ligaments and cartilage, invariably has a negative effect on joint mobility. Add this to the increased collagen content within skeletal muscle and any scar tissue that may have developed and the loss of muscle elasticity and joint mobility combine to reduce the potential flexibility at a joint of an ageing performer.

There also tends to be a reduction in bone density with age, especially in females beyond menopausal age. However, exercise can play an important role in maintaining bone density in both sexes.

In summary, age will affect your athletic performance, by just how much is down largely to you!

TAKE IT FURTHER

- WHO identifies that: in Japan the average healthy life expectancy is 74.5 years; in the UK it is 71.7 years; while in Russia it is 61.3 years (taking males and females together). In Table 2.9 is a list of the top ten countries for healthy life expectancy. Looking at diet alone, research the dietary habits of the countries identified to see if there is a potential link between diet and healthy life expectation.

Note: It might be types of food eaten, styles of cooking, time to eat or even quantity of foods eaten.

Country	Life expectancy (years)
Japan	74.5
Australia	73.2
France	73.1
Sweden	73.0
Italy	72.7
Spain	72.8
Greece	72.5
Switzerland	72.5
Monaco	72.4
Andorra	72.3

Table 2.9 *Top ten in the world for healthy life expectancy*

HOTLINKS

Research osteoporosis at **www.nos.org.uk** and explain the role of low-impact exercise in the strengthening of bones.

CASE STUDY
ACTIVITY IMPROVES YOUR VO₂ MAX

In the 1960s, Darren McGuire and Benjamin Levine from the University of Texas Southwestern Medical Center and Presbyterian Hospital in Dallas studied the physical fitness of five healthy men in their early 20s before and after three weeks of voluntary bed rest. In the late 1990s, McGuire and Levine revisited the same men, then aged 50 or 51.

This was the first time that scientists had studied the effect of age on non-athletes whose fitness had been so thoroughly tested when they were young.

The researchers compared old and new X-ray measurements of the volume of blood pumped with each heartbeat. They already knew that this volume increases with age, as the heart enlarges to force blood through age-stiffened arteries. But to the surprise of cardiologists, McGuire and Levine found that this increase in volume was more than enough to offset the decline in maximum heart rate. A 50-year-old's heart might not beat as fast as it once did, but it can pump
at least as much blood per minute.

So, VO_2 max declines with age but not as a result of the inability of the heart to deliver less oxygen. Consequently it must be related to the muscles' ability, or indeed inability to utilise that oxygen.

However, and what was startling to the researchers, was this:

'When the 50-year-old men began exercise programmes that gradually built up to between three and five hours per week, their average aerobic fitness improved so much that within six months it returned to what it was when they were 20. "We reversed 30 years of ageing with six months of training," says Levine.'

So this study showed that sedentary middle-aged people can vastly improve their VO_2 max simply by becoming more active.

(American Heart Association, 2001)

■ What conclusions about VO_2 max do you think McGuire and Levine drew from these results?

CASE STUDY
70+ AND STILL RUNNING!

John Keston, a retired Royal Shakespeare Company actor and opera singer began running at 55, initially to manage his high blood pressure. Fourteen years later, he became the oldest man ever to break the three-hour barrier in a marathon – a feat he came within a minute of repeating at the age of 71.

■ What conclusions would you draw from his performance as an athlete?

ExamCafé

Relax, refresh, result!

Revision checklist

▷ Know the definitions for and differences between health and fitness and the different role that exercise will play in achieving either

▷ Know what the contemporary concerns are (see previous chapter) and understand the positive effects that exercise can have on them

▷ Know the seven food groups and the main role of each of the seven

▷ Be able to apply the seven groups to the appropriate food for an ageing person and a healthy active athletic performer

▷ Know the necessity for optimum water balance

▷ Be able to compare trends on health in the UK with at least one other country

▷ Know the energy requirements for sporting activities and be able to plan diets for optimum performance, for weight loss and for maintenance of health

▷ Know the effects that ageing can have on athletic performance and how exercise can offset the ageing process

▷ Know the physiological reasons behind a potential loss of athletic performance for an ageing athlete

examiner's tips

Common mistakes for this question would be a failure to identify the type of athlete this diet was for and not explaining the food groups succinctly but only in general and vague terms.

Get the result!

Sample question and answer

Exam question

Correct nutrition is an essential consideration for any serious athlete in order to provide the energy necessary for training and competition.

Three food groups can produce energy. Name the three groups and identify the approximate percentages required by an athlete of your choice. You should explain the reason behind the given quantities. **(9 marks)**

Student answer

The three food groups that can produce energy are fats, carbohydrates and proteins.

For a long distance runner it would be important for him to ensure that he has lots of energy and most of his energy in a race would come from carbohydrates.

I would suggest that this athlete's diet would consist of at least 60% carbohydrates. If it was during an intense period of training then this could even increase to as much as 70%.

The athlete would need to have a significant amount of protein, not necessarily for energy but to help repair the muscle that is damaged while they run.

I would suggest that about 30% of the diet would come from protein.

I think that he should try to keep his fat intake as low as possible. He would get some fat anyway from the protein foods such as fish and meats and also from the way that the foods might be cooked.

If he could keep his fats down to about 10% that would be ideal.

Examiner says:

This is an excellent answer. The candidate has structured the answer well which means it is easy for them to ensure that they have answered all the necessary sections. It is also clear and easy for the examiner to mark.

The candidate has a clear understanding of the role of diet in athletic performance and also of the different roles that the food groups provide. This is displayed with the answer where he identifies the food groups and states the approximate desired proportions with reasons for each choice.

An excellent answer that would score all of the available 9 marks.

CHAPTER 3 EFFECTS OF EXERCISE – RESPONSES AND ADAPTATIONS OF THE BODY SYSTEMS

LEARNING OUTCOMES

By working through this chapter, you should:

- know the difference between a response and an adaptation
- know the main role of the systems covered
- know the basic anatomical components of the systems and also their physiology in relation to exercise
- know how the systems respond to exercise and how to control the exercise to control the responses
- know what would make the systems perform better and how to create the adaptations necessary

This chapter will focus on *physiological changes resulting from exercise*. Here we will look at the difference between responses and adaptations and why these changes take place at all within the *muscular-skeletal system*, the *cardiovascular system*, the *respiratory system* and the *neuro-muscular system*. We will examine the reason for the structural responses (short-term effects) and the functional responses that are carried out, as well as the structural adaptations (long-term effects) and the consequent functional adaptations which benefit performance. It is essential that a basic understanding of anatomy and physiology of the systems is gained for you to determine the way you want to improve their functioning and your fitness.

MUSCULAR-SKELETAL SYSTEM

In the context of this book the muscular-skeletal system covers striated, or voluntary or skeletal muscle, the bones they are attached to and connective tissue involved, such as ligaments and cartilage.

REMEMBER

There are three types of muscles in the body:

- voluntary/striated/skeletal – attached to the skeletal system
- involuntary/smooth/visceral – e.g. in the walls of the alimentary canal
- cardiac – in the walls of the heart.

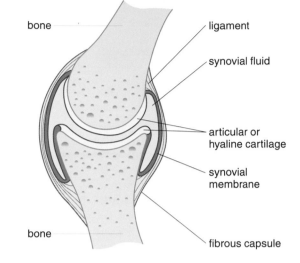

Fig. 3.1 *Parts of a* **synovial** *joint*

KEY TERM

synovial
describing a freely moveable joint that is surrounded by a tough membrane, such as the knee

There are two main types of striated muscle fibres: fast-twitch and slow-twitch. These are classified on the basis of their speed of contraction: type I (slow-twitch) and type II (fast-twitch).

Slow-twitch fibres, or type I fibres, are best suited to aerobic endurance type activities (low intensity, long duration) as they have a slower contraction time. Type II fibres are suited to high-intensity anaerobic exercise (maximal intensity, short duration). There are two types of fast-twitch fibres:

- Type IIa – or fast-twitch oxidative glycolytic fibres – are high-intensity fibres that also possess endurance characteristics. These fibres are suited to middle-distance athletes or games players.
- Type IIb – or fast-twitch glycolytic fibres – are the true fast-twitch fibres. These fibres are suited to maximal intensity but short duration activities such as 100 metres or the shot put.

We all have a predetermined percentage of fast- and slow-twitch fibres with the slow-twitch fibres generally making up the bigger proportion, as most activities that we do in everyday life are of a low intensity.

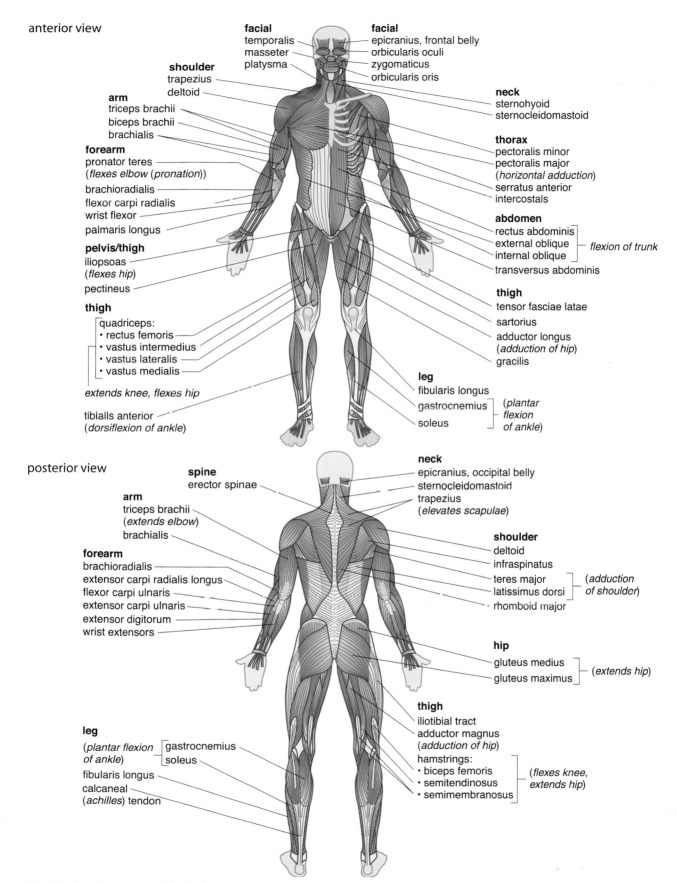

anterior view

facial
temporalis
masseter
platysma

facial
epicranius, frontal belly
orbicularis oculi
zygomaticus
orbicularis oris

shoulder
trapezius
deltoid

arm
triceps brachii
biceps brachii
brachialis

neck
sternohyoid
sternocleidomastoid

thorax
pectoralis minor
pectoralis major
(*horizontal adduction*)
serratus anterior
intercostals

forearm
pronator teres
(*flexes elbow (pronation)*)
brachioradialis
flexor carpi radialis
wrist flexor
palmaris longus

abdomen
rectus abdominis
external oblique ⎫
internal oblique ⎭ *flexion of trunk*
transversus abdominis

pelvis/thigh
iliopsoas
(*flexes hip*)
pectineus

thigh
tensor fasciae latae
sartorius
adductor longus
(*adduction of hip*)
gracilis

thigh
quadriceps:
• rectus femoris
• vastus intermedius
• vastus lateralis
• vastus medialis

extends knee, flexes hip

tibialis anterior
(*dorsiflexion of ankle*)

leg
fibularis longus
gastrocnemius ⎫ (*plantar
soleus ⎭ flexion of ankle*)

posterior view

neck
epicranius, occipital belly
sternocleidomastoid
trapezius
(*elevates scapulae*)

spine
erector spinae

arm
triceps brachii
(*extends elbow*)
brachialis

shoulder
deltoid
infraspinatus
teres major ⎫ (*adduction
latissimus dorsi ⎭ of shoulder*)
rhomboid major

forearm
brachioradialis
extensor carpi radialis longus
flexor carpi ulnaris
extensor carpi ulnaris
extensor digitorum
wrist extensors

hip
gluteus medius ⎫ (*extends hip*)
gluteus maximus ⎭

thigh
iliotibial tract
adductor magnus
(*adduction of hip*)
hamstrings:
• biceps femoris ⎫ (*flexes knee,
• semitendinosus   extends hip*)
• semimembranosus ⎭

leg
(*plantar flexion
of ankle*) ⎱ gastrocnemius
          ⎰ soleus
fibularis longus
calcaneal
(*achilles*) tendon

Fig. 3.2 Muscular systems of the body

Training does not change the fibre type, but it does maximise the abilities of the particular fibre type suited to perform the activity and it also encourages fibres to take on the characteristics of the type of training being carried out.

CASE STUDY
NOT ALL MUSCLE MASS IS BENEFICIAL

Lance Armstrong, a top cyclist and the youngest ever world champion of the sport, was diagnosed with cancer in 1996.

A combination of chemotherapy and inactivity during his treatment resulted in a significant loss of muscle mass, particularly in the upper body. Consequently when he began to train again he had lost almost 10 kg of weight. However, he was quickly able to regain his aerobic efficiency and muscular power. In cycling terms he was a superior athlete: increased VO_2 max (less mass for the inspired oxygen to have to fuel); less weight to carry up the mountain!

- Describe the type of training required for a trained athlete to return to fitness.

KEY TERMS

actin
the protein that forms (together with myosin) the contractile filament in muscle myofibrils

myosin
the fibrous protein that forms (together with actin) the contractile filament in muscle myofibrils

REMEMBER

- Mechanoreceptors and proprioceptors are sensory receptors that detect the extent of movement taking place in muscles and tendons.
- Thermoreceptors are sensory receptors that detect changes in body temperature.
- Chemoreceptors are sensory receptors that detect changes in the pH of the blood.
- Baroreceptors are stretch receptors that detect change in the stretch of various blood vessels.

RESPONSES

Muscular-skeletal responses to exercise include:

- fibre recruitment
- force production
- metabolism.

During exercise the body will recruit all three fibre types to perform a task depending upon the intensity and duration of the activity. Research indicates that regardless of the type of activity being performed it seems to be type I fibres that are recruited first. Other fibres are then recruited appropriately.

During light exercise mostly type I fibres will be recruited; during moderate exercise both type I and type IIa will be recruited; and then as intensity reaches maximum types I, IIa and IIb are recruited and contribute to the force produced.

KEY TERM

ATP
abbreviation for adenosine triphosphate, a chemical compound that is the body's energy currency

As exercise continues heat is produced from the release of free energy from ATP molecules. This heat will help to speed up the metabolic process, thus enabling the muscles to contract more quickly and with more force. Increased heat also helps to increase the elasticity of the muscle fibres and serves to increase the range of movement. This in turn means that the muscles can generate more force as well as reducing the likelihood of muscular injury.

SKELETAL RESPONSES

Greater flexibility at a joint occurs not just because of increased muscle elasticity but also as a result of responses within the joints. Increased heat aids the production of synovial fluid and also helps to reduce its viscosity: both factors aid friction-free movement. This is a reason why some people suffer a loss of joint mobility and consequent flexibility when the weather temperature drops.

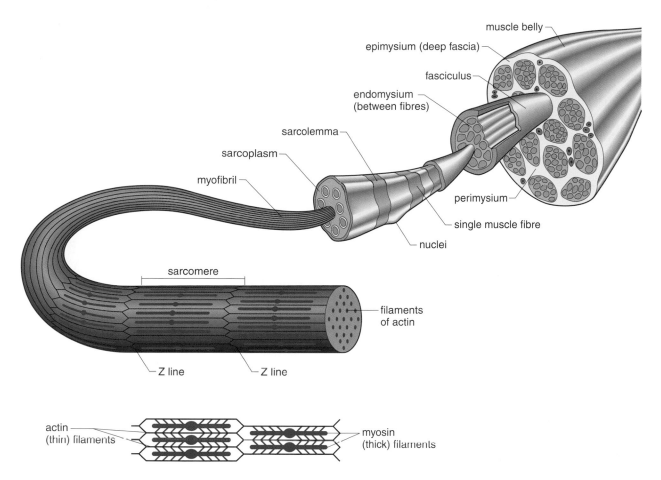

Fig. 3.3 *The component parts of striated muscle*

KEY TERM

myoglobin
the oxygen-binding pigment in muscle

MUSCULAR ADAPTATIONS

Adaptations result from a change to the environment and so any adaptations of the muscular system will be as a result of a specific change to their environment, such as the type of exercise carried out.

The type of training you do will affect the changes in your muscle fibres. Strength training will encourage an increase in both muscle size and strength with individual fibres being able to increase their size by as much as 45–50 per cent. Accompanying this increase in size is the potential for the muscle to develop a greater contractile force. The connective tissue around the muscle will also experience an increase in strength, which in turn can increase the stability of the joints.

The majority of research into muscular hypertrophy (growth of a muscle or increased size of a muscle girth) supports the view that it is as a result of the individual fibres increasing in size, rather than an actual increase in the number of fibres within the muscle that gives rise to this change. However, it would be inaccurate to state that all research supports this view with some studies claiming that an increased number of fibres results from resistance strength training. The research shows that an increase in the number of fibres can happen but it is not the case for all people or indeed all types of training.

Although men and women are able to develop musculature on a roughly linear scale, men have a naturally higher percentage of lean muscle mass prior to any form of strength training. This means that although percentage increases between men and women are comparable, men benefit from an increase in real terms. One of the main reasons for this is that the anabolic hormone testosterone is present in greater quantities in males. Also, the fact that not all men produce equal quantities of testosterone explains why some men enjoy greater and faster results from their strength training than others.

The visibility of your muscles is affected by their size and the amount of overlying fat. If you are leaner, your muscles will be more visible.

IN SUMMARY

The effects of exercise on the muscle systems are summarised in Table 3.1.

SKELETAL ADAPTATIONS

Bones also respond positively to stress. Weight-bearing activities provide the most obvious and widely accepted benefits of stress to bone structure. The increased stress encourages increased strength developing along the direction of the stress in the bone; for example a runner would experience an increase in strength vertically down the long bones that make up the upper and lower leg. However, there would be no corresponding increase in strength horizontally within the same bones as no stress would have been experienced there.

Non-weight-bearing activities have traditionally not been credited with aiding skeletal strength and development. Indeed, activities such as cycling have been cited in the past as contributing to increased bone brittleness in later life. This was blamed on a lack of 'good stress' to develop the strength in bones

▶ *A female body builder showing musculature*

The long-term effects of anaerobic training are to	The long-term effects of aerobic endurance training are to
■ increase the size of type II muscle fibres (hypertrophy)	■ increase the vascularisation of the muscle
■ increase the size of stored potential energy on the muscle such as phosphocreatin and muscle glycogen	■ increase the myoglobin within the muscle
■ increase the force that can be exerted by the muscle and the duration for which it can be exerted	■ increase the size and density of the mitochondria within the muscle
■ increase the tolerance of the muscles to lactic acid	■ decrease the levels of subcutaneous fat deposited within the muscles
■ increase the strength of the connective tissue, i.e. tendons and ligaments	■ increase the stores of muscle glycogen
■ make type IIb fibres begin to adopt the characteristics of type IIa fibres	■ increase the efficiency at which fat can be metabolised

Table 3.1 Effect of aerobic and anaerobic respiration on muscle

but also on the fact that continued demand upon the calcium stores in the body to facilitate muscular contraction left the bone mineral reservoirs low.

Recent research now indicates that even the act of a muscle pulling upon the bone via its tendon attachments leads to calcium deposits at the point of the stress. This serves to increase the strength of the bone at that point. This has been supported by many top tennis players who have far greater skeletal strength and bone density in their hitting arm than their non-hitting arm.

Weight-bearing activities can also encourage a nourishing and thickening of the hyaline cartilage, therefore aiding the cushioning of the joint. However, the benefits gained from weight-bearing activities must be considered in light of the potential damage caused by repetitive impact.

As we age, our bones may lose protein content as well as calcium. Both these factors lead to brittle bones, a condition which is potentially worse for women who are more prone to suffering from osteoporosis post-menopause. However, exercise can offset this by increasing the strength and density of the bones.

TASK

List the responses and the adaptations of the muscular-skeletal systems side by side.

Now list specific changes to the systems that would assist you in your performance. How would these responses and adaptations help you to perform better?

CARDIOVASCULAR SYSTEM

The cardiovascular system comprises the heart, blood vessels and blood.

Before looking at how the cardiovascular system responds or adapts to exercise it might be useful to have an understanding of its role and how it performs this role.

The heart contracts and relaxes. When it relaxes it fills with blood; when it contracts it pumps out the blood. The heart is divided sagitally (into left and right halves) with the two halves working in the same way but almost independent of each other. The right side

collects the deoxygenated blood from the body and pumps it to the lungs to be oxygenated. The left side receives the oxygenated blood from the lungs and pumps it around the body.

KEY TERMS

cardiac output (Q)
the amount of blood pumped out by the heart / left ventricle in one minute. Cardiac output = stroke volume (SV) x beats per minute (HR)

stroke volume (SV)
the volume of blood ejected into the aorta per beat measured in litres. Stroke volume = end diastolic volume – end systolic volume.

end diastolic volume
the volume of blood in the ventricle when finished filling

end systolic volume
the volume of blood remaining in the ventricle after contraction

venous return
the amount of blood returned to the heart / right atrium per minute

bradycardia
a resting heart rate below 60 beats per minute

hypoxic
a state where not enough oxygen is reaching the tissues

REMEMBER

- The pulmonary circulation involves the pulmonary artery carrying deoxygenated blood from the right side of the heart to the lungs to be oxygenated and the pulmonary vein returning the oxygenated blood to the left side of the heart.

- The systemic circulation involves the aorta carrying oxygenated blood from the left side of the heart to the rest of the body and the vena cava returning the deoxygenated blood from the body to the right side of the heart.

The bigger the heart the more blood it can hold. The stronger the heart the more blood it can force from the pumping chambers, the ventricles, with each beat.

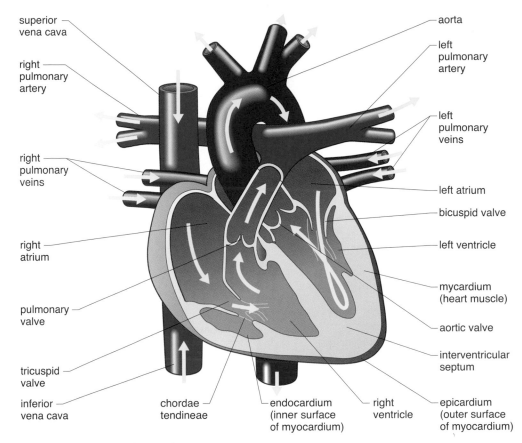

Fig. 3.4 The heart showing atria and ventricles

REMEMBER

■ The heart is the force behind the blood, helping to push it quickly and effectively to where it is needed.

■ The blood carries what the cells require, such as glucose, oxygen, hormones and antibodies, and removes what they do not need, such as excess heat and carbon dioxide.

■ If we are ill the body will create more white blood cells to help fight the infection. Similarly if we are continuously under **hypoxic** conditions through aerobic exercise then the body will create more red blood cells in order to carry more oxygen.

The heart gives force to the blood which in turn transports the requirements and waste of the cells. The blood travels through blood vessels en route to the cells. The blood vessels that feed from the heart are the largest arteries. They subdivide into smaller ones and eventually into capillaries. These are the smallest blood vessels in the body and it is these that actually carry the nutrient-rich blood into the muscles and to the cells. It is here where diffusion takes place. Consequently, the more vascular a muscle (the more capillaries there are in a muscle) the more blood – and therefore the more oxygen and nutrients – can be delivered.

RESPONSES

The responses of the cardiovascular system to exercise include:

■ increased **stroke volume**

■ increased heart rate

■ increased **cardiac output**

■ redistribution of blood flow to working muscles.

THE IMMEDIATE EFFECTS OF EXERCISE UPON THE HEART RATE

On some occasions athletes will experience an increase in heart rate even before the exercise or activity has begun. This is not, therefore, a physiological response to what has already happened but an anticipatory response in preparation for what is about to happen. In this case the anticipatory rise in heart rate is due to emotion or anxiety resulting in activation of the adrenal medulla and an increase in adrenalin in the bloodstream.

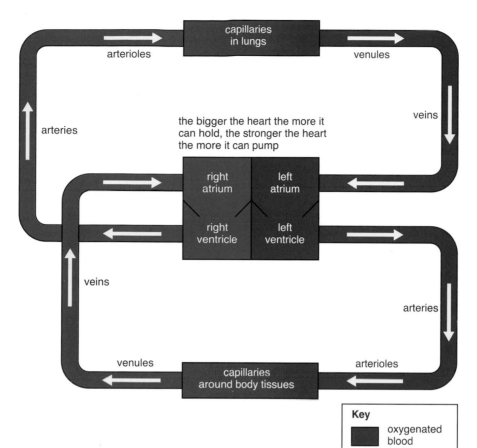

Fig. 3.5 Double circulation of blood from heart to lungs and body

THE HEART RATE DURING EXERCISE

Once exercise begins the heart rate rises rapidly due to:

- Chemicals such as lactic acid released by contracting muscles to stimulate nerve endings which transmit messages to the cardiovascular centre to increase heart rate.

- A similar message will be sent as a result in the detection of an increase in carbon dioxide levels.

- Nerve endings in the aorta and the carotid arteries register changes in oxygen and carbon dioxide content of the blood, and blood pH, and transmit messages to the cardiovascular centre to increase heart rate.

- Stretch of cardiac muscle and the sino-atrial node due to increased venous rate, and a rise in temperature of heart muscle causes an increase in heart rate.

During high intensity exercise (HR > 150), for at least 20 minutes, increased levels of circulating adrenalin also cause an increase in heart rate.

▶ *Heart rate can increase blood flow from 4–5 litres a minute to as much as 20 litres per minute.*

When an untrained person exercises they can experience a 400 per cent increase in cardiac output when compared to that at rest. This could be as much as 20 litres of blood per minute compared to 4 or 5 litres when at rest. This increase is mainly achieved through an increase in heart rate.

For a trained athlete the increase in cardiac output can be as much as 800 per cent that of resting levels. This is also partly as a result of an increased heart rate but also as a result of an increase in the stroke volume. The increased stroke volume can be as a result of an increased heart size (cardiac hypertrophy), which means that when **venous return** increases or speeds up during exercise the heart can hold a greater capacity (increased **end diastolic volume**) which means that more can be pumped out. Also, as a result of an increased force of contraction there will be more blood pumped from the heart (decreased **end systolic volume**).

THE EFFECTS OF EXERCISE ON BLOOD FLOW, BLOOD VELOCITY AND BLOOD PRESSURE

During exercise blood pressure within a muscle may increase up to 10 to 15 times its resting value. This flow is not constant, but falls sharply when muscles contract, and rises when they relax. This pattern of flow is caused by the rhythmical muscle contraction and relaxation, which alternately compresses the blood vessels to reduce blood flow, and then allows dilation of those vessels to increase flow.

During exercise, blood pressure is increased. This is due to:

- increased cardiac output
- constriction of the walls of the arterioles
- greater resistance in the contracting muscles
- constriction of blood vessels in the liver, the kidneys the digestive organs resulting in diverting blood into the dilated arterioles of the working muscles.

During static (isometric) exercise, the contraction of the muscle causes constant compression on the blood vessels. This is unlike the rhythmic contraction, which occurs during rhythmic (isotonic) exercise. This compression causes an additional restriction to blood flow in the working muscles, and will result in greater increase in blood pressure than in isotonic exercise. For this reason people with high blood pressure should avoid strenuous isometric exercise.

VASCULAR SHUNTING

If fully dilated, all the blood vessels in the body would hold approximately 20 litres of blood. However, the body only has 5 or 6 litres of blood. As different demands are put on the blood the body directs it to where it is most needed. This is achieved by a process which changes the size of some of the blood vessels, some getting bigger while others get smaller.

At rest only 15 to 20 per cent of cardiac output will be directed towards skeletal muscle. However, during intense, exhaustive exercise that figure may rise

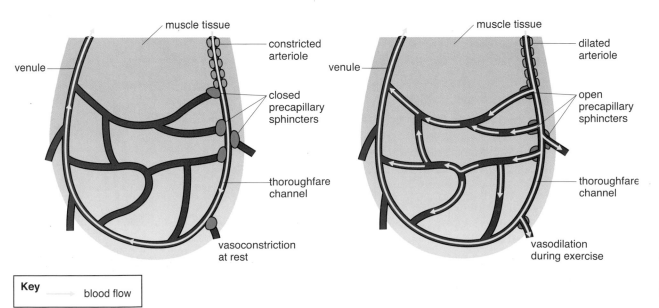

Figure 3.7 *Vascular shunting in striated muscle tissue*

to up to 80 per cent of cardiac output. Arterioles, in particular, are able to change their size by the greatest proportion in order to manipulate both blood flow and blood pressure. They either constrict (vasoconstriction) or dilate (vasodilation) rapidly, redistributing blood flow to meet the demands of exercise.

This increased flow to the muscles is a result of restricted flow to the kidneys, liver and stomach and is facilitated by vasoconstriction of blood vessels, which feed the non-demanding muscles while vasodilation occurs in the vessels demanding greater oxygen. This enables blood to be shunted to where it is most needed, a process called vascular shunting. The increased flow of blood to the muscles increases the exchanges of oxygen, the release of heat and the removal of metabolic wastes: lactic acid and carbon dioxide.

Blood redistribution takes several minutes; starting or stopping exercise abruptly doesn't allow these changes to occur smoothly. An abrupt start can leave you breathless and strain unprepared muscles. An abrupt stop can leave you light-headed when the blood pools in the working muscles, due to the sudden reduction of pumping action from the leg muscles to return blood to the heart.

The number of capillaries in muscles increases with training, while the blood becomes thinner (less viscous) and therefore better able to flow through the capillaries.

ADAPTATIONS

The adaptations in the cardiovascular system to exercise include increase in:

- size of heart
- stroke volume
- cardiac output
- number of capillaries.

HOW THE HEART ADAPTS

Almost certainly the most important adaptations to any athlete are those that take place in the heart. During exercise, it pumps blood containing oxygen, fluids and nutrients to the active muscles. Blood flow then removes waste products. The more blood pumped, the more oxygen is available to the exercising muscles.

Changes in the heart muscle occur gradually over the first four to eight weeks of consistent training.

Whether you train aerobically (low intensity, long duration) or lift weights (high intensity, short duration), your workout will get easier.

The heart can adapt structurally in the following ways:

- It can increase in size, particularly the left ventricle. This is called cardiac hypertrophy.
- The cardiac muscles can increase in thickness, so thickening the cardiac muscle in the heart wall, which means that there will be an increase in strength of contraction.
- There can be an increased vascularisation of the heart, meaning that the coronary arteries are able to deliver more oxygenated blood to the contracting cardiac muscle in the heart wall.

The heart adapts to aerobic exercise over time so it can pump more blood per stroke. As a result of this adaptation:

- The heart need not pump as frequently, assuming that demand has not increased. This would lead to a decrease in resting heart rate.
- The heart is able to pump more blood per minute (increased cardiac output) which means that the athlete can work harder, or longer, or both.

It is common for resting heart rate to have been reduced by 5–10 bpm within a few weeks of aerobic training. This is caused by an increase in stroke volume, as a result of an enlargement of the capacity of the ventricles, together with improved cardiac contractility.

For example, before embarking on an aerobic training programme an untrained person has a resting heart rate of 74 beats per minute (bpm) and a stroke volume (SV) of 70 ml. So cardiac output (Q) is as follows:

$Q = 70 \times 74 = 5180$ ml or 5.18 litres/min

After several months of following the training programme the athlete's SV has increased to 100 ml, so the athlete can achieve the same cardiac output with a resting heart rate of approximately 52 bpm, as:

$Q = 100 \times 52 = 5200$ ml or 5.20 litres/min

The benefits of these adaptations for the athlete are quite clear. As exercise results in an increase in heart rate the lower the initial, or resting, heart rate the greater the range the athlete has when exercising. The scope or range of the heart rate has increased. For example:

We use 220 minus your age as a guide to predicting maximum heart rate and we have two similar athletes in terms of size, weight and age – both are 30 years old, but both have different resting heart rate values. Athlete 1 has a resting heart rate of 72 bpm (roughly the national average). Therefore athlete 1 would have the following predictive capacity:

220 – age (30) = maximum heart rate (MHR) of 190 bpm

With a resting heart rate of 72 bpm his potential training range (the number of beats between his resting and maximal values) is 118 beats.

Athlete 2 has a resting heart rate of 46 bpm (lower than the national average). While athlete 2 would have the same MHR value of 190 bpm as athlete 1 his predictive capacity would be 144 beats.

When this is related to work rate and effect upon heart rate the difference becomes clearer.

If we assume that running at 10 km per hour has the effect of doubling the two athletes' heart rate from their resting values, athlete 1 would have a heart rate of 144 bpm, while athlete 2 would have a heart rate of 92 bpm.

Athlete 1 will be exercising at just 190 – 144 = 46 beats below his MHR, which would probably be at his anaerobic threshold, or very close to it, while athlete 2 would still be 190 – 92 = 98 beats below his MHR and would be comfortably within his aerobic capacity. Consequently athlete 2 could sustain the speed for longer.

It must be appreciated that the statistics quoted above are hypothetical and assume that work load has a linear effect upon both athletes. However, the purpose of the example is to illustrate the potential benefits to an athlete who is able to lower their resting heart rate.

TASK

Find out the resting heart rates of past or present sporting stars.

To help you, Miguel Indurain, the five times Tour de France champion is reported to have had a resting heart rate of around 30 bpm!

CIRCULATORY CHANGES

We have seen how the nervous system prepares the body for exercise by secreting hormones signalling dilation of the blood vessels in the heart and working muscles, and secretion of hormones in inactive tissue

for constriction of blood vessels. The more frequently the body is exposed to the stimulus that produces these responses the more rapidly and efficiently they will occur. With training, these systems act more efficiently and rapidly to redistribute blood, therefore improving performance.

The total number of red blood cells may increase slightly as a result of continued exposure to hypoxic situations. This can be exercise-induced hypoxia or atmosphere-induced hypoxia.

As we exercise and lose water our blood may increase in viscosity, effectively increasing the concentration of red blood cells. This will result in an increase in blood pressure, decreased efficiency in managing temperature, a decrease in the rate of metabolic processes and a general decrease in physiological functioning efficiency.

However, if we maintain good and regular hydration our bodies can respond to regular aerobic training by increasing the volume of water and dissolved proteins within the plasma. This will decrease the viscosity of the blood and reduce the concentration levels of the red blood cells. As a result of this the body may initially respond as if it has lost red blood cells and develop moderate anaemic symptoms such as lethargy. The positive benefit of this is that as blood is thinner more can reach the muscle tissue therefore increasing gaseous exchange and improving aerobic capacity.

IN SUMMARY

Red blood cell volume and haemoglobin content is higher in the trained athlete, which facilitates the transport of oxygen around the body.

However, although haemoglobin content increases, the increase in blood plasma is greater and consequently the blood haematocrit (the ratio of red blood cell volume to total blood volume) is reduced, which lowers the viscosity of the blood and facilitates its progress around the body.

TASK

What training would be ideal for you if you wanted to lower your resting heart rate? (see also Chapter 4)

*List in order the adaptations that would need to take place for **bradycardia** to occur. For each adaptation explain why it has taken place and how it will contribute to the result of lowering resting heart rate.*

RESPIRATORY SYSTEM

RESPONSES

The respiratory system's responses to exercise include:

- increased rate and depth of breathing
- increased gas exchange.

KEY TERMS

ventilation
the act of breathing

inspiration
breathing in

expiration
breathing out

respiration
the act of creating energy aerobically

diffusion
the movement of gases from one area to another. They will invariably move from an area of high pressure to one of low pressure

pressure gradient
the relative differences between the pressure within two adjacent areas

partial pressure (p)
the pressure exerted by a gas within a mixture of gases

As with the heart, the work rate of the respiratory system at rest is a mere fraction of what it is capable of.

Activity level	Ventilation rates per minute
Rest	– approximately 6 litres per minute
Steady state aerobic exercise	– approximately 80–100 litres per minute in young adult males – approximately 50–80 litres per minute in young adult females
Maximal aerobic exercise	– in excess of 120–140 litres per minute

Table 3.2 Activity levels of the respiratory system

These increases occur as a result of both an increase in the frequency of **ventilation** and an increase in the depth of ventilation.

As **respiration** deals with oxygen it is a simple assumption to make that our respiratory system determines our aerobic fitness. This perception is

further cemented by the frequent use of a person's VO_2max as a measure of their aerobic fitness level. (VO_2max is a measure of the maximum volume of oxygen that can be taken in and used per minute per kilogram of body weight.)

However, there are two key things to remember: firstly, the body expires up to 80 per cent of the inspired oxygen, (that figure may drop to 75 per cent during maximal aerobic exercise) and secondly the use of the term 'used' in the definition of VO_2max.

What this tells us is that the body is able to take in a considerable amount of oxygen but is not able to make use of all of it. To understand this we must first investigate the mechanics of **inspiration** and the related concepts of **pressure gradients** and **diffusion**.

DIFFUSION

Diffusion is the movement of molecules from a region of high concentration to a region of low concentration along a pressure gradient. The blood flow through the alveolar capillary network, and the exchange of air in the lungs due to the breathing mechanism, ensures that a pressure gradient exists in both oxygen and carbon dioxide concentrations between the blood and alveolar air. Oxygen breathed into the lungs diffuses into the alveoli, and then passes through into the capillary walls.

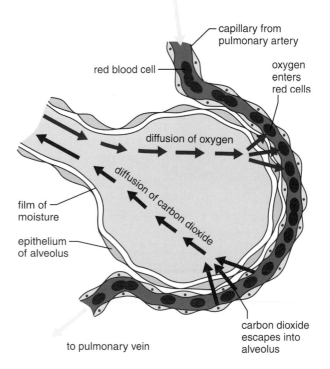

Fig. 3.7 Pressure gradient in alveoli

PARTIAL PRESSURE OF GASES

It is more accurate to talk about the **partial pressure** (p) of a gas, rather than its concentration, when considering a mixture of gases (such as atmospheric air). The partial pressure of a gas refers to the actual pressure it exerts within a mixture of gases, and is normally referred to in units of either kilopascals (kPa), or mm of mercury.

For instance, atmospheric air consists of approximately 20 per cent oxygen. It is more accurate to say that oxygen exerts a partial pressure of 20 kPa in atmospheric air. This is because, if we were to take a one litre bottle of compressed air and a one litre bottle of a thin air sample taken at altitude, both air samples would consist of 20 per cent oxygen, even though the compressed air would contain a greater amount of oxygen. Therefore, the pressure exerted by the oxygen in the compressed air sample would be much greater than the oxygen in the sample from altitude, and thus the partial pressure would be greater.

The partial pressure of the air in the alveoli of the lungs is approximately 13 kPa (which represents a concentration of approximately 13 per cent), and this is sufficient to virtually saturate the haemoglobin in the red blood cells passing through the alveolar capillaries with oxygen.

The ability for haemoglobin to become saturated with oxygen at relatively low oxygen partial pressures can be represented by the oxygen dissociation curve. The S-shaped curve is significant, in that it indicates that blood can become fully saturated with oxygen at low partial pressures.

For example, consider a situation of an atmospheric oxygen partial pressure of 5 kPa. The high affinity of haemoglobin for oxygen means that over 80 per cent of blood can become saturated, whereas if the relationship was linear, less than 40 per cent of blood would become saturated.

Exercise has the effect of displacing the oxygen dissociation curve to the right, as the blood pH falls (due to increases in carbonic acid and lactic acid), and body temperature rises. Both these factors reduce the ability of haemoglobin to carry oxygen.

THE MECHANICAL PROCESS OF INSPIRATION

Cause and effect

The process that we call breathing is a mechanical one that relies on a cause and effect relationship, i.e.:

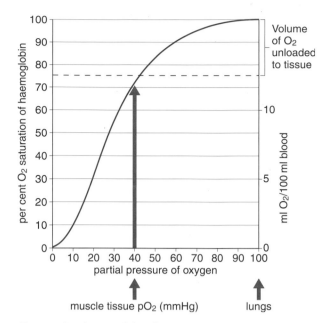

Fig. 3.8 Oxy-haemoglobin dissociation curve at rest

– Stimulation of the phrenic and intercostal nerves causes the contraction of the breathing muscles.

– During inspiration the contraction of the respiratory muscles, the diaphragm and the intercostal muscles increases the size of the thoracic cavity, allowing the lungs to expand.

– This causes a drop in pressure within the lungs to a level lower than in the atmosphere.

– This causes or creates a pressure gradient.

– Then air rushes into the lower pressure area of the lungs from the atmosphere.

– After inspiration is complete the lungs are full of air.

– This causes an increase in the pressure.

– As **expiration** begins the elastic recoil of the respiratory muscles causes the pressure within the lungs to increase further.

– It is now greater than that in the atmosphere.

– This has caused another pressure gradient.

Inspiration at rest is an active process while expiration is largely passive, relying predominantly on the elastic recoil of the primary respiratory muscles and the effect that this has on pressure within the lungs and surrounding atmosphere.

During exercise the body is able to call on secondary respiratory muscles such as the internal intercostals, pectorals, trapezium, latissimus dorsi, sternocleidomastoid and the abdominals. These all contribute to make the space within the thoracic cavity bigger and so create a greater pressure gradient, facilitating a greater volume of air and bigger quantity of gaseous exchange. The process of expiration also becomes a more active process.

Breathing at rest	Breathing during exercise
Largely passive	Largely active
Expiration is almost entirely passive	Expiration is more active
Breathing is slow	Breathing is faster
Breathing is shallow	Breathing is deeper
Smaller percentage of expired air is CO_2	Greater percentage of expired air is CO_2
Primary respiratory muscles only	Primary and secondary muscles used

Table 3.3 Summary of breathing

DEFINITIONS OF RESPIRATORY VOLUMES, VALUES AND MEASURES

The amount of air that is flushed in and out of the lungs varies substantially depending on the conditions of inspiration and expiration. Consequently, several different respiratory volumes can be described. Specific combinations (sums) of these respiratory volumes, called respiratory capacities, are measured to gain information about a person's respiratory status. The apparatus used to measure respiratory volumes is called a spirometer.

RESPIRATORY VOLUMES

The respiratory, or lung, volumes include:

Tidal volume (TV) is the respiratory volume. During normal quiet breathing, about 500 ml of air moves into and out of the lungs with each breath. This respiratory volume is referred to as the tidal volume.

Inspiratory reserve volume (IRV) is the amount of air that can be inspired forcibly beyond the tidal volume (2100 to 3200 ml).

Expiratory reserve volume (ERV) is the amount of air (normally 1000 to 1200 ml) that can be evacuated from the lungs after a tidal expiration.

Residual volume is the amount of air that remains in the lungs after expiration. Even after the most strenuous expiration, about 1200 ml of air still remains in the lungs. Residual volume ensures that the tissues of the lungs do not stick together, as would be the case if the lungs could be completely emptied. In such a case, it would be impossible to re-inflate the lungs. Total lung capacity is therefore the sum of the vital capacity and the residual volume.

RESPIRATORY CAPACITIES

The respiratory capacities always consist of two or more lung volumes and include:

Inspiratory capacity (IC) is the total amount of air that can be inspired after a tidal expiration; thus, it is the sum of the tidal volume and inspiratory reserve volumes.

Functional residual capacity (FRC) is the combined residual and expiratory reserve volumes and represents the amount of air remaining in the lungs after a tidal expiration.

Vital capacity (VC) is the total amount of exchangeable air. It represents the sum of the tidal, inspiratory reserve, and expiratory reserve volumes. In healthy young males, the VC is approximately 4800 ml.

Total lung capacity (TLC) is the sum of all lung volumes and is normally around 6000 ml in males. Lung volumes and capacities (with the possible exception of tidal volume) tend to be slightly less in women than in men because of their smaller size.

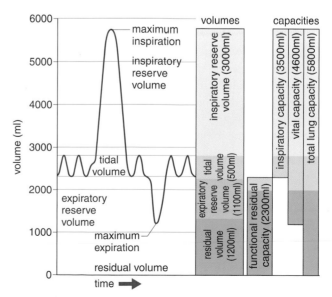

Fig. 3.9 A spirometer trace showing respiratory volumes and capacities

ANATOMICAL DEAD SPACE

Some of the inspired air fills the conducting respiratory passageways and never contributes to gas exchange in the alveoli. The volume of these conducting zone conduits, which make up the anatomical dead space, typically amounts to about 150 ml. This means that if the tidal volume is 500 ml, only 350 ml of this is involved in alveolar ventilation. The remaining 150 ml of the tidal breath is in the anatomical dead space. (The rule of thumb is that the anatomical dead space volume in millilitres in a healthy young adult is equal to the person's weight in pounds.)

If some of the alveoli cease to act in gas exchange (due to alveolar collapse or obstruction by mucus, for example), the alveolar dead space is added to the anatomical dead space, and the sum of the non-useful volumes is referred to as total dead space.

ADAPTATIONS

The respiratory system's adaptations to exercise include improvements in respiratory muscle performance.

The main limiting factor for an athlete participating in events lasting more than approximately four minutes is the ability of the cardiovascular system to deliver oxygenated blood to the muscles, and for these working muscles to utilise the oxygen to produce energy.

So it is safe to say that endurance performance is dependent upon oxygen transportation and utilisation but no matter how good the functioning of these are, improvements in performance will not happen unless we can get oxygen into the body. The respiratory system is responsible for receiving oxygen into the body and dealing with the waste products associated with muscle metabolism. Respiratory functioning does not usually hinder aerobic performance, and the adaptations that take place merely aid the improved cardiovascular functioning.

It is the ability of the muscles to extract oxygen from the blood, and the ability of the heart, lungs and associated structures to deliver oxygen to the muscles, that is the main determining factor for aerobic athletic ability.

Training has very little effect on lung volumes and capacities, although the capacities may show a slight increase. However, such measurements are not used as an indicator of aerobic fitness, as there is no correlation between lung volumes and athletic ability.

An aerobic training regime can increase the surface area of the alveoli, thus increasing the surface area available for gaseous exchange to take place. Training will also strengthen the muscles involved in breathing, i.e. the intercostal muscles and the diaphragm, which may slightly increase lung capacity, and will improve the breathing mechanism.

Following training, there is a reduction in both resting respiratory rate and the breathing rate during submaximal exercise. This appears to be a function of the overall efficiency of the respiratory structures induced by training. Surprisingly there are only very small increases in lung volumes following training. Vital capacity (the amount of air that can be forcibly expelled following maximum inspiration) increases slightly, as does tidal volume during maximal exercise. One factor to account for these increases is the increased strength of the respiratory muscles which may facilitate lung inflation.

TASK

Describe a warm-up that would encourage the structural and functional responses within the muscular, skeletal, circulatory and respiratory systems as described in this chapter.

NEURO-MUSCULAR SYSTEM

The brain controls the movements of skeletal (voluntary) muscles via specialised nerves. The combination of the nervous system and muscles, working together to permit movement, is known as the neuro-muscular system.

Messages are sent from the brain along the central nervous system until they are detected by neurons at the motor neuron pool. Every muscle in the body is represented by neurons which are connected to the central nervous system at the motor neuron pool.

Once detected the impulse is collected by dendrites which surround the nucleus of the cell. The collated impulse is then sent along the axon on its way to the muscle. Its journey is speeded up by the presence of an insulating sheath that runs along the outside of the axon, called the myelin sheath. The presence of the impulse on the axon at any point affects the sodium balance of the axon. There is a diffusion

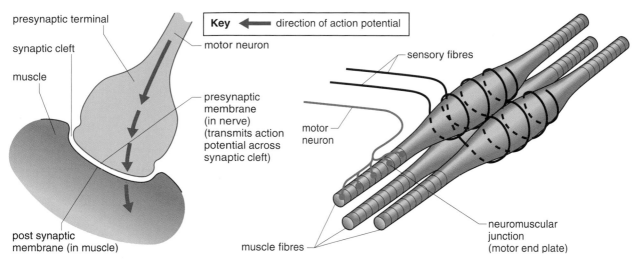

Fig. 3.10 *Transmission of an action potential across a neuromuscular junction*

of additional sodium ions which creates a positive sodium charge. This further assists in sending the impulse (which is called an action potential) towards the muscle.

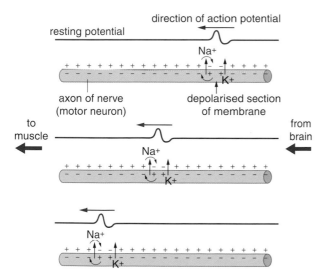

Fig. 3.11 *Action potential in a nerve reaching a muscle*

A typical muscle is serviced by anywhere between 50 and 200 (or more) motor neurons. Each motor neuron is subdivided into many tiny branches. The tip of each branch is called a presynaptic terminal. This connection between the tip of the nerve and the muscle is the motor end plate, or the neuromuscular junction. At this point if there is sufficient impulse – if the action potential is strong enough – then the muscle fibres stimulated will contract and they will contract maximally (all or nothing). If the action potential is not sufficiently strong then there will be no contraction at all.

RESPONSES

The neuro-muscular system's responses to exercise include:

- increased number of muscle fibres recruited
- increase in rate of fibre recruitment.

The type II muscle fibres are the first to be recruited because they have the lowest threshold for recruitment. If the intensity is increased to near maximal then the larger fast units will be recruited. In general, as the intensity of exercise increases in any muscle, the contribution of the type II fibres will increase.

So the brain recruits muscle fibres with regards to the required force. In the unfatigued muscle, a sufficient number of motor units will be recruited to supply the desired force. Initially desired force may be accomplished with little or no involvement of fast motor units. However, as slow units become fatigued and fail to produce force, fast units will be recruited as the brain attempts to maintain desired force production by recruiting more motor units.

Consequently as exercise duration is extended the body will need to recruit more motor units to generate the same force that was provided by fewer units at the beginning of the exercise. These additional units are those that control fast twitch muscles (type II) and so these units fatigue quicker.

ADAPTATIONS

Neuro-muscular system adaptations to exercise include:

- improved co-ordination
- increase in force production
- rate of force production
- increase in speed.

Training seems to enable the athlete to control the type and rate of motor unit recruitment.

In order for top-class power athletes, such as the shot putter or javelin thrower, to exert a maximal force they need to be able to recruit nearly all of their motor units simultaneously.

By comparison the firing pattern of endurance athletes becomes less synchronised. During continuous contractions, some units are firing while others recover, providing a built-in recovery period. Initial gains in strength associated with a weight training programme are due to improved recruitment, not muscle hypertrophy.

REMEMBER

Abbreviation	In full
MHR	maximum heart rate
RHR	resting heart rate
HRR	heart rate reserve
THR	training heart rate
RPE	recognised perceived exertion
HRM	heat rate monitor
RMR	resting metabolic rate
HR	heart rate

ExamCafé
Relax, refresh, result!

Revision checklist

▷ Know the difference between a response and an adaptation

▷ Know the main role of the systems covered

▷ Know the basic anatomical components of the systems and also their physiology in relation to exercise

▷ Know how the systems respond to exercise and how to control the exercise to control the responses

▷ Know what would make the systems perform better and how to create the adaptations necessary

▷ The cardiovascular system consists of the heart, blood vessels and blood

▷ The unique structure of the heart enables it to act as a dual action pump

▷ There are four stages to the cardiac cycle: atrial diastole where the atria (top chambers) fill with blood; ventricular diastole where the ventricles (bottom chambers) fill with blood; atrial systole when the atria contract forcing all remaining blood into the ventricles; and ventricular systole which forces blood out of the heart and into the circulatory system

▷ There are two circulatory networks: the systemic network (where blood is directed to the muscles and tissues of the body); and the pulmonary network (blood is directed from the heart to the lungs and back to heart again)

▷ The respiratory or lung volumes include tidal volume, inspiratory reserve volume, expiratory reserve volume and residual volume. Respiratory capacities include inspiratory capacity, functional residual capacity, vital capacity and total lung capacity

▷ There are two sites for gaseous exchange in the body:
  o at the alveolus
  o at the muscle cell

▷ Partial pressure is the pressure exerted by an individual gas when it occurs in a mixture of gases

▷ Training can improve lung function due to the small increases in lung volumes and capacities, the improved transport of respiratory gases, the more efficient gaseous exchange at the alveoli and tissues and improved uptake of oxygen

ExamCafé
Relax, refresh, result!

Refresh your memory

Revise as you go

1. Which blood vessels carry:

   a) oxygenated blood from the lungs to the heart
   b) deoxygenated blood from the heart to the lungs?

2. Define 'stroke volume', 'heart rate' and 'cardiac output'. State how they are related.

3. Give typical values at rest and during exercise for:

   a) stroke volume
   b) heart rate
   c) cardiac output.

4. How might these differ for a trained athlete?

5. Briefly outline the conduction system of the heart.

6. Explain the events of the cardiac cycle.

7. Explain the function of the sympathetic and parasympathetic nervous systems. How do they regulate the heart rate?

8. Define venous return. Explain the mechanism of venous return.

9. Explain the ways in which oxygen and carbon dioxide are transported in the body.

10. State two long-term effects of anaerobic training and two short-term effects of aerobic training on muscle tissue.

Get the result!

Sample question and answer

Exam question

Warming up is said to 'improve performance'. Identify **four** physiological responses to a warm-up and state how each aids performance. **(8 marks)**

Student answer

Once you begin to warm up there will be lots of changes that take place within the body. These are called responses because they take place quickly and will also disappear quickly. The reason that we do a warm-up is to make the body change in this way so that we can perform better. That is why a warm-up is said to 'improve performance'. If the changes were permanent then they would be called adaptations. One of the most obvious changes is that our heart rate will increase. This is because we need more oxygen in the body to make the energy that we need to perform. Other changes are that some blood vessels will get bigger, this is called vaso-dilation. At the same time some other blood vessels will get smaller which is called vaso-constriction. The capillaries in the face will open and enlarge and our faces will change colour. You will start to breathe faster as the warm-up continues and your stroke volume will also increase. Your muscles will get warmer and they will be able to stretch further. This will help to reduce the risk of injury.

Examiner says:

This is not an untypical type of answer. The candidate has a good understanding of why we warm up, they can distinguish between and define both responses and adaptations and they are aware of a number of responses that will occur while warming up.

However, the candidate has tried to score the marks available through quantity of writing rather than answering the question. Also, by answering in this way, i.e. in one long paragraph, it is difficult to see whether the candidate has referred to four responses and then justified them or not.

Examiner says:

The question clearly asks for four physiological responses (1 mark for each) and an explanation of the benefit gained for each response (again 1 mark for each explanation).

Student answer

Once you begin to warm up there will be lots of changes that take place within the body. These are called responses because they take place quickly and will also disappear quickly. The reason that we do a warm-up is to make the body change in this way so that we can perform better. That is why a warm-up is said to 'improve performance'. If the changes were permanent then they would be called adaptations. One of the most obvious changes is that our heart rate will increase. This is because we need more oxygen in the body to make the energy that we need to perform. Other changes are that some blood vessels will get bigger, this is called vaso-dilation. At the same time some other blood vessels will get smaller which is called vaso-constriction. The capillaries in the face will open and enlarge and our faces will change colour. You will start to breathe faster as the warm-up continues and your stroke volume will also increase. Your muscles will get warmer and they will be able to stretch further. This will help to reduce the risk of injury.

Examiner says:

Here is the answer again. Red is irrelevant, blue is not marked because it is not appropriate (may be a structural response) and black is marked correct.

Examiner says:

One mark awarded here.

Examiner says:

These may be structural responses and not physiological ones.

Examiner says:

One mark awarded here.

Examiner says:

Three marks awarded here.

Although the first lines of the candidate's answer is accurate information, it is not required to answer this question and so is a waste of time and scores no marks.

The first part of the answer that scores a mark is the reference to an increase in heart rate. The candidate then attempts to explain the benefit. Unfortunately the answer is not correct as increased heart rate speeds up delivery of the oxygen in the body.

The candidate then refers to two other responses, vaso-dilation and vaso-constriction. Although the explanation of these is correct they are structural changes, not physiological ones. No mention of the benefits that would be gained is made, which would indicate that the candidate is not really clear how to answer the question.

Changes to the capillaries in the face is a repeat of the vaso-dilation point; changing colour might have got a benefit of the doubt mark if the candidate had gone on to explain how this helps the athlete to cool down or lose heat but no explanation was given.

Breathe faster is correct and scores a second mark. Unfortunately increased stroke volume is a repeat of the increased heart rate mark. Neither of these points is followed up with an explanation of the benefits gained.

The candidate scores well in their last sentence but apparently by luck rather than judgement. 'Muscles getting warmer' scores a mark, as does 'they can stretch further' and the benefit gained of 'reducing injury' scores the final mark.

In total, the candidate has scored 5 marks which on the face of it is not too bad. However, without the last sentence that score would have fallen to 2 out of the available 8!

CHAPTER 4 FITNESS AND TRAINING

LEARNING OUTCOMES

By working through this chapter, you should:

- be able to define the different components of fitness and apply these to different sports
- know the different methods of training and apply these to particular sports by identifying specific training benefits/adaptations
- know what the principles of training are and be able to apply these to training programmes suitable for different people with different needs
- know why and when to carry out fitness tests and how to make these reliable and valid
- know the names and protocols of fitness tests for all the components of fitness

In this chapter we will focus on *fitness and training* by looking at the different *components of fitness* and relating them to activities and sports. We will look at the different *methods of training*, how they are performed and therefore what they can achieve, as well as their suitability for different activities and also for different performers at different physiological levels. We will look at the *principles of training*, identify them and how they need to be applied in order to ensure that you benefit from the work that you are doing but, perhaps more importantly, to ensure that you stay in control of the benefits that your training provides. We will also examine how different people at different times require adapted or even totally different training programmes or exercise regimes. We will examine the principles of training by applying the 'correct rules' in order to ensure that we get the appropriate adaptations. We will also consider the fine, and sometimes not so fine tuning that is necessary when designing training programmes for different people. Finally, we will look at how and why we can assess our state of health and fitness and also how we can be extremely specific as well as accurate in our information gathering process. Then we will examine the role of assessment in achieving and maintaining a level of fitness.

It will involve the application of previously discussed concepts in order to improve fitness.

We will first look at the different components of fitness, providing definitions for them and examples of their application in a sporting environment.

COMPONENTS OF PHYSICAL FITNESS

SPEED

Speed is defined as the time taken to move a body, part or whole, through a movement over a predetermined distance. It is often presumed to be a measure of maximum speed; however, all track events are a measure of speed, not just the 100 metre distance.

STRENGTH (MAXIMAL, STATIC AND DYNAMIC)

There are many different forms of strength:

- **Absolute strength** is defined as the maximum force that can be exerted once, regardless of body weight or size. An example of a sport requiring absolute strength would be rugby where the athlete makes a tackle with the greatest force that he can exert.
- **Dynamic strength** is defined as the ability to exert significant muscular force repeatedly. An example of a sport requiring this type of strength would be a 2000 metre rowing race where a rower exerts great force for up to 4 or 5 minutes.
- **Elastic strength** (similar to power) is defined as the ability to exert a force quickly and is calculated as strength multiplied by speed.
- **Explosive strength** is defined as the ability to exert a maximal force quickly or in one action. A shot putter would require elastic and explosive strength, as force and speed when added to trajectory keep the shot in the air for longer.
- **Relative strength** is defined as the maximum force that can be exerted in proportion to body weight. This is important for a boxer who needs to exert the greatest possible force within his weight category.
- **Strength endurance** (or localised muscular endurance) is defined as the ability of a muscle to resist fatigue while exerting a force, performing repeated muscular action over an extended period. A Tour de France cyclist, who performs the same pedal action up to 95 times a minute for over 5 hours a day, would most definitely require localised muscular endurance.
- **Static strength** is defined as the ability to exert a sustained force without significant movement.

▶ *Gymnasts clearly need a combination of many of the types of strength mentioned. The gymnast in the picture is demonstrating fantastic static strength at the moment; however, he needed to get into the position initially and he will need great elastic strength as he performs the bounds of the floor routine. To perform demanding moves consecutively will require dynamic strength…*

A gymnast who has to maintain their position in the crucifix on the rings would require tremendous static strength.

ENDURANCE (AEROBIC, CARDIOVASCULAR AND MUSCULAR)

To endure is to sustain and endurance is a measure of a component of fitness to sustain activity.

Aerobic endurance is the ability of the aerobic energy pathway to meet the demands of an activity. This may seem misleading because resting, walking and daily living activities are entirely aerobic and the body can sustain this level of activity for a very long time. However, within the context of sport and fitness aerobic activity is considered to cover any intensity below an individual's anaerobic threshold.

If an athlete is able to sustain the level of intensity just below their anaerobic threshold then they can delay the point at which they begin to work anaerobically, and therefore delay the onset of fatigue. However, perhaps a more important consideration would be the intensity at which an athlete begins to work anaerobically.

Athletes train to raise their anaerobic threshold while also training to be able to work for extended periods at higher percentages of their aerobic capacity. A 10,000 metre runner would require aerobic endurance in order to run at the highest possible intensity for as long as possible within the race.

Cardiovascular endurance is the ability of the heart, blood and blood vessels to work collectively to perform their function of fulfilling the needs of the cells in the body, by delivering oxygen and removing waste. Cardiovascular endurance is the ability of the body to deliver oxygen to working muscles and remove waste for an extended period of time. It is not lung capacity but cardiovascular efficiency that determines an athlete's fitness. It is a combination of having the red blood cells to carry the oxygen, the vessels for the oxygen-rich blood to travel through and a sufficiently sized and strong pump to deliver the oxygen. The marathon runner would need cardiovascular endurance in order to maintain the delivery of oxygen and removal of carbon dioxide and oxidisation of lactic acid for the duration of the 26 mile race.

Muscular endurance is the ability of a muscle to resist fatigue while exerting a force, performing repeated muscular action over an extended period.

FLEXIBILITY

Flexibility is defined as the range of movement available at a joint. It is determined by two factors: joint structure and muscle elasticity.

Any athlete would benefit from increased flexibility, as the greater the range of movement the greater the ease and efficiency of the movement; also as the range of movement increases then strength also increases.

▶ *Flexibility is a key component in athletic fitness*

BODY COMPOSITION

Body composition is used to describe the percentages of fat, bone and muscle that make up the human body. The percentage of fat (body fat percentage) is of most interest to athletes as this is invariably extra body tissue that needs to be fed with valuable oxygen and additional weight that needs to be carried with no positive benefit to the athlete. Because muscular tissue takes up less space in our body than fat tissue, our body composition, as well as our weight, determines how lean we appear. Two people at the same height and same body weight may look completely different from each other because they have a different body composition.

Somatotyping is a way of classifying different body compositional make-ups. Initially developed by Sheldon (1940) as a tool for predicting psychological behaviour, it has since been used by physiologists to classify a particular individual to an appropriate sporting environment.

- Ectomorphic body type is characterised by long arms and legs and a short upper body and narrow shoulders, and supposedly has a higher proportion of nervous tissue. Ectomorphs also have long and thin muscles. They usually have a very low fat storage, therefore they are considered as slim. An ectomorph would be ideally suited to a sport such as high jump.

- Mesomorphic body type is characterised by a high rate of muscle growth and a higher proportion of

▶ *Ectomorph body type*

muscular tissue. Mesomorphs have large bones and a solid torso combined with low fat levels, wide shoulders and a narrow waist. This body composition would be ideally suited to the 100 metre sprinting event.

- Endomorphic body type is characterised by an increased amount of fat storage, due to a larger number of fat cells than average and a higher proportion of digestive tissue. Endomorphs have a wide waist and a large bone structure, not ideally suited to many sporting activities except that of Sumo wrestling. However, exercise can limit the amount of body fat, and this body type also has the ability to build muscle mass relatively quickly.

▶ *Mesomorph body type*

No one will be 100 per cent one form of somatotype as there are percentages of all three represented in each of us. As such Sheldon devised a scale ranging from 1 to 7 for each of the somatotypes. If a pure somatotype were to exist then Sheldon's scale would read as follows:

pure endomorph: 7–1–1
pure mesomorph: 1–7–1
pure ectomorph: 1–1–7.

COMPONENTS OF SKILL FITNESS

CO-ORDINATION

This is the ability of the body to link movements together, either with other movements or in relation to an external object such as an opponent or a ball. The execution of a skill requires co-ordination; the greater the number of muscles and/or objects the harder the skill and the greater the degree of co-ordination required. For example, performing a 'lay up' in basketball requires significant co-ordination: first dribbling, then picking the ball up, moving it and shooting while taking the appropriate steps and protecting the ball before jumping prior to release.

BALANCE

In its simplest form balance is a measure of the ability to control the position of the body, either in a fixed position (**static balance**), or while moving from one position to another (**dynamic balance**). For example, the gymnast requires both static and dynamic

▶ *Endomorph body type*

balance: static balance as they hold a position within the routine, and dynamic balance as they move into the next position with control.

AGILITY

Agility is defined as changing position quickly and with control. It is similar to dynamic balance; for example, a netball player would require agility as they dodge quickly to get free from a marker.

REACTION TIME

This is the time taken from the presentation of the stimulus to the execution of the necessary subsequent action. For example, a sprinter hears the gun, interprets the sound and the necessary action to follow it and then pushes off from the starting blocks.

POWER

See also explosive and elastic strength. However, we must not always assume that power is a maximal effort. For example, cyclists use sustainable power as a far more accurate guide to measure training intensity than heart rate. They know their maximal power output and so can calculate the power output that they can sustain for any period as a percentage of their maximum.

▶ *Rugby requires all the components of fitness: co-ordination, balance, agility, reaction time and power*

TASK

A sport such as rugby would require almost, if not all, of the components of fitness. Categorise the components in order of priority, justifying your order.

TAKE IT FURTHER

Consider each component of fitness and a sport that would not require it. State why.

METHODS OF FITNESS TRAINING

AEROBIC/ANAEROBIC TRAINING

Aerobic or anaerobic training involves training that uses energy specifically or mainly supplied either aerobically or anaerobically. Aerobic energy is released in the presence of oxygen and if the muscles are starved of oxygen then anaerobic energy is released.

REMEMBER

■ One complete range of movement of an exercise, from the beginning to the end and back to the beginning again, is a **repetition** (**rep**). A collection of repetitions makes one **set**.

The energy systems within the body are quite complicated and only a simplified overview will be given here. The usable energy in the body is stored in molecules of adenosine triphosphate (ATP). The sources of energy provided by the food we eat have to be converted to ATP before they can be used by the cells of the body – for example in muscle contraction.

REMEMBER

■ Adenosine triphosphate (ATP) is a high-energy phosphate compound in which three molecules of phosphate are linked to one molecule of adenosine by an energy-rich bond.

adenosine triphosphate (ATP) formed from adenosine diphosphate (ADP) and a phosphate molecule

REMEMBER

- Phosphocreatine (PC) is a high-energy phosphate compound found in the cytoplasm of muscle cells. Energy stored in its bonds is used to make ATP when levels of ATP in muscle cells become depleted.

the bond between the second and third phosphate groups is rich in energy

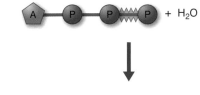

when a cell needs energy it breaks the energy-rich bond between the phosphate groups

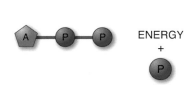

Fig. 4.1 The energy-rich bond in ATP is between the second and third phosphate molecules

The body has three systems that it uses to produce ATP:

- the phosphocreatine (ATP–PC) system (also known as the alactic energy system) (anaerobic)
- the lactic acid system (glycolysis) (anaerobic)
- the aerobic energy system.

All three energy systems are continuously producing ATP for the working body, though only one will be the predominant energy provider at any given time. It is working intensity and duration that determine which provider is the most dominant. The higher the intensity the more likely the dependence will be on the anaerobic energy pathways. The first two systems are both anaerobic energy systems as they can produce ATP when there is insufficient oxygen available for the complete breakdown of glucose. We all have different levels, or thresholds, at which the pathways are capable of being the dominant energy provider. Athletes will focus their training on shifting their own thresholds to better suit their performance.

All training methods can be adapted but many will have a natural predisposition to benefiting a particular energy pathway.

Long interval training sessions use both aerobic and anaerobic energy pathways, and are typically used by athletes involved in sports with efforts of one to six minutes and upwards, such as middle and long distance athletes and team game players.

System	Reaction	Description
phosphocreatine system (ATP–PC) (alactic system)	• Creatine phosphate energy system: ADP + creatine phosphate ⟶ ATP + creatine	anaerobic system where phosphocreatine (PC) is broken down to release energy to form ATP from ADP and phosphate. The levels of ATP are kept high
lactic acid system (glycolysis)	• Lactic acid energy system: Glucose ⟶ 2 ATP + 2 lactic acid + heat Glycogen ⟶ 3 ATP + 2 lactic acid + heat	anaerobic energy system in which ATP is made when carbohydrate is broken down into lactic acid
aerobic system	• Aerobic energy system: Glucose + oxygen ⟶ 38 ATP + carbon dioxide + water + heat Fatty acids + oxygen ⟶ 129 ATP + carbon dioxide + water + heat	energy system where oxygen is used to burn fats and glucose to produce ATP. Glycogen is used as a source of glucose first then fat. The latter is a slow process that is accompanied by a decline in performance level

Fig. 4.2 The three systems used to produce ATP

Sprint interval training sessions are specifically designed to stress the ATP–PC system, improving its capacity and increasing the muscle stores of ATP and PC. This obviously has a direct effect upon sprinters or any activity where bursts of speed are required.

Fast interval training sessions develop anaerobic endurance and therefore stress the lactic acid system. The buffering capacity of the body improves, which delays the onset of fatigue and decreases the effect of lactic acid. This training is of particular importance to 400 metre runners and sprint swimmers.

The aerobic system is stressed by performing slower intervals which improves the oxidative capacity of the body. Any endurance-based event, such as distance running or swimming, will benefit from this type of training, in addition to field games such as rugby and hockey. As this training relies on the phosphate energy system, and increases its capacity and restorative powers, an improved **alactacid source** is necessary for a sustained sprint or the stop-and-go action of many team sports.

> ### KEY TERM
>
> **alactacid source**
> a phosphocreatine source in muscle and nerve tissue, of high energy phosphate bonds

CONTINUOUS TRAINING

In continuous training the intensity is continuous or constant and associated with long distance/duration activity that, by definition, has to be of medium to low intensity. It is frequently used for developing endurance and uses the aerobic energy system. Continuous training is also used as a training intensity during the recovery period (see page 86) and because of this and the relatively low intensity it can be used for helping to perfect technique also.

This type of training uses large muscle groups of the body over a long period of time (between 30 minutes and two hours) and so is associated with weight or fat loss.

Good examples of continuous training activities include jogging, swimming, cycling or aerobic dance. The intensity of such exercise should be at approximately 60 to 80 per cent of HR_{max}, as outlined in the **Karnoven Principle**, so the body is not experiencing too much discomfort while exercising.

Unfortunately, with such long distance/high duration activity comes the potential for boredom and even repetitive stress injuries, particularly to the muscles and joints.

> ### KEY TERM
>
> **Karnoven Principle**
> a way of calculating a training zone based on exercise intensity related to maximal heart rate (see page 59). An athlete's critical threshold THR = RHR + (HRR × 0.6) where HRR = MHR − RHR and 0.6 is 60 per cent intensity

> ### REMEMBER
>
> - maximal endurance is measured by VO_2 max
> - maximal flexibility is measured by the sit and reach test
> - maximal strength is measured by the one repetition maximum test (1 rep max, 1RM)

INTERVAL TRAINING

This is a method of training where exercise (work) is interrupted by periods of rest (interval). The training session is split up around a **work** to **rest** ratio (**W:R**). An example of a work to rest ratio would be a football match that has 2 × 45 minute work periods with a 15 minute rest interval, written as 45 : 15, or 3 : 1.

Because there are different types of fitness, athletes have to train specifically to achieve the adaptations that they want. So the work period of the training session is calculated to a particular intensity and for a specific duration to achieve the desired adaptation. For example, to improve your maximal (strength, endurance, flexibility: see maximal tests below) you need to work at 90–100 per cent of your one repetition maximum. You will only be able to do this for a short period of time.

The rest period has to be long enough to enable the body to recover sufficiently that it can perform the next work period at the desired level of intensity/duration. Too little rest will prevent the training session from providing the desired effect.

The type of energy pathway used and the level of energy depletion experienced will determine the amount of rest time needed in order to fully replenish the pathway. The rest period can be calculated in order to allow the energy pathway that has been used to replenish itself.

Interval training is frequently associated with anaerobic activities only. However, it is rapidly becoming the basis of every athlete's training programme due to its adaptability and ability to provide qualitative benefits compared to the more quantitative benefits of continuous training, for instance.

Recovery time (s)	Muscle phosphocreatine restored
10	10%
30	50%
60	75%
90	87%
120	93%
150	97%
180	99%
210	101%
240	102%

Table 4.1 Approximate recovery rates for phosphocreatine

POWER TRAINING

Muscular power is determined by how long it takes for strength to be converted into speed. The ability to convert strength to speed in a very short time allows the athlete to exert a greater force than their strength levels alone would allow. For example, an athlete who has strong legs and can perform a squat with extremely heavy weights over a long duration may get less distance on a standing long jump than a weaker athlete who is able to generate a smaller amount of force but over a much shorter period of time.

Traditionally, training to enhance maximal power, or more accurately explosive or elastic strength, has used weight training as the medium, lifting at an intensity of between 90–95 per cent of the athlete's one repetition maximum (1 rep max or 1RM).

Traditional weight training exercises are replaced with those that resemble Olympic lifts, such as the 'clean and jerk' or 'snatch' with athletes either performing these movements as they are or as variations on the theme.

Although this is still a popular mode of power training there are other methods available to the athlete, most notably plyometrics (see page 81).

Power is determined by the force exerted by the muscle (strength) and the speed at which the muscle shortens:

power = force × velocity

Consequently, it follows that by improving either strength or speed of contraction then power should also be increased. It has long been established that muscles generate more force in contraction when they have been previously stretched. Plyometrics enables this to occur by taking the muscle through a forced eccentric (lengthened) phase before a powerful concentric (shortening) phase. This stimulates adaptations within the neuro-muscular system and produces a more powerful concentric contraction of the muscle group. This has important consequences for sprinting, jumping and throwing events in athletics, as well as in games such as rugby, volleyball and basketball where leg strength is central to performance.

Exercises that might form part of the plyometrics session include bounding, hopping, leaping, skipping, depth jumps (jumping onto and off of boxes), clap press-ups, throwing and catching a medicine ball. In short, any activity that requires a muscle to perform a significant breaking action prior to the more traditional positive or concentric action.

CIRCUIT TRAINING

Circuit training consists of a series of exercises arranged and performed in order. The circuit will be designed to develop a specific targeted component of fitness or specific sport-related skill.

Traditionally the athlete will move around a room performing a specific exercise at different parts of the room. These areas of the room and exercises make up exercise stations. The athlete will know the component of fitness that they are trying to develop and this will be reflected in the exercise duration at each station and also the recovery time between stations.

For example, if an athlete is working with 12 stations and aims to improve their aerobic fitness then they would work for at least 90 seconds at each station with a short break of 10 seconds between each station. If the circuit is arranged properly then the athlete will be exercising different body parts at each station. This enables the athlete to work at an intensity that they can sustain for the 90 seconds in the knowledge that the fatigued body part can recover while the next body part is worked. In this way it will take the athlete a few seconds short of 20 minutes to complete one circuit.

If the athlete wished to target anaerobic fitness benefits then they could perform the same exercise stations but working for 20 seconds at each station with 40 seconds recovery. This way they would work at a far higher tempo to last just 20 seconds as against 90 seconds in the first example.

There are two main types of circuit training:

FIXED LOAD CIRCUITS
Here each athlete performs a given number of repetitions at a station before moving on to the next station. The time taken to complete the circuit is recorded.

INDIVIDUAL LOAD CIRCUITS
Alternatively the athlete would perform for a designated amount of time at a station and would record the number of repetitions completed.

ADVANTAGES AND BENEFITS OF CIRCUIT TRAINING
Circuit training can be used to develop a variety of fitness components by adapting the available variables. It can be adapted further by working different body parts or the same body part at consecutive stations or by performing the skills of the sport.

It can be performed with little or no equipment in a confined space and can provide the athlete with a whole body workout in a relatively short period of time.

The circuit can be adapted to meet the specific fitness requirements of a given sport or activity.

REMEMBER
Overload is achieved in circuit training by:
- reducing target times
- increasing exercise resistance (difficulty of the exercise)
- increasing repetition numbers.

When planning a circuit there are several factors that need consideration. The fundamental consideration is – What targeted component of fitness or specific sport-related skill is the circuit required for? The exercises to include will depend on this. Other considerations are:

- the number of participants
- their standard of fitness
- the amount of time, space and equipment that are available.

Circuit training is often referred to as a form of interval training and is becoming increasingly popular as a mode of training.

press ups

star jumps

dorsal raises

shuttle runs

Fig. 4.3 *Circuit training*

STAGE TRAINING

Stage training is similar to circuit training. However, instead of immediately moving on to the next exercise, three sets of each exercise are repeated at one workstation (with short rest intervals) before moving on to the next.

WEIGHT/RESISTANCE TRAINING

Not to be confused with weight lifting, weight training involves exercising with a variable resistance. It is a predominantly anaerobic activity although by varying the intensity and duration of the training sessions it can be manipulated to provide numerous benefits, for example, muscular endurance, dynamic and maximal strength, power and body composition, and improved posture.

FIXED AND FREE WEIGHTS

Fixed weights refer to resistance machines. Each machine will be designed to work a particular muscle group and will allow movement in the necessary planes. Resistance is offered in several ways, such as hydraulics, weights and pulleys, incline/decline of the apparatus, elastic bands and so on. Machines are frequently called by the name of the exercise that they offer.

Free weights are the bars and bells that are traditionally associated with weight training. The disadvantages of free weights over fixed weights or resistance machines is that they require the athlete to learn the correct technique, they have a greater risk of injury and for safety reasons they require at least one or two training partners/spotters.

Although resistance machines provide stability for the body, a correct plane of movement, variable resistance and body size positions, are easily learnt and do not require spotters, they do have some disadvantages. For example, the resistance increments may be too large, the machine, although adjustable, may not fit the individual perfectly, they are expensive, you require a different machine for each exercise, they require a lot of space, and they do not develop the stabilising muscles because the resistance machines take the weight.

During weight training, subjects perform a series of resistance exercises designed to develop the fitness component they require in specific sport-related muscles.

When training with weights it is common to target specific muscles or muscle groups/body parts.

Exercises are known as 'isolation' exercises (work one specific muscle, e.g. the leg extension exercise works the quadriceps) or compound exercises (work muscle groups, e.g. the squat exercise works all of the main muscles of the trunk and the lower body).

ISOTONIC (TRADITIONAL) WEIGHT TRAINING

If a muscle contracts and changes its length to produce force, the contraction is isotonic. These types of contractions are normally what the athlete considers to be weight training, and can improve both strength, endurance and cardiovascular fitness.

This type of training can be carried out with free weights, or using multigym equipment, and can be tailored to improve muscular strength or endurance. Training with weights using specialist equipment (e.g. attached to pulleys) may mimic specialist movements involved in sports such as swimming, so that muscle groups may be strengthened by training out of the pool, in order to improve performance in it.

ISOMETRIC WEIGHT TRAINING

During isometric training, the athlete holds a maximum contraction for 5–7 seconds, recovers briefly, and repeats five times.

Isometric training is valuable only in sports like judo or gymnastics where you need to hold a position for several seconds. Since in isometric training strength gains are specific to the joint angle, the angles that are specific to the sport being trained for must be selected.

ISOKINETIC WEIGHT TRAINING

Isokinetic training requires expensive equipment, such as Nautilus®, HydraGym or CYBEX. These machines permit a person to work at a constant speed against a resistance or weight that changes as the muscular force changes throughout the movement range. These machines ensure that muscles are worked evenly at all stages of the movement and also permit the duplication of certain sports movements, such as throwing and kicking. Strength gains can be achieved faster with isokinetic training than with either isometric or isotonic training.

TASK

Select four components of fitness and explain how weight training could benefit each.

SPEED TRAINING

It would be easy to assume that as strength and speed equals power, so conversely increasing your strength and your power will improve your speed. There is a degree of truth in this but speed will only really begin to improve if the muscle fibres are stimulated to contract at a faster rate. The strongest muscles are not always the quickest ones!

Practising moving and accelerating faster helps to condition the neuro-muscular system to improve the firing patterns of fast-twitch muscle fibres (see page 48).

Two variations of basic speed training are assisted and resisted speed training:

Assisted speed training (also called overspeed training) helps to improve stride frequency through the use of equipment such as elasticated belts.

Resisted speed training helps to improve speed-strength and stride length, again by using equipment such as sledges or parachutes that are pulled.

Acceleration sprints are conducted for less than 5 seconds, with the athletes in a variety of starting positions – lying, sitting, kneeling or standing – depending on the sport. Because acceleration work does not allow enough time for maximum sprinting speed to be reached, it is necessary to extend the length of the sprint. This can be done in 20-second efforts, in which maximum speed is held for 5 seconds, after 10 seconds of gradual acceleration.

FARTLEK TRAINING

This form of training has some similarities to both continuous and interval training. The translation from Swedish is 'speed play' and it involves training at different intensities or on different terrains. It is a form of endurance conditioning, where the aerobic energy system is stressed due to the continuous nature of the exercise. However, it can be adapted so that the higher intensities stress the anaerobic energy systems and also their speed of recovery.

Like continuous training, Fartlek is generally associated with long distance, duration training. Fartlek sessions are usually performed for a minimum of 45 minutes, with the intensity of the session varying from low intensity walking to high intensity sprinting. Traditionally Fartlek has taken place in the countryside where there is varied terrain, but this alternating pace method could occur anywhere and you could use an area local to you.

This type of training can be very individual and the athlete can determine the speed or intensity at which they wish to work. Since both aerobic and anaerobic systems are stressed through this method of training, a wealth of sportspeople can benefit. It is particularly suited to those activities that involve a mixture of aerobic and anaerobic work, such as field games including rugby, hockey or soccer. It can also be fun and offers variety and change compared to what some regard as the monotony of continuous jogging.

CROSS TRAINING

This is a mixture of a variety of training methods and styles which are employed to provide psychological relief from boredom (applying the principle of variance) but it also provides physiological benefits. Different ranges of movement and intensities are exercised so preventing **DOMS (delayed onset muscle soreness)** and forcing the neuro-muscular system to develop new and more efficient energy release pathways and avoiding physiological plateaus.

KEY TERMS

DOMS (delayed onset muscle soreness) post-exercise muscular soreness caused by the healing process of damaged myofibrils

CORE STABILITY TRAINING

Core stability training is becoming increasingly popular as coaches and athletes begin to appreciate the benefits derived from strengthening this area of the body. The core muscles of the body are the foundation for all other movement.

The core muscles are within the torso and generally attach to the spine, pelvis and muscles that support the scapula (see Figure 3.2, page 49). When these muscles contract, they stabilise the spine, pelvis and shoulders and create a solid base of support. The stronger this base the better the platform that other muscles, particularly those of the arms and legs, have to work from. Consequently, they can generate more forceful contractions. Training the core muscles of the body can also correct postural imbalances and reduce the risk of injury.

As with any type of strength and conditioning training, the muscles that make up the core must be trained specifically and appropriately for their task. Their predominant role is that of stabiliser; they do

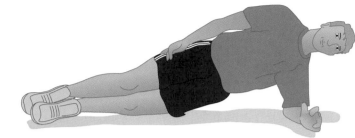

abdominal bracing for external obliques

abdominal bracing for rectus abdominis

Fig. 4.4 *Core stability training*

not usually exert significant forces but will have to work for long periods of time. They will be using static, or isometric, contractions with the aim of developing very good endurance of low-level forces.

Abdominal bracing is the main technique used during core exercise training. It involves the contraction of the abdominal muscles. It is important to breathe normally throughout this type of exercise. Do not hold your breath but breathe evenly. Other exercises that develop core strength include exercises on a stability ball, medicine balls, wobble boards and Pilates exercise programmes.

PLYOMETRIC TRAINING

For a muscle to cause movement, it must shorten (concentric contraction). There is a maximum amount of force that a muscle can generate while contracting concentrically. However, if the muscle is lengthened (eccentric contraction) just prior to the contraction, it will produce greater force through the storage of elastic energy. This effect requires that the time between eccentric contraction and concentric contraction (amortisation phase) be very short because the stored elastic energy, created by the eccentric contraction, is lost very quickly. The process is frequently referred to as the 'stretch shortening cycle', and is one of the underlying mechanisms of plyometric training.

Plyometrics is a type of exercise that utilises a rapid eccentric movement, followed by a short amortisation phase, and then followed by an

press-ups with claps for pectorals, deltoids and triceps

Fig. 4.5 *Plyometric training*

explosive concentric movement, which enables the synergistic muscles to engage in the myotatic-stretch reflex during the stretch-shortening cycle.

Plyometric exercises use explosive movements to develop muscular power and also co-ordination. Plyometric training will improve the neuro-muscular link. The result will be an increase in power but not necessarily an increase in maximal strength.

It should also be noted that plyometric training leaves the athlete at an increased risk of joint and soft tissue injury and very much more susceptible to post-exercise DOMs.

SAQ (SPEED, AGILITY, QUICKNESS)

Speed, agility and quickness are essential ingredients in a great many sporting activities and as such athletes incorporate this form of sports training into their programme to enhance these components. SAQ is patented by a company called 'SAQ International'. The system has gained national and international success and is used by many top teams across the world, notably in the UK, US and Australia.

The key difference between SAQ and traditional speed training is that the emphasis is on the neuro-muscular system. Messages are sent to the muscles through nerves. By developing and honing the neurological firing patterns, the brain and body learn to work together much more efficiently. The theory behind this type of training is that by improving the athlete's neuro-muscular system the initial movements will be more automatic and more efficient resulting in a more explosive and precise action. For example, by getting the feet moving faster the brain will have to send more frequent impulses to the muscles.

SAQ is perhaps most famous for incorporating horizontal ladder drills and emphasising correct running technique and posture. The programme also uses explosion training, resisted running, contrast training and assisted running:

- explosive training is done using short speed bursts
- resisted running involves recruiting more muscle fibres than normal
- contrast training involves no resistance but persuades the body to recruit more muscle fibres as if the resistance was being applied
- assisted training increases the frequency at which the brain sends impulses, in response to the increased muscle fibre recruitment and increase

in muscular power output. The short speed bursts can be achieved with tennis ball drops and/or reaction drills.

As part of developing the 'whole package' this training system incorporates exercises to improve the athlete's reaction time by practising responses to common stimuli, such as sight or sound.

STRETCHING

Stretching is recognised as being the best way to increase or maintain muscle elasticity. There is, however, debate as to the best types of stretching to use, what else stretching can achieve and the best time to do stretching.

It is important to understand the physiological processes occurring when a muscle is stretched. The stretch takes place in two places, in the sarcomere and within the connective tissue (see Figure 3.3, page 51). The muscle fibres that are being stretched, which is not all, will experience a decrease in the overlap between the two main protein filaments within the sarcomere, namely the actin and myosin. As the fibres are stretched this overlap will decrease as the filaments themselves are stretched and realigned. The remainder of the force of the stretch will be absorbed within the connective tissue, namely the tendons.

Located within the muscles are different types of proprioceptors (such as the muscle spindles and golgi tendons). These send messages back to the brain, via the central nervous system, which will instigate a resistance to the stretch; the degree of resistance will be matched by the degree of the stretch.

The aim of stretching is to recruit as many sarcomeres as possible and then to 'reprogramme' the proprioceptors to accept a more stretched muscle as the norm.

Generally, stretching will fall under two categories, either static or dynamic (i.e. stationary or moving) each of which can also be subdivided two categories, either passive or active (passive meaning that the stretching is being done to you while active means that you are performing the stretch yourself).

The following are examples of static and dynamic stretching.

active static stretch of hamstrings

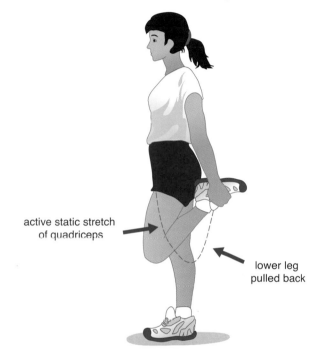

active static stretch of quadriceps

lower leg pulled back

Fig. 4.6 *Stretching a muscle*

STATIC STRETCHING

This is recognised as the safest mode of stretching as you maintain control of the movement. The muscle is taken to its current elastic limit and held in position; over time the muscle spindles and golgi tendons send a message to the brain that the new stretched position is not as severe as first identified.

The benefits of the stretch are not as pronounced as in other forms of stretch and it is not sports-specific, which has led many physiologists to question its role in warming up in order to prevent injury.

BALLISTIC STRETCHING

Ballistic stretching uses the momentum of a moving body or a limb in an attempt to force it beyond its normal range of motion. This type of stretching involves bouncing into (or out of) a stretched position using the stretched muscles as a spring to pull you out of the stretched position, e.g. bouncing down repeatedly to touch your toes.

It has often been considered as dangerous because of the short period of time that the sarcomeres are stretched. The danger is that the sarcomeres and the proprioceptors are not able to adjust, and the muscles respond by tightening up rather than stretching. The muscles should be thoroughly warmed and pre-stretched with a more controlled static stretch first, to avoid injury.

It is not considered suitable as a general stretching exercise because it can lead to an increased susceptibility of DOMS and, if performed incorrectly, to injury. However, it is sports specific and can lead to significant momentary gains in elasticity. It is best suited to short duration, high intensity explosive events such as the 100 metre or shot put events.

DYNAMIC STRETCHING

Dynamic stretching involves stretching the muscles through a full range of momentum and gradually increasing reach, speed of movement, or both. The major difference between dynamic and ballistic stretching is that ballistic stretching uses momentum to forcibly stretch the muscle while dynamic stretching uses controlled movements to enhance the stretch.

ACTIVE STRETCHING

An active stretch is one where you assume a position and then hold it there with no assistance other than using the strength of your muscles.

PASSIVE STRETCHING

A passive stretch, or relaxed stretch, is one where you assume a position and hold it with some other part of your body, or with the assistance of a partner or some other apparatus, for example, bringing your leg up high and then holding it there with your hand.

▶ *Flexibility exercises help stretch muscles, protect against injury and allow the maximum range of motion for joints*

PROPRIOCEPTIVE NEURO-MUSCULAR FACILITATION (PNF) STRETCHING

PNF stretching is currently the fastest and most effective way known to increase muscle elasticity and flexibility. It is a combination of passive stretching and isometric stretching in order to achieve maximum static flexibility. The muscle group is passively stretched, then contracts isometrically against a resistance while in the stretched position, and then is passively stretched again through the resulting increased range of motion. PNF stretching usually employs the use of a partner to provide resistance for the isometric contraction and then later to passively take the joint through its increased range of motion.

PRINCIPLES OF TRAINING

The principles of training are the rules that are applied to the methods of training in order to achieve the specific adaptations required to improve performance.

FITT (FREQUENCY, INTENSITY, TIME, TYPE)

Frequency, Intensity, Time, Type (FITT) describes how often you train. As exercise plus recovery provides the potential for improvement then it follows that the more often, or frequently, that you train the more you can improve. This is true only up to the point at which you train before you have fully recovered. If your body does not fully recover and you begin training then you will start regressing.

INTENSITY

Intensity is the variable that is likely to determine the outcome of your training. Unfortunately, the 'no pain, no gain' advocates have created an environment where many people believe that there is only one training intensity and that is maximal. Yet different training intensities will most certainly produce different training adaptations (see Table 4.2).

TIME OR DURATION

This is the length of the exercise period. Again, this is closely related to the training intensity as the greater the intensity the shorter the duration and vice versa. The duration has to be sufficient to create the necessary stimulus for the desired adaptations.

TYPE

This is the method of training specific to the sport games player. If you want to improve your aerobic and cardiovascular endurance then a 6 mile continuous training run might seem to be appropriate. However, although it would offer some benefits to you, unless you intend to run at a constant intensity throughout the duration of the game then it would not be totally appropriate. Fartlek training might be.

RECOVERY

Recovery is the amount of time to enable a full anabolic period (recovery) and is dependent upon the intensity and duration of the catabolic phase (exercise period). Getting the right amount of recovery is essential. The recovery period is when the adaptations in the body occur. Too much recovery and the body will begin to experience reversibility. Too little recovery and the body begins to regress. Other factors that need to be considered are the experience of the athlete and exposure to similar types and levels of training and the parts of the body exercised. For instance, a 60-minute heavy weight training session focused on the quadriceps might take as much as

HR training intensity (% of MHR)	Training adaptation	Weight training (based on % of 1RM)	Training adaptation
60%	critical threshold	60%	localised muscular endurance
60–70%	baseline aerobic/cardiovascular benefits	70–80%	dynamic strength
70–80%	anaerobic threshold	80–85%	increased mass/body shaping
80–90%	lactate tolerance	85–90%	power
90%+	VO_2 max	90–95%	maximal strength

Table 4.2 How different intensities can produce a very different end product

4 days to recover from, while a 4-hour cycle training ride could be repeated the following day.

APPLICATION OF FITNESS

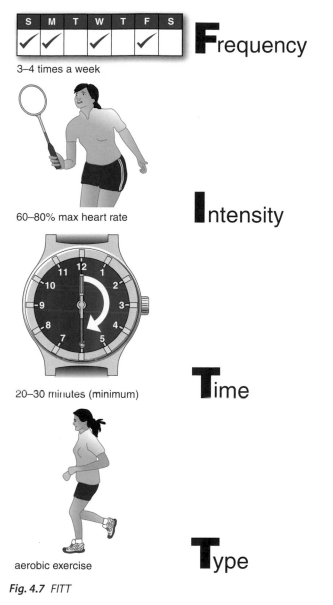

S	M	T	W	T	F	S
✓	✓		✓		✓	

Frequency

3–4 times a week

Intensity

60–80% max heart rate

Time

20–30 minutes (minimum)

Type

aerobic exercise

Fig. 4.7 *FITT*

SPECIFICITY

It is important to be aware of what the athlete is aiming to achieve and to choose specific and appropriate activities for training. Training should be mirroring significant aspects of the activity or sport.

INDIVIDUAL NEEDS

Every athlete will have their own individual needs and the focus of the training should be on these. For instance, if you are a football player, what is your position or role in the team? What are the fitness demands made on you? Both centre half and a full back are defenders yet they both have different fitness demands, so their needs are different and their training needs to reflect this. The training should reflect other factors such as gender, experience and levels of performance.

PROGRESSIVE OVERLOAD

Progressive overload is the need to increase training demands upon the body in order to encourage it to adapt further. Increases in training can come in a variety of forms: increasing training frequency, duration, intensity; decreasing rest periods within the training session. However, it is important that increases in training come in manageable increments and the limit of no more than 5 per cent a week is a good rule of thumb.

REGRESSION/REVERSIBILITY

The body adapts to its new environment; if that environment is a new training regime then the adaptations will be positive in terms of improved fitness. However, the new environment might be a less active phase caused either by injury-enforced lay-off or simply through too long a time between training sessions. The result will be that the body or part of the body will revert to pre-exercise levels of fitness.

VARIANCE

By varying your training not only will you avoid the monotony and potential boredom of performing the same routine over and over again, you will also help to avoid overtraining.

OVERTRAINING

Overtraining (often confused with overload) should be avoided, by allowing full recovery from the previous training before any more takes place. Occasional overtraining is manageable but repeated overtraining will lead to a decline in performance, loss of enthusiasm and motivation, reduction in muscle size, an inability to sleep, irritability and mood swings, and an increased susceptibility to illness and injury.

APPROPRIATENESS OF PROGRAMMES TO DIFFERING CLIENTS

Understanding the principle of individual needs means that every training programme will be tailored to one athlete.

YOUNG AND OLD

It is generally accepted that childhood is the best time to take part in regular sporting activity. Interests in sport, and abilities that are gained as a result of participation, are strong indicators that these may continue into adulthood. The converse is also true: if sport and physical activity is low in childhood, it is likely that this will be the case throughout life. Such inactivity may also lead to childhood obesity, which is likely to remain throughout adolescence and adulthood.

Exercise is associated with a reduction in the likelihood of the occurrence of cardiovascular heart disease, high blood pressure, and mature onset diabetes in later life, and participation is therefore to be encouraged during childhood. However, the effect of overtraining pre-pubescent children can also be extremely harmful. Repetitive training can cause injuries to bones and joints, as a result of incomplete bone growth in children. Other factors, also related to incomplete growth, are also affected, such as the fact that smaller heart size and lung size together with the larger surface area of the body compared to adults means that children are not as mechanically efficient as adults, and cannot control their body temperature as efficiently.

In summary, exercise for young children should be enjoyable and fun. However, it is important to stress the teaching of correct technique at an early age. This will prevent the occurrence of injury and will enable the child to refine his or her techniques to achieve possible elite sport performances in later life.

AGEING

It is a common assumption that beyond a certain age an athlete's fitness measures will gradually deteriorate, and performance levels will decrease. In some sports athletes were thought to be past their prime once they had reached their 20s. In recent years, the performances of a number of athletes have suggested that this assumption may not be absolutely true.

Linford Christie became an Olympic champion in his 30s, Merlene Ottey is another who remained at an elite level beyond an age that is generally accepted as normal, winning an Olympic medal at the age of 36 years. A number of boxers, notably George Foreman and Evander Holyfield, have made relatively successful come-backs in their 40s.

Unfortunately the use of performance-enhancing drugs has brought into question the achievements of many top-class performers; however, there is ample evidence to challenge the view that athletic performance should automatically drop off past 30 years of age.

Despite these exceptions, it is generally accepted that beyond 30 years of age, a degenerative process does occur, which tends to have a detrimental effect on an athlete's fitness measures. However, much of this degenerative process can be offset by maintaining activity levels, which, together with high motivation, may explain the performances of older elite athletes.

Strength tends to decline with age, as a result of the degeneration of the nerves supplying the muscles. Also, extra collagen fibres are laid down between the muscle fibres, which reduces the elasticity of the muscle, with a resultant decrease in movement efficiency. However, as with other capacities, it is possible to maintain strength with regular training.

Endurance also tends to decline as a result of extra collagen fibres in the cardiac muscle tissue, leading to a reduction in cardiac output. Maximum heart rate also tends to decline, which reduces the VO_2 max value of the athlete. Extra collagen fibres are also responsible for a reduction in elasticity of lung tissue, which has the effect of further reducing the endurance capabilities of the athlete. However, this can largely be offset through the natural enlargement of the heart resulting from years of aerobic training. There also tends to be a reduction in bone density with age, especially in females beyond menopausal age.

However, exercise can play an important role in maintaining bone density in both sexes. A general stiffening of the blood vessels, together with any cholesterol deposits in the walls of arteries, reduces the blood supply to many organs, and reduces the exercise capacities of the athlete.

It is important to remember that regular exercise can offset many of the effects of the ageing process, as studies have shown that many older athletes who have continued to train have shown only small declines in their exercise capacities.

TRAINED AND UNTRAINED

It is important to remember that improvements in fitness measures are a result of weeks or months of training, not a result of a single bout of exercise. The adaptations which occur will depend on the nature of the training. A 5 per cent increase in training load is widely recognised as being the very maximum increase that an athlete should experience. So the training load that an experienced athlete could endure would be far greater than for a novice athlete. The novice would be overtraining and likely to experience DOMS as well as susceptibility to injury if they were to attempt to copy a training programme of an experienced elite athlete.

ACTIVE AND SEDENTARY/ HEALTHY AND UNHEALTHY

The comparison between active and sedentary/ healthy and unhealthy performers would be similar to the differences between trained and untrained athletes, except the gap would be far greater. It is also absolutely essential that someone who has not undertaken physical activity, let alone been classed as being unhealthy, should undertake a thorough medical examination prior to undertaking any exercise. The exercise programme should be planned by an experienced professional.

FITNESS ASSESSMENT

The priority when tests are being performed should always be the health and well-being of the participants, and therefore any ethical considerations should be taken into account before commitment to fitness testing. When any type of testing is undertaken, it must be remembered that many things contribute to performance, and fitness tests are looking solely at one aspect. Other factors to be considered when testing include:

motivation – is the athlete really pushing themselves in the tests? Some tests require the athlete to work to near exhaustion.

testing environment – does it offer the athlete the best opportunity to perform? Are the tests truly replicating the sporting environment accurately?

In order to maximise the validity of a specific test, it may be necessary to repeat the test several times in order to minimise the possibility of human error.

Also tests are frequently criticised for not taking into account sports-specific movements or skills.

Before undertaking a fitness test you should be fully aware of:

- what you want to discover. Are you aware of the specific areas of fitness that you wish to discover?
- the validity of the test. Does the test chosen enable you to discover exactly what you want to know and is it reliable?
- the protocol of the test. Are you fully aware of how to run the test accurately?
- the current state of the athlete. Is the athlete up to the test both mentally and physically? Have they filled out a PAR-Q (Physical Activity Readiness Questionnaire)?
- informing the athlete. Is the athlete fully aware of the test that they are about to undertake and have they consented to it?

RATIONALE OF ASSESSMENT

There is a variety of reasons why athletes and coaches might undertake fitness testing; however, there are also a number of factors that need to be considered if the tests are to be worthwhile.

REASONS FOR TESTING

The following list provides a number of reasons why fitness tests might be carried out:

- to identify the strengths and weaknesses of the athlete
- to provide baseline data for planning and monitoring performance
- to provide the basis for applying the training principles
- to assess the value of different types of training and help to modify training programmes
- to predict physiological and athletic potential
- to provide comparisons with previous tests and other elite performers in the same group
- to enhance motivation
- to form part of the educational process.

MAXIMAL VERSUS SUB-MAXIMAL TESTS

Fitness tests come under two broad categories, those that are maximal and those that are sub-maximal.

Maximal tests tend to be progressive, making the athlete work progressively harder, until maximal effort occurs. Examples of maximal tests are the treadmill and bicycle ergometer VO_2 max tests, in which the speed or slope of the treadmill, or cycling resistance, are progressively increased until the athlete cannot continue. The same principle applies to the Multistage Fitness Test, in which the athlete runs progressively more quickly along a 20 metre course in time to a series of bleeps.

Sub-maximal tests tend to use heart rate response to exercise or power output as an indicator of the athlete's fitness. This is possible because oxygen uptake and heart rate tend to show a linear relationship (until relatively heavy exercise loads come into play). Therefore many tests, such as the Harvard Step Test, use heart recovery rates as an indicator of aerobic fitness values.

VALIDITY AND RELIABILITY

Numerous fitness tests can be carried out; however, they need to be both valid and reliable to give them any value.

The validity of a fitness test will depend on whether it measures a fitness component relevant to the sport. For example, timing a 100 metre race might seem an appropriate way to test speed. However, does the test measure speed alone or do reaction time, acceleration and anaerobic capacity play a significant part in the results?

The ability to reproduce a test under exactly the same conditions offers a measure of reliability. Does the test measure accurately the necessary components with the only variable being that of fitness? For example, performing the NCF Multistage Shuttle Fitness Test outside on a grass pitch might seem appropriate. However, weather and surface changes, place of the test on the field and getting the distance between the cones accurate are all variables that might make the results of the test worthless.

TECHNOLOGY IN TESTING

Technology plays an undisputed role in sport, both for the athlete, as they seek to get an edge over their opponents, and for the manufacturer who can use the sports arena as a testing ground for their products in the hope of mass commercial appeal thereafter.

From the athlete's perspective technology can aid them in a variety of ways: better, lighter, stronger equipment, better training aids and supplements

and also better access to the measure of their own performances.

FITNESS TESTING

The use of technology in fitness tests has taken this area of training to a very different level. As laboratory tests become more accessible, e.g. home lactic/anaerobic threshold testing packages, heart rate, power output monitors and so on, then so continues the development of laboratory tests for the elite.

▶ *The technological revolution has brought many useful tools for elite athletes*

Elite athletes may require greater objectivity in their results if they are to compare themselves accurately with other elite performers in their group. Specialised laboratories have therefore been established which dedicate themselves to sports testing. One such laboratory is the Human Performance Centre at Lilleshall, another is the National Sports Medicine Institute at St Bartholomew's Hospital, and an example of some of the tests they now administer on the elite sports performer is illustrated in the photograph.

With gas analysis, biomechanical analysis and the facility to make use of very advanced equipment, it is now possible to undertake fitness tests that are totally reliable.

CASE STUDY
HIGH-TECH DATA

For under £400 it is now possible to buy a polar heart rate monitor and power output sensor. This sensor and monitor, which is also a watch, can be attached to a bike to provide a wealth of information. On completion of the training ride the monitor will download to a PC information regarding pedalling cadence, altitude, speed, heart rate and power output. Not only does it inform the athlete of the power he or she is producing, but it analyses it further so the power produced by either leg at any stage of the cycling circle is given. The athlete can now analyse what would be the most efficient pedalling style by comparing heart rate and power with altitude and cadence, all for the comparative cost of a home game video console.

- Does technology create more pressure or less pressure for modern-day athletes?

PROTOCOL OF RECOGNISED FITNESS TESTS

Completing a physical activity readiness questionnaire (PAR-Q) is a valuable task if a programme of fitness is about to be undertaken. For most people, physical activity should not pose any problems. The questionnaire has been designed to identify the small number of people for whom physical activity might be inappropriate or who should seek medical advice concerning the type of activity most suitable for them.

APPLY IT!

Figure 4.8 shows an example of a PAR-Q. Create your own questionnaire that would provide you with the information that you believe would be necessary to allow people to undertake exercise under your care.

TESTS FOR DIFFERENT COMPONENTS OF FITNESS

STRENGTH

The one repetition maximum test (1 rep max or 1RM) is a recognised test for maximal strength. Here the athlete performs one repetition with the greatest possible resistance. By definition this will be the greatest resistance that they can perform in one complete repetition without struggling or losing form. Similarly a 12RM test could be used to measure dynamic strength and a 25RM test could measure localised muscular endurance.

Anaerobic capacity (defined as the amount of time for which maximum output can be maintained) is measured using the Wingate Test. Each athlete is required to perform a maximal 30 second bout of exercise (sprint) on a bicycle ergometer, which has been specially linked to a microcomputer. During the bout of exercise the computer records the peak power reached, which relates to the body's explosive power as well as the mean power. This is an indication of the body's ability to sustain high intensity effort. The percentage of fatigue sustained can also be recorded.

Those athletes who are able to sustain and achieve high levels of power throughout the test are those with the greatest ability in anaerobic events.

The Wingate Test can also be used to predict anaerobic power values, such as peak and average anaerobic power.

POWER

Simple tests for power include the standing board jump and the Sargent jump.

A standing board jump involves the distance travelled from a stationary two-footed jump.

In the standing Sargent jump the athlete stands sideways against a wall or vertical object. His or her maximum vertical reach height is measured before he or she performs a stationary two-footed jump reaching as high as possible. Their maximum reach height is subtracted from their maximum jump height to give a value indicating their leg power. A standing Sargent jump is a better indicator of power as less jumping technique is required.

Physical Activity Readiness Questionnaire (PAR-Q)

PAR-Q is designed to help you help yourself. Many health benefits are associated with regular exercise, and the completion of PAR-Q is a sensible first step to take if you are planning to increase the amount of physical activity in your life.

Common sense is your best guide in answering these few questions. Please read them carefully and check **YES** or **NO** opposite the question if it applies to you. If yes, please explain.

YES **NO**

☐ ☐ 1) Has your doctor ever said you have heart trouble?
         Yes, _____

☐ ☐ 2) Do you frequently have pains in your heart or chest?
         Yes, _____

☐ ☐ 3) Do you often feel faint or have spells of severe dizziness?
         Yes, _____

☐ ☐ 4) Has your doctor ever said your blood pressure was too high?
         Yes, _____

☐ ☐ 5) Has your doctor ever told you that you have a bone or joint problem(s), such as arthritis that has been aggravated by exercise, or might be made worse with exercise?
         Yes, _____

☐ ☐ 6) Is there a good physical reason, not mentioned here, why you should not follow an activity program even if you wanted to?
         Yes, _____

☐ ☐ 7) Are you over 60 and not accustomed to vigorous exercise?
         Yes, _____

☐ ☐ 8) Do you suffer from any problems of the lower back, i.e. chronic pain, or numbness?
         Yes, _____

☐ ☐ 9) Are you currently taking any medications? If YES, please specify.
         Yes, _____

☐ ☐ 10) Do you currently have a disability or a communicable disease? If YES, please specify.
         Yes, _____

If you answered NO to all questions above, it gives a general indication that you may participate in physical and aerobic fitness activities and/or fitness evaluation testing. The fact that you answered No to the above questions, is no guarantee that you will have a normal response to exercise. If you answered Yes to any of the above questions, then you need written permission from a physician before participating in physical and aerobic fitness activities and/or fitness evaluation testing.

_____   _____   _____

Print Name   Signature   Date

Please Note: If you contract a communicable disease, it is your responsibility to inform the staff of the Fitness Centre of this condition and your membership may be suspended until this condition is cured or in a state of remission.

Fig. 4.8 *Physical Activity Readiness Questionnaire (PAR-Q)*

SPEED

The simplest measure of speed is a 30 metre sprint. A 30 metre flat area is marked out with sufficient space for the athlete to accelerate up to full speed before reaching the beginning of the 30 metre area. The time to cover the 30 metres is the speed travelled. The main drawback in this test is that it may prove difficult to record accurately, especially if you do not have access to expensive lighting and camera equipment.

FLEXIBILITY

The sit and reach test can be easily administered and provides a good indication of the flexibility of the hamstring muscles and the lower back. This involves the athlete sitting down on the floor with his or her legs out straight and feet flat against a sit and reach box. Without bending the knees, bending forwards with arms outstretched, the athlete pushes the cursor on the sit and reach box as far down as possible and holds for 2 seconds. The score is recorded.

Fig. 4.9 Sit and reach test

ENDURANCE

VO₂ MAX

VO_2 max (not to be confused with cardiovascular endurance) is defined as the maximum amount of oxygen that an individual can take in, transport and utilise per minute per kilogram of body weight.

A simple prediction of VO_2 max can be made through the NCF (National Coaching Foundation) multistage fitness test. This is a progressive shuttle run test as it is easy to start with and gets increasingly difficult.

An athlete is required to run a 20 metre distance as many times as possible, keeping in time to the bleeps emitted from a tape. Each shuttle of 20 metres should be timed so that the athlete reaches the end line as the bleep is emitted. The difficulty increases with each level attained, and the speed of running will need to be increased accordingly. The athlete runs for as long as possible until he or she can no longer keep up with the bleeps set by the tape. If the 20 metre shuttle is not reached before the bleep is emitted then the athlete should withdraw from the test, ensuring that the level and shuttle number attained have been recorded.

The multistage fitness test gives a reasonable prediction of VO_2 max, but it is purely a prediction and not a truly objective measure of the volume of oxygen that the body can take in, transport and utilise. Gas analysis is perhaps the most accurate measure of this.

In gas analysis an athlete uses one of any laboratory ergometers (treadmills, cycle or rowing machines tend to be the most popular), while breathing through respiratory apparatus which is linked to a computer. The computer analyses the relative concentrations of oxygen and carbon dioxide inspired and expired. Since the concentrations of these in the surrounding environment are known, it is fairly simple to calculate the amount of oxygen consumed and the amount of carbon dioxide produced over time. The athlete continues to work at increasingly higher intensities, until a time is reached when oxygen consumption does not increase further with increasing workloads. This is the athlete's aerobic limit, and any further increments in workload will be met through anaerobic means. This is the point of maximal oxygen uptake, and the amount of oxygen being consumed can now be recorded.

VO_2 max can be measured in absolute terms, i.e. 1/mm for non-weight bearing activities such as swimming, cycling and rowing, or relative to body weight in ml/kg/min (millilitres of oxygen per kilogram of body weight per minute). The higher the value of VO_2 max, the more efficient is the body at exercising under aerobic conditions.

The Cooper 12 minute run is another endurance test used to predict VO_2 max. It only requires a stopwatch and a 400 metre track. An athlete runs or walks continuously for 12 minutes, maintaining a constant pace throughout. A prediction of the VO_2 max can be calculated using the following formula:

$0.0225 \times$ metres covered $- 11.3$

So, for 3000 metres, for example:

$0.0225 \times 3000 - 11.3 = 56.2$ ml/kg/min

CARDIOVASCULAR ENDURANCE

The Harvard step test is a good measure for cardiovascular endurance. The athlete steps up on to a standard gym bench once every 2 seconds for 5 minutes (150 steps).

One minute after finishing the test take the pulse rate (bpm) – Pulse 1

Two minutes after finishing the test take the pulse rate (bpm) – Pulse 2

Three minutes after finishing the test take the pulse rate (bpm) – Pulse 3

This test uses heat recovery rates as an indicator of aerobic fitness.

Another test for endurance is the onset of blood lactate accumulation (OBLA) test. This lactate threshold is the point at which the body appears to convert to anaerobic energy production. Below the lactate threshold the body works aerobically and prolonged exercise can take place, with a blood lactate volume of 2–3 mmol per litre of blood. Exercise above the lactate threshold (which usually occurs at 4 mmol per litre of blood) can only usually be sustained for approximately one minute. For example, think of how your legs feel at the end of a flat-out 400 metre run!

The test is performed in four stages where athletes are required to run at speeds of 8, 9, 10 and finally 11 miles per hour. At the end of each stage blood samples are taken by a small prick on the finger, and analysed for blood lactate. The point at which blood lactate rises significantly indicates the point of onset of blood lactate accumulation, and the running speed which corresponds to this is recorded. Improvements in endurance ability can be observed where lower lactate levels are recorded for the same intensity of exercise; this shows that the body has adapted to cope better with this intensity of exercise through buffering lactic acid.

LOCALISED MUSCULAR ENDURANCE

A test for muscular endurance will assess the ability of one muscle or muscle group to continue working repeatedly. A simple test to measure the endurance of the abdominal muscle group is the NCF abdominal conditioning test. Athletes are required to perform as many sit-ups as possible, keeping in time to the bleeps emitted from a tape. Count the number of sit-ups completed correctly, and time the duration of the

work period. Athletes should withdraw from the test when they can no longer keep in time to the bleeps, or when technique deteriorates noticeably.

AGILITY

Agility can be measured through the Illinois test which measures an athlete's ability to change direction quickly. The athlete runs around cones on a marked-out course (see Figure 4.10).

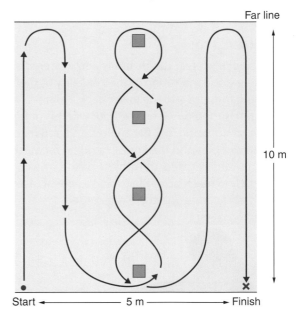

Fig. 4.10 Agility course for an athlete involves changing direction quickly

The athlete begins in a prone position behind the base line. When he or she starts the time is recorded. The course should be covered as quickly as possible and the test performed three times in order to calculate an average.

BODY COMPOSITION

Body fat is measured in a variety of ways:

- Hydrostatic weighing measures water displacement when the body is submerged in water.
- Bio-electrical impedance is another popular objective measure whereby a small electrical current is passed through the body from wrist to ankle. As fat restricts the flow of the current, the greater the current needed the greater the percentage of body fat.
- By measuring of skinfold using callipers.

Skinfold measures are the simplest measure of body fat.

- On the left side of the body, take measures at the following sites: biceps, triceps, sub scapular, supra iliac.

- Add the totals together in millimetres and record your results.

- At this stage, you may wish to make some other measures such as length of bones and overall height, muscle girths or circumferences, and **condyle** measures at the joints.

> ### KEY TERM
> **condyle**
> the knuckle of any joint

As well as measuring these physical or health-related factors, it is also possible to assess skill-related components.

TASK

Research how each of the following can be used to calculate an athlete's body composition. Then evaluate which you think would be the best test.

Body Mass Index (BMI)

Hydrostatic weighing (also known as hydrodensitometry or underwater weighing)

Dual-Energy X-ray Absorptiometry (DEXA)

Near Infrared Interactance

Total Body Potassium (TBK)

Whole-body Air-Displacement Plethysmography (BodPod)

Magnetic Resonance Imaging (MRI)

Total Body Electrical Conductivity (TOBEC)

Computed Tomography (CT)

Total Body Protein (TBP)

TASK

Rank in order of importance three components of fitness for you in your sport.

Devise a fitness test that would measure each of the three components that would score at least 9 out of 10 for both validity and reliability for you in your sport.

Predict your fitness levels for the three components.

APPLY IT!

Carry out the three tests you described in the task below. How did your predictions compare with the actual results?

TAKE IT FURTHER

- *Compare and contrast the reliability of the RPE scale (recognised perceived exertion) with that of the heart rate.*

- *You will need a heart rate monitor for this activity. First of all, calculate your critical threshold (at 60 per cent of MHR) using Karnoven's Principle (see page 69). Now, grade your running speed on a scale of 1–10 (where 1 is walking speed and 10 is maximum sprint speed). Run for 20 minutes at what you perceive to be 0.6 (60 per cent) while wearing the HRM. DO NOT check the HRM during the run.*

- *After the run compare what you perceived to be 60 per cent with the data from the HRM. How accurate were you?*

ExamCafé
Relax, refresh, result!

Revision checklist

▷ Know and be able to define the different components of fitness

▷ Be able to apply the components to different sports

▷ Be able to identify and rank the importance of the components to your own sport

▷ Know the different methods of training

▷ Be able to apply the methods to particular sports and specific training benefits/ adaptations

▷ Know what the principles of training are

▷ Be able to apply the principles of training to training programmes suitable for different people with different needs

▷ Know why and when to carry out fitness tests

▷ Know how to make tests reliable and valid

▷ Know the names and protocols of fitness tests for the components of fitness

Get the result !

Sample question and answer

Exam question

Identify **two** contrasting sporting events and name the most appropriate fitness test for each event. Identify the main component of fitness for **one** of the events chosen. Select a fitness test that would be suitable for that component but not for that athlete and explain why. **(3 marks)**

Student answer

The component of fitness for my chosen event of 800 metres freestyle is VO_2 max. A fitness test that is suitable for measuring VO_2 max is the bleep test. It is not valid because a swimmer does not run and this test measures your VO_2 max while running.

Examiner says:

Nearly an excellent full mark answer that is badly let down by a poor use of appropriate language.

The candidate clearly knows where the marks are allocated and has structured the answer clearly and appropriately.

The activity/sport is stated and the component of fitness is also appropriate. This gets the first of the three available marks.

The choice of fitness test would be suitable for the component of fitness but not for the identified athlete and would have scored the second mark and also the third mark for a succinctly explained justification.

However, the candidate failed to name the test properly. To call it the 'bleep test' is lazy and fails to score the mark. It also prevents the candidate from scoring the following mark.

So what could have been a maximum scoring answer of 3 out of 3 has actually scored a low 1 out of 3.

UNIT 1
PARTICIPATION IN SPORT AND RECREATION

PART B
OPPORTUNITIES AND PATHWAYS

In this section we take a more sociological view of the current provision for sport and recreation. This begins with a review of how competitive sport has developed in the UK and how this development has shaped the current provision of both sport and recreation.

CHAPTER 5 *THE DEVELOPMENT OF COMPETITIVE SPORT*

LEARNING OUTCOMES

By working through this chapter, you should:

- understand the role of festivals in the history of sport
- understand the emergence of rational sport as a result of the Industrial Revolution
- understand the characteristics of sport in the twentieth and twenty-first century
- understand the concept of deviance in sport

FESTIVALS OF SPORT

Pre-industrial society was characterised by limited leisure time and sports were closely associated with the church calendar of holy days and festivals. Most people lived and worked in isolated rural communities and there was little travel. Pre-industrial society was split into two basic sections – the gentry and the peasants. These two groups generally kept well apart though there was some overlap in sport. The gentry who were the landowners had more time for play, less discomfort and better food and housing.

KEY TERM

pre-industrial society (in the UK)
the period of time before the Industrial Revolution, in the second half of the eighteenth century and the first half of the nineteenth century

ANCIENT ORIGINS

Most early sports were used in preparation for war or to develop hunting skills and because of this many were referred to as combat sports, such as archery. The Greeks and the Romans were the first to establish sporting festivals that served as celebrations as well the functional use of preparing men to fight.

After the Norman Conquest of 1066 in Britain a new social order began to establish itself. It was a time of unrest, instability and war. There was a need for all men, whatever their rank and class, to maintain their fighting fitness. The development of combat sports followed.

The gentry trained their skills through the joust and tournament. These took place in confined areas (royal showgrounds), often with purpose-built grandstands to allow spectators to watch the action. The contests were very much festivals with colour and pageantry but they acted as important social meeting places, also. However, after the invention of gunpowder, which made the heavily armoured horsemen out of date, these festivals and tournaments were held less often and gradually died out.

CASE STUDY   JOUSTING

The joust was brought to the UK during the Norman Conquest. Its main role was to train knights on horseback. Originally the tournament took the form of a mock battle with soldiers, both on horseback and on foot, fighting in an enclosed area. They used blunted weapons, though injury and death were still common. By the end of the fourteenth century these mock battles had been replaced by the more individual and spectacular joust, a duel between two knights. These were complex contests with rules and judges called heralds who adjudicated and kept the score. The competitions ran along the idea of a knockout – the winner of each heat going forward to the next round until the best two knights of the day would meet in the final.

- Why was jousting confined to the upper classes?

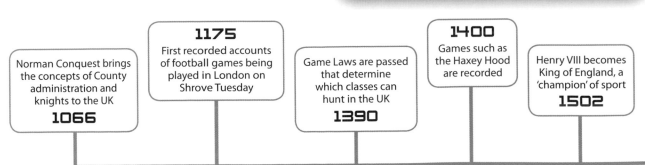

1066 Norman Conquest brings the concepts of County administration and knights to the UK

1175 First recorded accounts of football games being played in London on Shrove Tuesday

1390 Game Laws are passed that determine which classes can hunt in the UK

1400 Games such as the Haxey Hood are recorded

1502 Henry VIII becomes King of England, a 'champion' of sport

Fig. 5.1 Pre-Industrial sport timeline

Archery was the requisite military skill for the lower classes. The longbow was an essential part of English military strategy. A succession of English kings made it compulsory for all men to own a bow and to practise on Sundays. Competitions were often set up by the local gentry to help motivate this practice and these too became social gatherings.

FESTIVAL GAMES

The time available for sport during the **Middle Ages** was often restricted to holy days. Travel was difficult and so recreational activities were local and used ready-to-hand materials. Recreational activities changed throughout the year. In winter, mass games such as mob football were played. These were often violent contests with few rules. In summer, gentler, more individual and athletic-type activities were followed, such as smock races and sledge hammer throwing. It is important to recognise that sport and recreation reflected the split of pre-industrial society into two basic sections – the gentry and the peasants. In general the gentry played more individual and sophisticated activities such as real tennis while the peasants were restricted to the so-called mob games.

KEY TERMS

Middle Ages
the historical period from 400 to 1500 AD

invasion game
a game where players seek to avoid one another in order to score while invading the 'territory' of the other team

The sporting year began sometimes as early as New Year's Day and Plough Monday (the first Monday after Christmas) when games were held. The real celebrations came slightly later with spring fertility festivals. The highlight of spring was Shrove Tuesday when all around the British Isles violent forms of

football and other **invasion games** were played as a last release of aggression before Lent. May Day was often marked by games in which young men chased women, again a tradition concerned with the ritual of fertility. Whitsuntide was the high point of the sporting year with much dancing and games. This was a slack time for agriculture and animals and crops were left to graze and grow. The church often provided space as well as time to play these games with the local gentry offering patronage and donating prizes.

POPULAR RECREATIONS

Mob games such as the Haxey Hood in Lincolnshire, the Ashbourne Shrovetide football game and Hurling in Cornwall are all examples of what are referred to as popular recreations. These are called mob games as they involved huge numbers of players; teams were often over 100 a side. They often involved whole villages and teams were selected on criteria such as 'uppers' and 'downers' (one or other side of a river), or alternatively single men against married men.

▶ *A mob game of football*

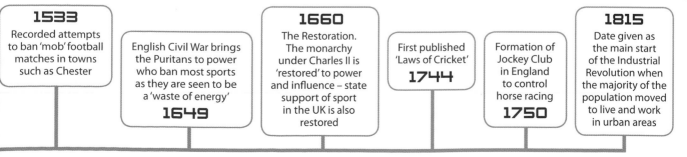

1533
Recorded attempts to ban 'mob' football matches in towns such as Chester

English Civil War brings the Puritans to power who ban most sports as they are seen to be a 'waste of energy'
1649

1660
The Restoration. The monarchy under Charles II is 'restored' to power and influence – state support of sport in the UK is also restored

First published 'Laws of Cricket'
1744

Formation of Jockey Club in England to control horse racing
1750

1815
Date given as the main start of the Industrial Revolution when the majority of the population moved to live and work in urban areas

CASE STUDY
ASHBOURNE ROYAL SHROVETIDE FOOTBALL

Shrovetide football is a game which is at least four hundred years old, and is still played each year on Shrove Tuesday and Ash Wednesday in the Derbyshire town of Ashbourne. It is a mob game with two teams of Up'ards and Down'ards (decided on whether you were born north or south of the river that runs through the centre of the town). There are few rules. The game is played between two millstones set in the bank of the river three miles apart that act as the goals. The game begins each day at 2.00 pm when a ball gets tossed into the mob, and can last till 10.00 pm. The game can go anywhere in the town apart from the cemetery, churchyard or memorial gardens. The royal connection comes from 1928 when the Prince of Wales started the game, a tradition maintained by the current Prince of Wales who also started the game in 2003!

■ How does such a sport function with so few rules?

TASK

Use the Internet to see if you can find any popular recreation or festival games that are linked to your local area. They can be historic or contemporary.

TAKE IT FURTHER

How did sport in the pre-industrial era reflect the pre-industrial society?

THE OLYMPIC GAMES

Sport is very popular around the world and major events like the Olympic Games and World Cup football are televised and followed in every country.

The Olympic Games have their origins in Ancient Greece, where they were held every four years as part of a religious ceremony to the god Zeus. During the latter part of the nineteenth century a number of people including Dr William Penny Brookes and Baron Pierre de Coubertin began to work towards re-introducing an Olympic festival. An early attempt had been made in the Cotswolds where a local barrister,

Robert Dover, had established a long running Olympick Games held every Whitsuntide. Brookes himself had developed a similar festival held at a small Shropshire town called Much Wenlock.

The Much Wenlock Olympian games are still held every year. Based on these models and his study of the sport in British schools, de Coubertin launched the modern Olympic Games in Athens in 1896, also setting up the **International Olympic Committee (IOC)**. The IOC is responsible for organising the summer and winter Olympic Games every four years.

De Coubertin had wider objectives for the games: he hoped they might help prevent war and develop more international friendship. The games for most of the twentieth century were amateur, with performers competing purely for enjoyment. Sportsmanship was the central point to the games. However, the increasing commercialisation of sport has seen this eroded and Olympic gold medal winners are now very attractive to sponsors and the media.

KEY TERM

International Olympic Committee (IOC)
the governing body for the Olympic movement

HOTLINKS

Check out the IOC website:
http://www.olympic.org/uk/index_uk.asp

The IOC organises each Games every four years, choosing the host city and co-ordinating the huge amounts of money it now takes to stage the Games. Most of the IOC's income comes from selling the festoon (the five ring logo) to multinational sponsors and media rights to broadcasters.

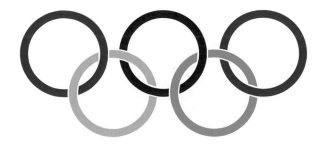

Fig. 5.2 The Olympic rings, one for each of the continents united in sport

TASK

The Haxey Hood game involves groups playing for possession of a rolled cloak. In Hurling a small ball is kicked and thrown over a pitch over 14 square miles in size.

See if you can research and find out more facts about these historic games.

EXAM TIP

Be prepared to use and describe at least two different popular recreations in your examination answers.

INTERNATIONAL SPORTS FESTIVALS

At the start of the twentieth century most of the popular sports began to establish international sports bodies and these in turn began to organise international fixtures and competitions. These tend to be run along the lines of two models: a festival approach where countries play in a series of games and events over a period of up to three weeks, or a knock-out format where rounds are played with the winning team progressing through to the next round.

The big events such as the FIFA World Cup and the Commonwealth Games are now run on a similar pattern to the Olympics every four years – other events such as the Athletics and Cricket World Cup are run on a shorter rotation. Like the Olympics, all international sports festivals rely on funding from sponsors and media rights.

TAKE IT FURTHER

Can you identify the common characteristics that all global games now follow in the twenty-first century?

REMEMBER

- Sport in pre-industrial Britain was linked to a need for war preparation.
- Early sports were divided by social class and background.
- The church and local gentry were important in the organisation of festival games.
- The modern Olympic games are a combination of ancient and modern festivals.
- Pre-industrial sport was unruly, mob-like, violent and restricted by geography.
- Rational sport was formal, standardised and played across the whole country.

THE EMERGENCE OF 'RATIONAL SPORT' AS A PRODUCT OF THE INDUSTRIAL REVOLUTION

SPORT AFTER THE INDUSTRIAL REVOLUTION

Sport in the post-industrial phase is characterised by the development of **codification** and administration. The Industrial Revolution was the period in history when the majority of people living in the country moved from rural areas to living and working in cities and urban areas. With that the influence of the rural elements from the popular recreation era steadily declined (modern sport is also urban sport). In this time of change came opportunity, especially for entrepreneurs and professionals who emerged as a new social class (the middle classes) with a very important influence on the development of sport.

Codification involved the creation and maintenance of a set of national rules. The developing transport system meant that teams and individuals could travel out of their local areas to compete on a national scale. This highlighted the problems of local versions of games and local rules. In most cases, each sport appointed a national governing body (NGB), which standardised the rules for the sport. The NGBs then began to develop more area fixtures and competitions.

KEY TERM

codification
the creation and maintenance of national sports rules

These are some of the factors that influenced the progress of sport as a result of the changes in the way people lived and worked in the post-industrial period:

Urbanisation meant large populations moving into the cities and towns where there was a lack of space for recreation.

Industrialisation led to life based around the factory system and machine time. The old 'holy' days were largely lost and work was no longer organised around the seasons – every week was a busy time.

Working conditions initially were very poor for the lower classes, with long shifts and little free time. The twentieth century saw a gradual increase in free time; legislation brought in the Saturday half day, the Ten Hour Act and early closing for shop workers.

Economics characterised by the systems of capitalism and industrial patronage led to the formation of work and church teams, which often developed into professional clubs. Sport had become part of the entertainment business and many entrepreneurs saw that money could be made from it.

The development of rationalised sport began in **public schools** (fee-paying schools attended by the upper classes) and was spread by old boys, church and schoolmasters working in local communities. Active manly recreations were seen as a means of social control, keeping both schoolboys and the working classes out of trouble, while at the same time developing skills and virtues that would be

TAKE IT FURTHER

Explain how societal changes during the Industrial Revolution had a major influence on the development of sport.

useful to the ever-expanding British Empire.

THE EMERGENCE OF CODIFICATION

Organised games began to appear in public schools at first as spontaneous recreations and, for the most part, were disapproved of by the teachers. However, as the games became more developed it was recognised that educational objectives could be passed on through participation in games. Sports became a feature of all public schools. The main sports were football and cricket (and rowing at schools situated on suitable rivers). These activities were physically demanding and relied on co-operation and leadership.

KEY TERM

public school
a private, independent, fee-paying school

CASE STUDY PUBLIC SCHOOL FOOTBALL

Each school developed its own version of a football game. The format of the game differed according to the environmental and social make-up of the school. Where there were large numbers of boys in the school, large-scale mob games were developed. At Eton School the playing area was initially restricted because the school was bound by a large wall and consequently they incorporated the wall into their game – the Eton Wall Game. Later when the school expanded and gained more grounds a second more expansive game – the Eton Field Game – was introduced. Rugby School had large playing fields and the game they developed reflected this with players able to kick and run with the ball. At Winchester School, their game was played in the river meadows, where the pitch was long with a low net run down one of the touch lines, probably to stop the ball ending up in the river.

■ Why was it not a problem that each school had a different version of football?

The Industrial Revolution created a new affluent social class – the middle class, resulting in a huge market for private education. Sport became a central part of the new schools that were built and opened to satisfy this demand. The development of sport within the schools systems was to play an important part in the further development of sport not just in Britain but across the globe. The boys who left the public schools spread the games cult across the world.

C – Colonial Many former public school boys took up posts in the colonial service, helping to administer and govern the British Empire. They took with them their sporting kits, initially playing amongst their own community, but gradually the games and sports filtered through into the indigenous populations until they became established.

A – Army Another career for many school-leavers was as commissioned officers in the armed forces. Initially the officers used sport as a recreation to fill the long hours, but the social control and moral value of keeping the working-class soldiers occupied was not lost on them. This played an important part in spreading the cult still further.

T – Teaching Many former pupils became teachers, especially in the now expanding grammar schools. Often, they simply repeated the programme of games and physical recreations they had followed in their own school days.

P – Patronage Patrons supported sporting events and competitions, for example by providing funding for trophies or land for pitches.

U – University This was a very important stage. Cambridge and Oxford Universities (often shortened to Oxbridge) provided students further time and resources to pursue sporting activities. One major problem was the plethora of different rules for various games. In order to allow everyone to play, compromise rules were required and this was the first step towards the rationalisation of sport.

I – Industry Once they had finished school, many boys returned to find work in their fathers' factories and businesses. Their love of sport provided the catalyst for teams, clubs and societies to be set up within the work environment and many were linked to these factories and businesses. At first there were some social limits and only managers and office staff could join but gradually the working classes were also admitted. Many teams, such as Manchester United, Arsenal, Stoke City and West Ham, were formed in this way.

C – Church Much of the boys' education in school was based on religion, so it was not surprising that many took up careers in the church. Muscular Christianity promoted the use of sport as a vehicle for teaching morals and Christian virtues. Many clergy used it in its most practical form, encouraging sports and setting up teams both here and abroad. Again there are examples in modern football – Aston Villa, Everton, Southampton and Wolverhampton Wanderers have church origins.

C – Clubs The first impulse for many old boys enthusiastic about their sport was to form clubs so they could continue to play with each other and take part. The Old Etonians is an example of this type of club, but many were formed and still exist today.

A – Administration When their playing days were over, many men joined governing bodies and developed their sports by helping to formulate national rules.

EXAM TIP

An effective way of memorising this impact is the mnemonic CAT PUICCA.

THE ROLE OF OXBRIDGE

The role of Oxford and Cambridge Universities was key in the development of modern sport and is often referred to as 'the melting pot'. This reflects the process whereby the prospective students brought to university many different rules for the same game and it was here that there was an attempt to rationalise the rules and create one standardised set. A good example of this was the Cambridge rules of football drawn up by a committee of undergraduates in 1848.

The Oxbridge rules did not fully solve the problem and it was the formation of governing bodies beginning with the formation of the FA (Football Association) in 1863 that finally established **rational sport**.

The new governing bodies not only governed and controlled their own sports in the UK but, due to the status of the British Empire, many of our governing bodies became the world's sports regulators. The Lawn Tennis Association and the Royal and Ancient Club (golf) are examples. The competitions these two bodies set up (Wimbledon and the Open Championship) became world-renowned events.

▶ *Varsity matches between Oxford and Cambridge Universities contributed to the development of modern sport*

KEY TERM

Blue
a person who has represented either Oxford or Cambridge University in their sport (blue is the colour of the team blazer: light for Cambridge; dark for Oxford)

REMEMBER

■ In the nineteenth century the combination of the physical and moral was of paramount importance and playing honourably was more important than winning.

TAKE IT FURTHER

Explain why the world plays sport that originated in the UK.

SPORT IN THE TWENTIETH AND TWENTY-FIRST CENTURIES

INTO THE TWENTIETH CENTURY

By the beginning of the twentieth century sport had evolved to match the urban/industrial society. It was now governed by independent bodies who regulated their sport and oversaw competitions including national leagues and challenge cups. Their net of influence spread far and wide over most of the globe and international competition began. The commercial side of sport was evolving, with professional performers and '**spectatorism**' creating commercial clubs and purpose-built stadiums.

THE DEVELOPMENT OF PROFESSIONAL SPORT AND 'SPECTATORISM'

The other major development was that the working classes generally were given Saturday afternoons off and consequently this became the time for sport. Church and factory teams soon emerged and many entrepreneurs, with an eye for making money, set

up teams. The demand for regular fixtures was twofold: so that players could play each other and a match could attract spectators. With the money from the spectators the clubs were able to pay their players. The more spectators they attracted the more money there was to pay players and pay for better players. Soon an elite group of professional teams, mainly from the Midlands and North of England, came together to form the Football League in 1888. Cricket's County Championship developed in a similar way into a regular system of fixtures with points and a championship. In rational sport few played and many watched, which contrasted directly with the popular recreation of the seventeenth and eighteenth centuries, where many played and few watched.

KEY TERMS

rational sport
sport with set rules and national organisation (the progress of which coincided with the development of modern society in the UK during the nineteenth century)

spectatorism
sport as a spectacle where people pay to watch sport

THE OLYMPIC CASE STUDY

In the past the Olympic Games were used to promote all that was good in sport. All competitors were amateurs competing purely for enjoyment and, although the winner received a medal, it had no monetary value. However, as the modern games moved into the second half of the twentieth century, television coverage opened up a huge global audience. This had the effect of making the games very attractive to commercial sponsors.

The first Modern Olympic Games were held in Athens in 1896. They were founded by Baron de Coubertin, a French aristocrat. He had studied the Ancient Olympics, but drew most of his inspiration from the English public schools. He travelled extensively during the 1880s and 1890s researching for a programme to reform French education. He was concerned that the French were physically degenerating and wanted to revitalise the youth of the nation through physical activity. It was on these travels that he also fostered the idea of developing an international sports movement.

De Coubertin had read the novel *Tom Brown's Schooldays* and was drawn to Rugby School to search

REMEMBER

- Cambridge and Oxford Universities played an important role in the development of sport.
- They were the first place where compromise rules were developed.
- They also developed regular fixtures – Varsity matches.
- **Blues** became important role models and teachers.

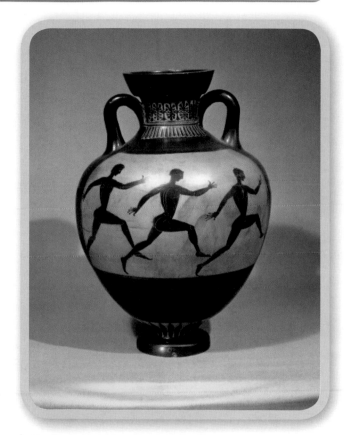

▶ *Greek amphora depicting Ancient Olympic Games*

out the concept of **athleticism**. He was convinced that the English public school tradition of games-playing had been responsible for the great growth in England's power in the nineteenth century and he wanted to export this ideal to France.

KEY TERM

athleticism
describing the characteristics that were attributed to the experience of playing competitive sport in nineteenth-century public schools, characteristics that included manliness, a sense of fair play, leadership and bravery

De Coubertin saw two benefits for sport:

- it developed physical health required to defend your country
- it integrated populations, bringing together social classes.

This amateur ideal behind the Olympics was further enhanced by de Coubertin's motto for the early games:

The important thing at the Olympic Games is not to win, but to take part; for the essential thing in life is not to conquer but to struggle well.

There is a record of Olympic-style festivals held in the UK as early as 1620 when a Cotswold lawyer, Robert Dover, established the 'Cotswold Olimpicks'. The events of the early games were an extension of the traditional Whitsuntide festivals that had been held in the Cotswolds for centuries. Activities included horse racing, coursing, running races, throwing the sledge hammer, wrestling, shin kicking, fencing, dancing and tumbling. The term 'Olimpick' was first printed in 1636. It was used many times in early accounts of Dover's games. Many commentators made direct comparisons between events and practices at the original Olympics in Greece and what occurred at Chipping Campden. For Dover the term simply meant:

'the gathering of all types of people to take part in healthy outdoor activities and friendly competitions.'

(Burns, 2000)

The Olimpick Games continued as an annual event until 1642 when the new Puritan movement in Britain that resulted from the Civil War suppressed many sporting and cultural festivals. They were restored as part of the Festival of Britain in 1951 and events included tug of war, running races, shin kicking and a exhibition of backsword play. It was such a success that it was decided to restore the Olimpick Games to an annual event and in 1965 the Robert Dover's Games Society was formed to conserve the traditions of the games.

CASE STUDY OLIMPICKS AT DOVER'S HILL

The Cotswold Olimpicks is still held every year at Dover's Hill just outside Chipping Campden in Gloucestershire on the Friday following the Whit Bank Holiday. There is a small fee to watch the games and you can join in some of the events, including shin kicking!

Another, more famous English Olympics is still held at Much Wenlock, Shropshire, and began in 1850. Their guiding light was Dr William Penny Brookes, a local GP, who set up an Olympian Society in the town – mainly as a way of keeping people out of the ale houses. The society organised an annual sporting festival attracting participants and spectators from throughout England. It also promoted PT in the local elementary schools. Penny Brookes and de Coubertin met and corresponded over a number of years about the possibility of promoting the Olympic movement. De Coubertin actually visited the Much Wenlock games in 1890 and after Penny Brookes' death in 1895 he became the driving force in resurrecting the Olympics. Although Penny Brookes was listed as an honorary member of the 1894 Congress for Olympic Games, he was unable to attend because of ill health. Regrettably he died just four months before the realisation of his life-long ambition, to launch the first International Olympic Games held in Athens in 1896, and so did not see his dream come to fruition.

- ■ What role did the early Olympic festivals play in shaping de Coubertin's vision for the Modern Olympic Games?

THE BIRTH OF THE MODERN GAMES

In 1894 de Coubertin arranged an International Congress primarily to discuss the issue of amateurism. He skilfully changed the focus of the meeting to raise the issue of Olympic revival and a decision was made to set up an International Olympic Committee. Demetrius Vikelas, president of the Greek Gymnastic Society, was elected as the first president of the IOC. The Congress also decided that the Modern Games, like their ancient model, should be held every four years. The first Games would be held in Athens in 1896 and in Paris four years later. There was discussion on whether the ancient site of Olympia could be used but it was felt that this area was too remote and the Games needed the facilities and infrastructure offered by a capital city like Athens. This idea has been retained and all the Modern Games have been held in major cities, though the Athens 2004 Olympics did stage some events at Olympia. Also the site is still used by the Olympic Movement to ignite, with the rays from the sun, the Olympic flame as it starts its journey to the next host city.

▶ *Olympic flame on its journey from Olympia to the host city*

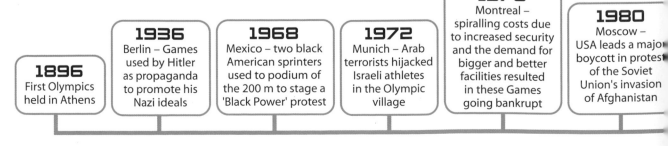

1896
First Olympics held in Athens

1936
Berlin – Games used by Hitler as propaganda to promote his Nazi ideals

1968
Mexico – two black American sprinters used to podium of the 200 m to stage a 'Black Power' protest

1972
Munich – Arab terrorists hijacked Israeli athletes in the Olympic village

1976
Montreal – spiralling costs due to increased security and the demand for bigger and better facilities resulted in these Games going bankrupt

1980
Moscow – USA leads a major boycott in protest of the Soviet Union's invasion of Afghanistan

Fig. 5.3 The Modern Olympic timeline

The congress did not simply want to duplicate the Ancient Games – they wanted it to have a modern character and the 'spirit of Olympism' to be the emphasis of the games. Other rules were agreed:

- Each participating country should hold preliminary heats or contests so only true champions would take part in the games.
- Members of the IOC would be representatives of global Olympism rather than their own countries.
- Each participating country had to establish a National Olympic Association.

APPLY IT!

Many of de Coubertin's ideals are still very much evident in the mission statement of the current Olympic Movement:

'To contribute to building a peaceful and better world by educating youth through sport practised without discrimination of any kind and in the Olympic spirit, which requires mutual understanding with a spirit of friendship, solidarity and fair play.'

CASE STUDY
THE FIRST MODERN OLYMPIC GAMES – ATHENS 1896

The first Games in 1896 attracted about 245 athletes (all men) in 43 events. At the Athens 2004 Games, more than 10,000 athletes took part in 300 events. Female athletes made up a third of the total number of competitors. The US dominated the medal table as they so often do in the modern games. The Greek nation were depressed at the thought that they may win no medals – but the story of these first Games was a race that re-enacted the ancient story of the marathon. The race was run from Marathon to Athens (estimated at 26 miles), was watched by more than 100,000 people and was won by a Greek runner, postman Spiridon Louis.

- Use the Internet to find out more about the history of the marathon race.
- Can you comment on how the success of the Olympic Games in the twentieth century has influenced the organisation and scope of other sports events?

THE RISE OF SPORT AS A BUSINESS

With the rise of quicker travel, especially by air, and the move to digital-via-satellite and broadband broadcasting, sports competitions have become global events. The Olympic Games now boasts a TV audience of over 4 billion. These huge audiences are why media corporations are willing to pay huge amounts of money to secure the exclusive rights to screen events. They also make the events very attractive to sponsors who can pay to have their logos and brands seen around the stadiums and on the players' clothing. This 'shop window' that is created through the globalisation of sport may sometimes be used by countries, groups and individuals for political or propaganda purposes.

GLOBALISATION AND ITS EFFECTS

Sport is now played the world over. Many of the sports that were developed in the UK at the end of the nineteenth century spread around the world and many countries now play sports such as association football, cricket and rugby, though some sports have been adapted to better suit the environment and culture of the society. For example, Australian Rules and American Football are both based on rugby but they have very distinctive characteristics of their own.

1984
Los Angeles – 'Tit for Tat' boycott led by the Soviet Union over security concerns in the US. Also referred to as the 'hamburger' Olympics due to the over-commercialism

1988
Seoul – 100 m Gold medallist Ben Johnson is stripped of his medal and title after failing a drugs test North Korea

1996
Athens – controversy over the centenary Games being awarded to Atlanta and not Athens – Atlanta also home city of major Olympic sponsor, Coca-Cola

2006
Athens – on the eve of the opening ceremony two Greek sprinters fail to attend drugs tests and are suspended

► *'Black Power' political protest at the 1968 Olympics*

Any person or country that wants to make a point is guaranteed maximum exposure at these sporting events. One memorable example of this was the period between 1960 and 1990 when the two super-powers of the US and USSR spent huge amounts of money trying to outdo and better each other in all sporting disciplines. A win at the Olympics proved, it was said, that one political system was better than the other. Each country also chose to **boycott** the Olympic Games and used their power and influence to persuade other countries not to take part. This seriously affected the Olympic Games of 1980 and 1984, which were boycotted by other nations too, as a form of political protest.

KEY TERM

boycott
withdraw from taking part, especially where nations do not allow their athletes to compete at a sports meeting in order to make a political point

AMERICANISATION AND COMMERCIALISM

Sport is now seen as big business and in order to compete and develop the sports community increasingly turns to the private sector for finance. This system of funding through sponsorship and media fees first developed in the US and has now crossed the Atlantic in a process referred to as 'Americanisation'. This move to private funding has also changed the main ethic in sport, from the traditional recreational ethic of playing for the love of the game (an amateur focus) towards a more commercial 'win at all costs' attitude. This has brought a move towards an 'open' focus where performers are free to earn money from their sport. The Rugby Union's move towards a professional premiership in the late 1990s is a good example of the way traditional amateur sports have become more commercialised.

Most of the credit for this reliance on commercial funding is laid at the hand of Peter Uberroth who led the organising committee for the 1984 Los Angeles Olympic Games. Due to the security problems of the 1972 Munich Games and the fact that the Montreal Games of 1976 went bankrupt, both the US federal government and the California state government withdrew their funding and sponsorship during the run-up to the 1984 Games in LA. This left Uberroth with the dilemma of how he could find the money to pay for the Games. His solution was twofold: for the first time in Olympic history he offered the TV broadcasting rights to just one company; and then he also leased the festoon (the five ring logo) to commercial sponsors who bought the right to produce an 'official Olympic product' and display the logo or associate themselves with it. This proved to be a major success: not only did Uberroth raise enough money to pay for the Games but, for the first time, the Olympic Games recorded a profit. The 1984 Games became known as the 'Hamburger Games' due to the overt profile given to the sponsors and in particular to McDonald's. This approach created the model for the organisation of all future Olympic Games, and indeed for global games in general.

▶ *Sponsors pay to have their branding seen at the Olympics*

CASE STUDY
THE OLYMPIC PARTNER PROGRAMME (TOP)

After the financial success of the 1984 Olympics, the IOC set up the 'Olympic Partner Programme' which offers international companies the opportunity to become a commercial partner of the Olympic Games. This agreement gives the companies exclusive rights to use the Olympic logo on their products. For the 2012 London Games the price to become a TOP sponsor is around £50 million and it is projected that the TOP sponsors will contribute £750 million towards the running of the Games. Commercial sponsorship now equates to 40 per cent of all Olympic revenue.

- Can you explain the significance of the five rings and their respective colours from the festoon?

The presence of the media has turned sport into a commodity that can be bought and sold. Television companies pay huge amounts of money to cover sports, and advertisers and sponsors back the Olympics because they know the benefits of the exposure they will get through global coverage will be invaluable. Individual athletes train and prepare for sport in the knowledge that the media will give them a stage on which to present their talents – also, it can be a lucrative way to earn a living.

KEY TERM

shamateurism
describing the custom of pre-1990 athletes who were amateur but received unofficial payments in the form of either commercial scholarships or state bursaries

However, the pressure of having to train and compete at the highest level has made enormous demands on the athletes in terms of time and expense. It was in the 1970s that the concept of '**shamateurism**' emerged, whereby performers kept their amateur status but often received 'unofficial funding' rather than prize money. This in turn led to a change in emphasis within the sport with the win ethic replacing the recreational ethic. To many performers, sport had become a career rather than a leisure pursuit. Commercial pressures increasingly permeated all sports. By 1981 the IOC had removed the term amateur from the Olympic Charter.

The Olympic Games receive most of their funding from US TV networks that pay in excess of $400 million to secure the exclusive TV rights. This kind of financial influence gives the TV companies control over many factors. For example, we are now used to having to stay up late to see key events such as the 100 metre final so that it fits with the prime-time television slot on the east coast of America.

APPLY IT!

The Olympic Charter
The Olympic Charter is the codification of the Fundamental Principles, Rules and Bye-laws adopted by the IOC.

Check out the IOC website and read through the summary of the Olympic Charter.

REMEMBER

- The rise of spectatorism and its influence on sport in the twentieth century
- The continued development of commercialisation and Americanisation in UK sport
- The influence the 1984 Olympics have on future global games

TASK

Can you identify examples of Americanisation and the influence of commercialism on other global sports events?

EXAM TIP

For your exam you will need to give examples of Americanisation and the influence of commercialism on global sports events.

DEVIANCE IN SPORT

All sports have rules and deviance occurs when participants break these rules. This cheating is an important issue in modern sport. Cheating is not a new concept – we know that the ancient Olympians took tonics to try to improve their performance. Some people would argue that cheating is an important element in sport and that without it sport would be dull. Sport has many written rules but there are also unwritten ones and these make an investigation into deviance more complicated.

THE CONCEPT OF SPORTSMANSHIP

The Olympic ideal is based around the philosophy of sportsmanship – people conforming to the written and unwritten rules of sport. The idea of fair play means that you treat your opponents as equals and, although you want to beat them, you will do so only by adhering to the rules and a code of conduct that has been developed in the sport through tradition. This includes shaking hands and congratulating the other team or opponents at the end of the game. Cheating not only destroys the game but also detracts from your personal achievement. A win through cheating is a hollow victory where you may gain the extrinsic rewards, but not the more fulfilling intrinsic ones.

GAMESMANSHIP

The alternative dynamic in sport is known as gamesmanship – where you use whatever means you can to overcome your opponent. The only aim here is to win, and for most people it is not a question of breaking the rules, but more about bending them to your advantage.

REMEMBER

- Sportsmanship is playing within the rules – gamesmanship is bending the rules in order to win

THE PROFESSIONAL FOUL

Some behaviour in sport is said to be dysfunctional – it destroys the sporting ethics of fair play and equal competition. Increasingly in some sports players are deliberately trying to injure or obstruct players so that they will get the right result – a win. Examples include:

- stamping in rugby – the injured player has to leave the field for treatment, giving one team an advantage
- 'sacking' in American Football – defensive players attempting to 'sack' the opposition quarterback, the key playmaker, who will not be able to play if he is deliberately injured
- the professional foul in football – an attacker is deliberately fouled to prevent him from scoring

- sledging in cricket – verbally abusing an opponent in an attempt to break their concentration.

TAKE IT FURTHER

Discuss why the ethic of sportsmanship has been replaced by gamesmanship in recent times.

PERFORMANCE-ENHANCING DRUGS

Drug abuse has been one of the main areas of deviance in sport over the last few years. It is not clear whether the actual level of drug taking has increased or whether we are now more aware of it because testing systems have improved. It is also difficult to decide where the line should be drawn between illegal drugs and legal supplements. Many athletes have tested positive but claim that they only took cough mixture or other such products that can be obtained without prescription.

Taking performance-enhancing drugs is the ultimate in gamesmanship – taking something to increase your performance and increase your chances of winning. There is a range of performance-enhancing drugs that athletes can take. Most originated as genuine medical treatments but their side effects have been used by athletes to improve their athletic performance illegally. The range and availability of these types of drugs are constantly increasing, making control very difficult.

The increase in the rewards of winning may have meant that the temptation to cheat has become too great for many athletes. This appears to be very true in one of the most prestigious athletics events, the 100 metre sprint. Starting with Ben Johnson in 1988, most of the world's top sprinters such as Linford Christie, Tim Montgomery and more recently Dwaine Chambers have all tested positive and received bans for taking performance-enhancing drugs.

Most media attention has been focused on the use of steroids. These are artificial male hormones that allow a performer to train harder and longer. In the past they had been difficult to trace as they are not taken immediately before a performance but athletes take them during their preparation phase, usually in the 'closed' season. A breakthrough in detection came when the authorities started to test athletes at any time in the year.

As already discussed, there is a very fine line between what can be considered as a legal supplement and what is an illegal drug and this has caused many dilemmas for both athletes and authorities alike. A substance is only illegal if it is on the IOC Medical Commissions list of banned substances. It may be possible that athletes with access to highly qualified chemists and physiologists may be able to keep one step ahead by taking substances that have not yet been banned.

KEY TERM

doping
taking drugs in order to enhance sporting performance

WADA AND THE FIGHT AGAINST DRUGS

The World Anti-Drugs Agency is an international agency that attempts to bring together governments, IOCs and ISFs. WADA was set up in 1998 when the international sports bodies and several state governments agreed that **doping** had become a global problem and not one that could be left to individual national governing bodies and ISFs.

The main concerns were:

- athletes now spend so much time away from their 'home' country and traditionally athletes can only be tested by their 'home' sports body
- one court case could bankrupt a whole sport (as in the case of the British Athletics Federation and the Diane Modahl case).

REMEMBER

Diane Modahl:
British middle distance runner

1994 Banned after a sample failed a drugs test. However, investigation finds sample had been mishandled by Portuguese test centre. Diane cleared and received a large sum of money in compensation for earnings lost while banned. UK Athletics Governing Body suffering financial problems as a result.

Fig. 5.4 *The UK Sport website promotes the fight against doping in sport*

Pledge: To use the UK's role as a world leader to promote drug-free sport and help create a sporting environment in which doping is not tolerated
Testing and Results Management
To have in place a comprehensive testing programme for the UK that acts as a suitable method of deterrence and detection, and that affirms athletes' performances as drug-free.
Education and Research
To continually enhance the Drug-Free Sport prevention strategy and Education and Information Programme, assisting athletes and support personnel in making responsible and informed choices about competing drug-free.
National and International Policy and Standards
To ensure that UK Sport, and the UK's sporting community, is in full compliance with the World Anti-Doping Code, and to use our influence internationally to ensure such standards are adhered to worldwide.

Table 5.1 *The UK Sport Manifesto for Drug-Free Sport has a three-part approach (summarised here)*

WADA'S MISSION

To promote and co-ordinate at international level the fight against doping in sport in all forms.

In 2006 UK Sport launched what it considers to be the world's most comprehensive and up-to-date online drug information service. Athletes can log on to the website and check out any medicines or supplement they may be considering taking.

The database will allow athletes, coaches, team doctors and other support staff the opportunity to check the status of most UK licensed pharmaceutical products or licensed substances according to sport's anti-doping bible – the Olympic Movement Anti-Doping Code (the list published by the IOC and WADA of what is prohibited in sport).

FUTURE DEVELOPMENTS

Though the level and scope of drugs testing continues to grow across the globe, there is still a feeling that the dopers and drug abusers may be one step ahead. The recent case involving US sprinter Marion Jones and BALCO, a Los Angeles-based laboratory that had been supplying her with a steroid nicknamed the 'clear' as it was undetectable,

is an example. She has been forced to give back the gold medals she won at the Sydney 2000 Olympic Games. Genetic engineering is considered to be the new threat to sports ethics, especially as four uses of genetic engineering in sport have already been identified:

- drugs can be fine tuned to suit an athlete's genetic composition
- genetic information can be used to identify sporting talent
- an athlete's genetic composition can be modified to improve performance
- the cells of a newly fertilised egg can be adapted to produce 'super' athletes.

EXAM TIP

Searching the web for the archives of newspapers and looking at broadsheets such as the Times *and* Telegraph *is a good way of researching your examples of deviance in sport. You will get extra credit in the exam for using up-to-date examples.*

ExamCafé
Relax, refresh, result!

Refresh your memory

Revision checklist

▷ Sports in pre-industrial Britain were linked to a need for war preparation

▷ Early sports were divided by social class and background

▷ The church and local gentry were important in the organisation of festival games

▷ The Modern Olympic Games are a combination of ancient and modern festivals

▷ The Universities of Cambridge and Oxford played an important role in the development of sport as they were the first place where compromise rules were developed

▷ The twentieth century saw the rise of 'spectatorism' and this changed the organisation and philosophy of sport, the spectator becoming the priority

▷ The influence of the 1984 Olympics led to the increased development of commercialisation and Americanisation in UK sport

▷ Understand the concepts of sportsmanship and gamesmanship

▷ Be able to offer reasons why performers take performance-enhancing drugs

▷ Explain the role WADA pays in attempting to alleviate deviance in international sport

▷ Be able to discuss the future of deviance in sport

Revise as you go

1. What were the main characteristics of mob games?

2. How did the agricultural year in pre-industrial Britain affect the time available for sport?

3. In pre-industrial Britain how did the social background of a person affect the type of sports activities they took part in?

4. What role did sport play in the nineteenth-century public schools?

5. What is the link between the nineteenth-century public schools and the global spread of sport?

6. How did rational sport differ from mob games?

7. What effect did industrialisation have on the way people lived?

8. What changes in society led to the development of national Sports Governing Bodies in the latter half of the nineteenth century?

9. How did the relationship between spectators and performers change in the twentieth century?

10. What were de Coubertin's motives behind setting up the Olympic Games?

Get the result!

Sample question and answer

Exam question

Festival games dominated the pre-industrial era. Describe and explain the main characteristics of these festival games. **(7 marks)**

Student answer

Before the industrial revolution festival games and sports were occasional in that they were only played occasionally during the year. Games were normally held on the holy or festival days such as Shrove Tuesday. This was the day that all the peasants were given freedom from work.

Before factories were built and people moved to live in towns there was a lot of space, and the festival games were often played on huge pitches. The Ashbourne Football game is played on a pitch which is three miles wide.

Because all the peasants had the same day off work the festival games were mob-like with hundreds on each team.

Although the gentry did not play in the festival games they would support them and also gamble on the outcomes. This support could include donating prizes for the winners or providing equipment and land for the games to play on. The Haxey Hood game is played on fields given to the villagers by Lady de Mowbray.

To reflect the society of the time, festival games had few rules and those that did exist were not written down but were passed on by word of mouth. The lack of rules also meant that the games were often very violent.

Examiner says:

This answer scores full marks as it has fulfilled the question set. Not only has the candidate described the key characteristics but they have gone on to explain them and if possible back up the points they make with a named example. They have also written down more points than needed to gain full marks and this is a good tip.

Sample question and answer

Exam question

Outline the main values and characteristics associated with public school athleticism.

(5 marks)

Student answer

The first public schools in the UK were all boarding schools. Only people who could afford the fees could send their sons there. There were none for girls. The sons of upper class people went there to be educated as leaders of society, such as politicians, lawyers and doctors. They also played team games such as rugby and football. The teachers thought they could teach leadership and teamwork through games as well as keeping the boys fit and healthy. It was a way of teaching discipline through the rules of the game as well as loyalty and pride when playing a sport for their school. These were the foundations of athleticism, where taking part in sporting activities and setting an example of how games should be played were thought to be good role models for the rest of society. Fair play and taking part were more important than winning.

Examiner says:

The first few sentences are not directly relevant to the question. It may have been better to start with the definition of athleticism.

Examiner says:

The mention of leadership and team games in the context of teaching would get the candidate his or her first mark. However, it would have been worth including that team games kept the boys from leaving the grounds of the school or getting into trouble.

Examiner says:

Setting an example and providing a role model are good points for 1 mark.

Examiner says:

Fair play and taking part as a priority over winning are important points in the concept of athleticism, earning the candidate 2 more marks. This gives a total of 4 out of 5 marks.

CHAPTER 6 PERFORMANCE PATHWAYS

LEARNING OUTCOMES

By working through this chapter, you should:

■ understand the concept of the sporting pyramid and its four levels (foundation, participation, competition, elite)
■ identify the role of key UK agencies
■ describe the traditional and contemporary pathways in UK sport
■ understand the concepts of talent identification and development

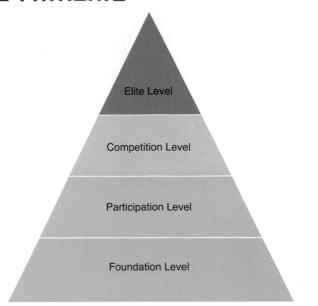

Fig. 6.1 *The participation pyramid. The higher up the pyramid performers are, the greater their training and support needs*

The aim of this chapter is to identify the pathways that are open to performers in sport. The most common pathway is represented in the so-called sporting pyramid. Performers move up the pyramid until they reach their potential. For a few this will mean reaching the elite level; that is, playing at an international or professional level. As this will only be a few it's clear to see how the pyramid analogy was developed. We will also investigate the role of the key sports agencies in how they support performers as they move up the pyramid. Traditionally in the UK, performers have started off playing at school and then moved into club sport. Under the current National Framework for Sport the key UK sports agencies are looking to create more opportunities for people to progress up the pyramid. Selecting those that can achieve the elite level in sport is a complex issue and we will investigate the concept of talent identification and talent development.

THE SPORTING PYRAMID

The different levels of sport can be represented best in a pyramid (see Figure 6.1). Such a concept is used by many sports organisations to develop a continuum of participation from the foundation level (also known as the grass roots level) to the elite level. In theory, the broader the base of the participation pyramid the greater the elite pool from which selection can take place. The link from the base to the elite level has many aspects, for success in sport creates role models who can inspire those at the base level of the pyramid, especially younger performers and athletes. This provides motivation for them to get involved in sport and to progress up the levels of the pyramid.

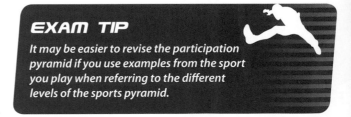

EXAM TIP

It may be easier to revise the participation pyramid if you use examples from the sport you play when referring to the different levels of the sports pyramid.

THE SPORTING PYRAMID LEVELS

There are four levels of performance within the pyramid:

■ The foundation level, also known as the grass roots level, is mainly associated with introducing young children to sport and encouraging their learning the fundamental motor skills. In the UK schemes such as TOP Sport and Dragon Sport have been used by sports councils to promote participation amongst children.

■ The participation level refers to sport undertaken primarily for fun and enjoyment, and often at basic levels of competence. However, many very competent sports people take part in sport purely for reasons of fun and health and fitness.

■ The competition level, also known as the performance level, reflects a more structured form of competitive sport at club or county level, or indeed at an individual level for personal reasons.

- The elite level applies to performers at the highest national and international levels.

TASK

Can you identify the key differences between participation and performance levels?

It may be useful to think of people you know who are at the different levels of the sports pyramid.

Can you reproduce the pyramid for your sport? Give examples of clubs and performers for each level.

Where would you place yourself on the pyramid? Add this information to your diagram.

TAKE IT FURTHER

Produce a pyramid for a technical sport, such as trampolining or gymnastics, and a pyramid for recreational sport, such as golf or snowboarding. How does the width of the pyramid levels differ between these sports?

THE ROLE OF KEY UK SPORTS AGENCIES

The development and organisation of sport in the UK has not followed a regular pattern. Individuals, groups and clubs have always been free to develop their sport as they liked and the government has never involved itself directly in the organisation of sport at either local or national level.

Today there are three key agencies that oversee sport in the UK: UK Sport, Sport England (or Sport Scotland, Sports Council for Wales (Sport Cymru), Sports Council Northern Ireland) and the Youth Sport Trust.

UK SPORT

UK Sport is responsible for the management of elite sport in the UK. Its mission is to work in partnership to lead sport in the UK to world-class success.

It does this through two main goals:

1 Primary goal: to support and help deliver success at the Olympic and Paralympic Games. A 'no compromise' approach is taken, targeting resources and activity primarily at those sports and athletes capable of delivering medal-winning performances.

2 World Class Performance Programme: funds performance and subsistence costs of UK elite athletes (the money comes from the National Lottery).

HOTLINKS

Research one regional elite training centre in the UK and share your findings with your group.

REMEMBER

- UK Sport has the primary role of investing in and supporting the nation's Olympic and paralympic ambitions.

SPORT ENGLAND

Sport England is the government agency responsible for advising, investing in and promoting community sport to create an active nation. Their current key aim is to get 2 million people more active in sport by 2012. They also distribute money from the Lottery Sports Fund to assist in the provision of sport and recreation through local schemes.

Their latest strategy is a Promoting Sport Tool Kit package, which is a collection of simple-to-use tools to help sports clubs, County Sports Partnerships and local authorities to promote sport and active recreation more effectively, more easily and more cheaply to the community.

There are parallel agencies in each of the other three home countries: Sport Scotland, Sports Council for Wales (Sport Cymru) and Sports Council Northern Ireland. All play a similar role to that of Sport England in that they have direct responsibility for raising participation in their region. Sport England also manages and oversees the County Sports Partnerships, which are responsible for the strategic co-ordination of sport at county level. They run participation events, help co-ordinate coaching and volunteering activities and manage qualifications, such as Step into Sport.

One of Sport England's key objectives at the start of the twenty-first century was to reverse the massive decline in sports participation. The fall-off in participation generally occurs at the time young people reach the age of 16. The aim of Sport England is to get young people to stay involved in some form of sport after they leave compulsory schooling. They have developed a number of programmes:

- Helping club development so that local clubs are able to attract young people, mainly through links to schools
- Supporting community sports provision
- Helping National Governing Bodies (NGBs) to develop effective competition frameworks aimed at young people
- Developing volunteering opportunities for young people to get involved in leadership and coaching.

HOTLINKS

Sport England recognise 105 sports in England. Check their website **www.sportengland.org** to see if your sport is included.

TAKE IT FURTHER

Check the equivalent websites for Scotland (http://www.sportscotland.org.uk), Wales (http://www.sports-council-wales.org.uk) and Northern Ireland (http://www.sportni.net/). Is there any difference between the sports included?

KEY TERM

Sport England
an agency whose primary role is to sustain and increase participation in community sport. It is the government's key delivery partner and a lottery distributor for community sport

Sport Scotland, Sports Council for Wales and the Northern Ireland Sports Council have the primary role of sustaining and increasing participation in community sport in their own regions.

YOUTH SPORT TRUST

The Youth Sport Trust (YST) has responsibility for all sport and activity that involves young people in and out of school. The Youth Sport Trust plays a central role in supporting the Department for Children, Schools and Families (DCSF) and the Department for Culture, Media and Sport (DCMS) in the delivery of a range of national strategies promoting PE and school sport.

The YST has been instrumental in introducing, developing and overseeing the following initiatives:

- TOP programmes – these provide a sporting pathway for all young people aged 18 months to 18 years

▶ *A club sportsground can offer excellent facilities for a school team*

▶ *Specialist Sports College with a wide range of sports activities and opportunities*

- Specialist Sports Colleges – secondary schools with a specialist status in sports, which means they get extra funding to be able to offer their own pupils, and those in the wider community, access to a greater range of sports activities and opportunities
- School Sport Partnerships – groups of schools working together to develop PE and school sport opportunities for young people
- Physical Education, School Sport and Club Links (PESSCL) strategy – a joint initiative between government departments and the YST with the aim of enhancing the take-up of sport amongst 5–16-year-olds. The government and the YST have set ambitious targets whereby they aim to have 85 per cent of all school-aged children able to access high quality PE and sport for 2 hours a week by 2008 and 4 hours by 2010.

There are a number of strands to the initiative:

Step into Sport – aimed at encouraging 14–19-year-olds into sports leadership and coaching

Gifted and Talented – designed to help young elite athletes reach their potential

- National Competitions Framework – aimed at building a world-class system of competitive sport for young people. This is facilitated by employing competition managers who manage competitive school sport at a county level and encouraging NGBs to produce school sport-specific competitions.

EXAM TIP

Revise the role of the key sports agencies – the key information could be included in a revision table that covers all of the three key agencies.

TASK

Can you research and describe examples of the YST work in your own area? If your school or college has a sports co-ordinator, he or she might be a good place to start researching for information and leads.

HOTLINKS

For more information on the Gifted and Talented strand of the PESSCL strategy check out the website: **www.talentladder.org**

REMEMBER

- Step into Sport is a joint initiative delivered by the Youth Sport Trust, Sport England and Sports Leaders UK. It provides opportunities for young people aged 14–19 to get involved in leadership and volunteering in sport. Participants in the scheme can experience sports leadership, gain leadership qualifications, help children in primary schools organise festivals of sport and take up volunteering placements in their communities.

CASE STUDY SCHOOL SPORTS PARTNERSHIP

A typical School Sports Partnership consists of

1 Partnership Development Manager (PDM)
8 School Sport Co-ordinators (SSCOs)
45 Primary and Special School Link Teachers (PLTs)

■ Have you got a local School Sports Partnership?
Find out which schools are involved and draw up
a table that gives your own local example.

EXAM TIP

*Don't be afraid to use local examples
in your exam answers.*

The PDM is a full-time position usually based at
the sports college which acts as the hub for the
partnership. They manage the partnership and help
develop links with community clubs and facilities.
The SSCOs are based in secondary schools. Their
role is to improve the opportunities in sport for their
pupils, and they cover both curricular and extra-
curricular sport, intra- and inter-school competition
as well as playing a role in making links with local
clubs. PLTs are based in primary and special schools
with the aim of improving the quality of PE and
school sport within their school.

TRADITIONAL PATHWAYS

Historically in the UK, there have been two main
pathways for aspiring athletes and performers to
follow, as shown in Figure 6.2.

The pathway a young person took was largely
determined by the sport, though in sports such as
rugby and netball, both approaches were running
simultaneously. In recent times there has been more
emphasis on the club structure since the funding
and support managed by UK Sport is done through
governing bodies and clubs. However, there has

been a move to rectify this and restore the balance.
The PESSCL strategy and role of the specialist sports
colleges has gone some way to bringing the two
pathways closer together. Another interesting
statistic, reflecting a dominance in the traditional
pathway, is that 50 per cent of all British Olympic
medal winners over the last 50 years have come from
the private education sector which constitutes only
7 per cent of the total British population.

The school sports system has traditionally included a
mix of friendly and competition-based fixtures, with
most senior schools offering young people the chance
to represent the school in a range of sports. There are
a large number of school sports associations such as
the English School Football Association that run both
regional and national sports competitions. Inter-house
and inter-form sport within a school, as well as sports
days and swimming galas, have also been offered by
most schools. The criticism of the school sports system
is that it can only usually cater for a relatively small
percentage of the schools' population. On average, only
around 5 per cent of pupils at a school are involved in
competitive sport.

The pathway has traditionally moved from school to
regional and county representation in most sports,
and a number of sports also run national teams in
various age groups. The majority of school sport is
still run by volunteers who are usually teachers giving
up their own time to coach, referee and support
school teams. There have been moves to facilitate
school sport through full- and part-time positions
but there will always remain some fluidity in the
provision of school sport.

A major concern has been the massive decline in
participation in sport after the age of 16 years, the
so-called post-school gap.

APPLY IT!

*Research your own sport at school level.
Are there any national competitions and is
there a specific school sport association?*

*Can you produce the sport pathway for your
sport at school level?*

Education

Club

***Fig. 6.2** Pathways for aspiring athletes and performers*

Fig. 6.3 *The School Sports pathway*

UNIVERSITIES

In the past universities have provided opportunities for all levels of performers. Many, such as Loughborough and Bath, have allowed elite athletes to train in conjunction with their academic course and many have also offered sport-specific degrees.

The university sports competitions, especially UAU (Universities Athletic Union) and BUSA (British Universities Sport Association), have also allowed individuals and teams to compete to a high level. The annual Varsity games between Oxford and Cambridge in a range of sports is still an important part of the sports calendar. Universities have also offered scholarships and bursaries to help students fund their sports training and development. This was especially useful in the tradition of amateur sports such as rugby union and athletics. Inter-mural sports programmes have also been a popular feature at most UK universities, allowing a greater range of the student body to participate in sports competition at a lower level. Most universities also provide

an extensive range of sports facilities, often at a discounted admission price for students.

THE GOVERNMENT'S SPORTING AGENDA

The government has recently developed and published a range of documents and policies that set out its objectives for sport in the twenty-first century. These are described below.

NATIONAL FRAMEWORK FOR SPORT

The National Framework for Sport is a joint policy document developed by the government and the key sports agencies that sets out the vision for sport in England. Its subtitle is Making England an Active and Successful Nation – a Vision for 2020, and this summarises the main focus of the strategy that it outlines. The key aim is an attempt to change the culture of sport and physical activity in England in order to increase participation across all social

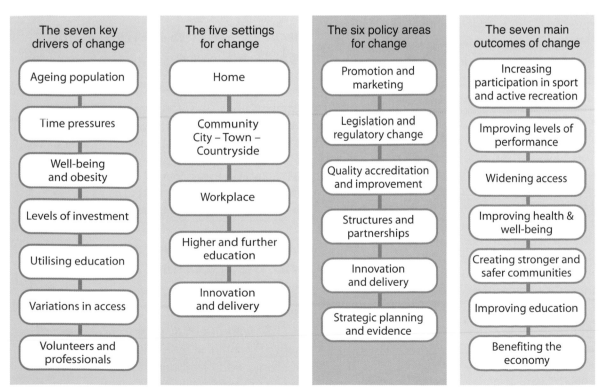

Fig. 6.4 *The National Framework for Sport in England*

groups. The framework identifies 20 priority sports and a further 10 development sports for which plans have been produced in order to provide clear pathways for people to get involved and, where possible, progress all the way to the elite level.

At the heart of the framework is a conceptual model which challenges all involved in sport in England to consider what the issues are and to drive towards the changes needed in terms of culture and provision in order for England to become a successful sporting nation, both in terms of mass participation and in achieving sports excellence.

GAME PLAN

In December 2002 the UK government published 'Game Plan', a strategy for delivering its sport and physical activity objectives for the nation. Game Plan set out two overriding aims:

- A major increase in participation in sport and physical activity, primarily because of the significant health benefits from being active and to reduce the growing costs of inactivity faced by the nation (especially the alarming rise in obesity).

- A sustainable improvement in success in international competition, particularly in the sports which matter and appeal the most to the public, primarily because of the national 'feel good factor' associated with winning and succeeding.

Game Plan set the ambitious targets of:

- 70 per cent of the population being reasonably active by 2020

- British and English teams and individuals to sustain rankings within the world's top five, particularly in more popular sports.

Part of this refocusing is the development of seamless pathways to ensure that energy is focused on the end result. The UK government and its sport agencies hope that the new streamlined structure of sport in England reduces bureaucracy and ensures that all the agencies are clear in their role. The overall aim is to release the sporting potential (including volunteering, coaching, effective leadership and officiating) in as many people as possible. The systems is now referred to as a 'sports relay race' (see Fig. 6.5).

The Youth Sport Trust are at the grass roots level to start the race, encouraging young people to get into the habit of participating in sport and active recreation. They then pass the baton on to Sport

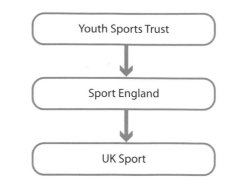

Fig. 6.5 *'Sports relay race'*

England whose role is to sustain this interest in sport and also attempt to persuade anyone who has dropped out to re-engage in sport and active recreation. Sport England, in turn, hand on a very small number of highly talented individuals to UK Sport.

A SPORTING FUTURE FOR ALL

'A Sporting Future for All' was a policy document published by the government in 2000 which set out the government's vision for sport at the start of the twenty-first century. It set out objectives for sport within education, community sport, sporting excellence and the ultimate aim of modernising England's sporting organisations. It was superseded by the government's National Framework for Sport, which was published in 2004.

SPORTS SEARCH PROGRAMMES

The national framework recognises that identifying potential sports talent in young people should be a priority in the run-up to the 2012 London Olympic Games. One of the programmes that has been developed is Sports Search. This is an online system run by a non-profit-making organisation. It allows every 11–17-year-old in the country to assess their suitability to take part in over 150 sports and activities as well as giving links to clubs and facilities where they could pursue these sports (see page 129).

TALENT IDENTIFICATION AND DEVELOPMENT

THE CONCEPT OF TALENT IDENTIFICATION

Talent Identification (Talent ID) is the process of identifying potential sports talent in young people and then providing supportive pathways that allow them to progress and fulfil this talent.

Identifying potential is not an easy task. Most of the current systems use physical characteristics and capacities that have been mapped against specific sports. However, achieving success in top-level sport also requires high levels of desire, determination and mental toughness – these are less easy to measure and identify.

Talent ID tends to work best in closed-loop sports – these tend to be repetitive in nature and include rowing, canoeing, cycling, weight lifting and swimming. In such sports there is a clear link to defined physical characteristics which can be identified in young performers. Open-loop sports, such as tennis and football, require constant decision making, response organisation and spatial awareness as well as a range of physical and technical abilities. So, talent ID in open sports tends to be less accurate.

HISTORY OF TALENT DEVELOPMENT IN EAST GERMANY AND AUSTRALIA

East Germany is often credited as being one of the first nations that developed the concept of talent identification. A relatively small country, East Germany had a population of only 16 million but for 40 years it was at the forefront of international sport. A newly created country in the aftermath of World War II, East Germany decided to use sport, and specifically success, at the Olympic Games as a shop window – that is, gaining international recognition. Talent identification became an integral part of school sport at primary level. This formed the first part of the state-sponsored elite sports programme in which every child was screened for sporting potential at the age of 7. Results were analysed by the National Sports Federation and those that scored well on the biometric and sporting tests were invited to attend local training centres several times a week. If children made good progress they would then, at the age of 10, be transferred to a sports boarding school where more time could be devoted to sports training. These sports boarding schools, which were also linked to elite sports clubs, put their students through a punishing regime which involved 6 hours of sports coaching and 2 hours of academic study a day for 6 days a week.

The majority of elite athletes were based at high-performance centres or sports institutes and it is this model that has been adopted in some guise around the world. After graduating from the sports boarding schools athletes could now devote themselves

▶ *Sport in post-war East Germany*

full-time to preparation at one of the eight national centres. Here they had access to top-class facilities, the best coaches and a huge array of sports science and technical support.

The Australian Institute of Sport (AIS) now functions in a similar way to the East German high performance centres. Following Australia's disappointing performance at the 1976 Olympics in Montreal, the Australian government undertook a review of its elite sports system. The outcome was a central focus for identifying and nurturing the country's sporting talent.

The AIS was opened in 1981 and now offers scholarships to over 600 elite athletes in 32 separate sports, employs 75 full-time coaches and offers athletes top-class training facilities along with sports science and medical back-up. There are now a further seven satellite institutes based in all of Australia's state capitals.

One of the most successful sports science experiments developed by the AIS was 'Sports Search', a talent identification programme. Initially piloted in rowing, this programme developed a bank of fitness and basic body measurements that could be used to identify a best-fit sport for each participant. This programme was rolled out in a national talent search visiting every Australian high school between 1994 and 1996 in the run-up to the 2000 Sydney Olympics. Those that were identified as having potential talent were invited to sports specific screening at the nearest institute of sport. Though successful, there was some criticism that this programme was very elitist as only 2 per cent of those tested were invited to the second phase of testing.

TAKE IT FURTHER

What are the benefits of the elite sports institute system of nurturing talent?

TALENT DEVELOPMENT IN THE UK

In 2000 the UK government produced its vision for sport for the forthcoming decade in the document entitled 'A Sporting Future for All'. This set out the plans for talent identification and development in the UK. Within the National Framework for Sport, a partnership between UK Sport, the UK sport institutes and the national governing bodies has been developed in order to facilitate the systematic identification of talent and the advance of fast track development programmes in targeted sports towards London in 2012.

The **English Institute of Sport** (EIS) has identified that it takes 6–8 years for a promising athlete to reach a medal-winning potential. It has, for the first time, employed dedicated talent ID specialists who are travelling the country looking for potential talent. There has been a specific focus on the new Olympic sports: basketball, handball and volleyball.

Another 2012-focused initiative is Project Swap Shop – a talent transfer programme where existing elite athletes are given the opportunity to try a different Olympic sport.

SPORTING GIANTS – TALL SPORTS PUBLIC APPEAL

In a bid to discover talent for the targeted sports of rowing, handball and volleyball, a public appeal was launched. Women over 180 cm and men over 190 cm were invited to attend an initial talent screening; those chosen were then fast tracked on to a programme for Olympic development.

CASE STUDY TALENT DEVELOPMENT IN TENNIS

The Lawn Tennis Association has in place a comprehensive talent pathway with a clear aim of getting more British tennis players into the world top 100 rankings. It has financed and established a network of High Performance Centres (HPCs) around the UK that are linked to county accredited satellite clubs. Its long-term aim is to ensure that talented tennis players are no more than 30 minutes' drive from a high-level performance environment where they can train and receive coaching and sports science support.

■ Can you research a talent pathway for your own sport? Check out your sports National Governing Body website.

Talent Camps
aimed at players aged 8–14, run locally with an aim to identify potential talent

Satellite Clubs
aimed at under 10s and acting as feeder clubs into the regional HPC's

HPCs
offering training and support for talented young players aged 10–16, players will also receive funding to allow international travel for both training and competition

National Tennis Centre (Roehampton)
the research and development hub for British Tennis, Highest level performers will be based here. Players at each level are managed by regional talent and performance managers

WORLD CLASS PROGRAMME

Once identified, potential elite athletes in the UK become part of the national lottery-funded **World Class Pathway**. This has three levels:
■ World Class Talent – identifying athletes with the potential to progress
■ World Class Development – assisting talented athletes who have competitive capabilities

▶ UK gymnast, Beth Tweddle, in action on the uneven parallel bars

▶ UK rowers, Matthew Pinsent and James Cracknell, competing in the Men's Coxless Pair

As athletes move up the World Class Pathway they get increased access to these EIS-supported facilities.

The funding of sport in the UK is prioritised to ensure the most effective use of lottery funds and to achieve the overall aim of the UK becoming one of the world's top five sporting nations.

APPLY IT!

Beth Tweddle, the Great Britain and World Champion gymnast, trains 6 hours a day for 6 days a week.

Matthew Pinsent, four times Olympic Gold Medallist rower, trained 5 hours a day (2 × water sessions and 1 × gym session) for 6 days a week.

What does it take to be a champion in your own sport?

KEY TERMS

English Institute of Sport (EIS)
One of the UK sport institutes, it aims to advance athlete development programmes

World Class Performance Programme
the lottery-funded elite sports support programme for athletes in the UK

World Class Pathway
UK Sport's programme for identifying talent and supporting elite athletes

- World Class Podium – supporting athletes with medal-winning potential both financially and by providing top-class facilities.

Elite sports performers also require the support of an ever-increasing range of sports specialists – psychologists, dieticians, physiotherapists – as well as video and computer equipment to help improve technique. In the UK, such services are now provided through a number of specialist sports centres around the country forming a national network under the banner of the EIS. Their aim is to enable our top athletes to use high quality facilities for training.

The primary role of each EIS High Performance Centre is to assist national governing bodies and their top performers (identified through the **World Class Performance Programme**) to reach their targets in terms of championships and medals. This will be achieved by providing both athletes and coaches with a comprehensive network of services at each centre, which in turn will bring together the best sports scientists, medical professionals and support personnel to provide the best environment in which to work.

Region	High Performance Centre
East	Hertfordshire Sports Village, Hatfield
East Midlands	Loughborough University
London	Lee Valley Athletics Centre, Edmonton
North-east	Gateshead International Stadium
North-west	Sport City, Manchester
South	Bisham Abbey, NSC
South-west	University of Bath
West Midlands	Lilleshall, NSC
Yorkshire	Don Valley Stadium/EIS Sheffield
Scotland	University of Stirling
Northern Ireland	University of Ulster/ Jordanstown Campus
Wales	University College of Wales

Table 6.1 *The EIS High Performance Centres delivering excellence programmes across the UK*

The network centres will also act as a vehicle for accessing an overseas network of facilities and services, including warm-weather training, acclimatisation, altitude and winter sport venues.

ATHLETE AWARDS

The essential living costs cover rent/mortgage, bills, food, basic cleaning and maintenance, general clothing, phone, Internet and mobile costs, household and personal insurance, Voluntary National Insurance contributions and a stakeholder pension.

The sporting costs covers a contribution to personal sports travel, equipment and training costs, including running a car, training clothing, conditioning equipment, gym membership, domestic competition costs, HR (heart rate) monitor and a laptop computer.

CASE STUDY EIS AT LOUGHBOROUGH UNIVERSITY

Loughborough University has been chosen to be part of the English Institute of Sport network. These institutes are charged with supporting sports performers and their coaches who are working at the very highest level, or who have the potential to do so.

Loughborough University and Sport England have developed a package of sports facilities (athletics, badminton, gymnastics, hockey, netball and swimming) to supplement the already extensive resources.

As a regional High Performance Centre the facility is required to offer the following mandatory services to athletes in their region in addition to generic support facilities:

- acclimatisation accommodation
- conditioning suites
- sports massage
- physiotherapy
- sports medicine.

- How do you think the facilities and services offered by a regional HPC such as Loughborough help develop the elite performers that are based there?

CASE STUDY UK SPORT

Athlete category	Award
A	£23,930
B	£17,948
C	£11,965
A – Under 21	£14,879
B – Under 21	£12,129
C – Under 21	£ 9,379

Table 6.2 *These awards are made to athletes each year by UK Sport*

- How do these awards given by UK Sport compare to the wages of performers in professional sports in the UK?

▶ *Regional English Institute of Sport Arena at Sheffield*

TAKE IT FURTHER

See if you can find out what the average salaries are for footballers, golfers, cricketers and rugby players. Then compare these with awards for athletes.

OTHER TALENT DEVELOPMENT PROGRAMMES

Talent identification programmes include:

Sports Search – an online system which allows 11–17-year-olds to try out their suitability for over 150 sports. This system also signposts clubs and pathways where choices can be followed up.

HOTLINKS

The Sports Search website can be found at:
www.sportsearch.org.uk

School Games – annual 'Olympic-style' events funded by the UK government and lottery that aim to give young people experience of a big championships. Athletes compete for regional teams.

Gifted and Talented Performance – run by the Youth Sport Trust and targeted at 14–17-year-olds in a range of sports and held at HPCs, they offer training and support from top-class athletes such as Dame Kelly Holmes.

Talented Athlete Scholarship Scheme (TASS) – a government-funded programme that supports elite athletes who are also following academic study programmes in further and higher education. Athletes are given awards that help them continue their training and development. TASS bridges the gap in the sports talent development pathway between junior representative sport and the world class programme for talented performers aged 16–25. Performers eligible for TASS support are identified by their respective NGB. The athletes don't actually receive funding but they are able to access a range of services offered by their NGB or educational institution (this could include free access to gyms, free physiotherapy and so on).

► *Kelly Holmes amongst the young adults she supports at YST*

HOTLINKS

The TASS website can be found at:
www.tass.gov.uk

Sports Aid – a charity that provides talented young sports performers with direct funding to help them train and prepare for their sports. The funding is aimed at young people aged 12–18 (especially those that cannot access other forms of support funding). To be eligible for a Sports Aid grant performers need to be nominated by their NGB, having met sports-specific criteria.

HOTLINKS

The Sports Aid website can be found at:
www.sportsaid.org.uk

Advanced Apprenticeship in Sporting Excellence (AASE) – a programme piloted in football and now also available for 16–18-years-olds in cricket, tennis, aquatic sports and rugby union. It is a scheme that allows young potential professional performers to combine education, training and sport-specific qualifications. The apprentices train and play for a professional club but are also released for 10 hours a week to enable them to study an academic programme at a local college. At the end of the two years the aim is to get a professional full-time contract at the club. This programme is funded through the sports governing bodies and player associations, and is independent from the UK Sport World Class Performance Programme.

ExamCafé

Relax, refresh, result!

Refresh your memory

Revision checklist

▷ There are four levels of the participation pyramid: foundation level, participation level, competition level and elite level

▷ The traditional pathways open to performers in the UK were through school and club systems

▷ Three key agencies manage the participation pyramid in the UK: UK Sport, Sport England and the Youth Sport Trust

▷ The Youth Sport Trust is primarily responsible for increasing the quantity and quality of PE and school sport

▷ Sport England is primarily responsible for sustaining and increasing participation in sport and recreation

▷ UK Sport is primarily responsible for the development and support of world-class elite athletes

▷ You should be able to describe and explain the concepts of talent identification and talent development

Get the result!

Refresh your memory

Revise as you go

1. Describe the four parts of the participation pyramid.

2. What is the role of UK Sport?

3. How do the UK Sports Institutes support elite athletes?

4. Explain the three levels of the World Class Programme.

5. What legacy has the East German elite sport system had on sport in the UK?

6. Describe the Australian support of elite sport performers.

7. Explain the role of the Youth Sport Trust.

8. What is the key focus of Sport England's work?

9. Outline the traditional pathways that have been open to performers in the UK.

10. Explain the concept of talent identification.

11. Can you describe two methods of talent identification that have been used in UK sport?

12. Explain why closed-loop sports are best suited to talent identification.

13. Outline the kind of support elite athletes require in the twenty-first century.

14. How is elite sport funded in the UK?

Exam question

Define the term Americanisation and explain how it is affecting sport in the UK. **(5 marks)**

Student answer

Americanisation refers to the increasing commercialisation of sport in the 21st century. Sports in the UK are now adopting the American model of funding and organising professional sport. This basic model was developed by Peter Uberroth at the 1984 LA Olympics and results in a reliance on money to run sport coming from commercial sponsors and media contracts.

Sport in the UK is now seen as a business and this is growing. Professional teams in all the main sports of football, rugby and cricket are sponsored by companies; this gives the companies recognition and advertising. To sponsor the shirts of a team in the Premiership now costs several million pounds a year.

TV channels now try to outbid each other to gain exclusive rights to sports and/or specific sports competitions. This can be good for the sports as it brings in lots of money but it also gives the TV channel lots of power and they can dictate when games are played. It may also mean that big events like England cricket games are only available on satellite TV channels. The TV companies can make some of the money back by selling adverts that will be shown at breaks during the games; this could result in sports like football having to develop more breaks into the game to satisfy the advertisers and TV companies.

The overall effect of this Americanisation is the fact that in England cricket now gets 90% of its revenue from commercial sponsors and TV contracts. This is fine as long as the game is attractive to sponsors and TV but this puts a lot of pressure on the cricket governing bodies to do this and has resulted in them having to bring versions such as 20-20.

Examiner says:

This question requires candidates to do two things: explain what Americanisation is and then explain the effect it is having on sport in the UK. This answer does cover both parts. At the start the candidate gives a sound definition of the term. They then move on to explain the effect it is having on sport in the UK with good examples also being given. They finish strongly with a short paragraph which definitely does answer the question.

CHAPTER 7 LIFELONG INVOLVEMENT

LEARNING OUTCOMES

By working through this chapter, you should be able to:

- explain the concept of mass participation
- develop an understanding of the constraints on participation
- identify the role of the Sport for All Campaign
- build knowledge and understanding of reformative policies
- appreciate factors in designing models for the development of the long-term athlete (Long-Term Athlete Development)

In this chapter we concentrate on the bottom of the sports pyramid, and how more people can be encouraged to follow a healthy lifestyle that includes active sport and recreation. We begin with an investigation into the concept of mass participation. You will need to define the term and also understand the constraints on achieving it. We will discuss specific groups of the population that find it difficult to access sport and recreation and then also investigate the reformative policies that agencies such as Sport England have set up in an attempt to increase participation. We will end the chapter with a look at the long-term athlete development models that have recently been adopted by most sports in the UK.

▶ *Modern mass participation sport includes marathon running*

LIFETIME SPORTS

THE CONCEPT OF MASS PARTICIPATION

The opportunity to take part in sporting activity and physical recreation should be a basic human right; however, many people suffer constraints that prevent them from taking part. The aim of mass participation is to break through these constraints, whatever they may be, and to encourage as many people as possible to take up active lifestyles.

There are many benefits from a society promoting mass participation. Some are said to be intrinsic – physical activity promotes mental and physical health; it is a positive use of spare time and an important emotional release. Other benefits are said to be extrinsic – people will be fitter and healthier, making less strain on the health system. It is suggested that crime and anti-social behaviour are reduced if

people are engaged in physical activity, there will be economic benefits from increased numbers taking up active lifestyles and this may be attractive to investors and companies looking to relocate.

LIFETIME SPORTS

Lifetime sports are ones that can be pursued throughout life and include sports such as badminton and golf. The key is that these are self-paced: you can play at your own level or choose an opponent of similar ability. The main emphasis should be on low energy output and fun and enjoyment. The philosophy is that schools should be introducing young people to potential lifetime sports and activities so that they carry the interest on through to adulthood. In practice, most schools still concentrate on invasion games such as football and netball.

LEADERSHIP AND VOLUNTEERING SCHEMES

Performers in sport require coaches and administrators to organise, officiate and lead their sport. Sport England recognises that if it wants to promote participation it must also encourage more people into leadership and volunteering. Currently around 1.2 million individuals regularly coach sport in the UK (1 in 50 of the UK population) and there are 6 million sports volunteers actively involved in the UK. It is important to remember, however, that the large majority of coaching in the UK is carried out by non-qualified unpaid part-time volunteers.

There are a number of schemes that have been developed in an attempt to encourage more people into sports leadership and volunteering:

- Sport Leaders awards – these are overseen by the organisation Sport Leaders UK. The awards are primarily aimed at school and college students.
- Step into Sport is a joint initiative delivered by the Youth Sport Trust, Sport England and Sports Leaders UK. It provides opportunities for young people aged 14–19 to get involved in leadership and volunteering in sport.

▶ Golf is a lifetime sport though it is rarely taught in schools

▶ Many people drawn into leadership roles in sport are volunteers

SPORT ENGLAND'S PARTICIPATION SEGMENTS

Sport England has divided the sports participation market into four segments. For each segment there is a targeted strategy to reduce drop-out in sport, increase participation, change attitudes towards physical activity for the better and motivate people to start participating.

BENEFITS OF INCREASED PARTICIPATION

The government and key sports agencies believe that participation in sport and physical activity can help achieve the following outcomes:

- help people achieve healthier lifestyles
- create safer communities
- promote positive behaviour and confidence
- improve educational attainment
- help build social networks within communities
- reach out to and engage with disaffected and hard to reach people.

CASE STUDY
THE COST OF INACTIVITY

The UK National Audit Office produced a report in 2001 that suggested obesity costs the National Health Service £500 million a year. They also calculated that the wider costs to the UK economy and the reduction in productivity costs the country a further £2 billion.

- Find out how much the UK government spends on sport and health in a year. How do these figures compare and do you think the balance is right?

Before we consider the constraints on mass participation it is important to set out the basic requirement for accessing an active lifestyle. The basic requirements include fitness, ability, resources and time (see Figure 7.1).

Lifestyles have changed dramatically over the last few decades – the development of better and more accessible transport (especially the car) and other technological developments in the work place

Segment	Approx % of population	Description	Sport England's action plan
Sporty types	20	Those who participate in sport and are keen to continue	People who will play sport almost regardless of public policy intervention: safeguard provision of sporting opportunities, and develop pathways to elite sport
Mild enthusiasts	16	Those who participate in sport but could do more	People who know the benefits of sport and could be encouraged to do more: increase access, reduce drop-out, and foster enthusiasm
On the subs bench	44	Those who do not currently participate but could be persuaded if it was made easy enough	People who may have little time/ energy and feel they are not 'sporty' enough: remove barriers, offer incentives, and take sport to them
Couch potatoes	20	Those who do not participate and who don't want to, and those who have a negative attitude to sport (often established at an early age)	People who have little interest in sport/fitness and like 'putting their feet up': raise awareness, promote health benefits, and change attitude to physical activity at young age

Table 7.1 Sport England's participation segments

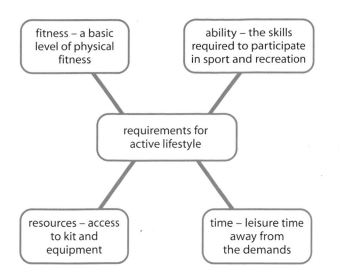

fitness – a basic level of physical fitness

ability – the skills required to participate in sport and recreation

requirements for active lifestyle

resources – access to kit and equipment

time – leisure time away from the demands

Fig. 7.1 *The basic requirements for accessing an active lifestyle*

and home have meant a move towards a more sedentary lifestyle for most of the population. Work and leisure now require much less physical activity than they used to. There are now concerns about the lack of fitness amongst young people and the rise of diseases such as obesity and cardiovascular problems.

CONSTRAINTS ON MASS PARTICIPATION

CULTURAL FACTORS

Many people do not have equal access to physical activity, often as a result of discrimination due to cultural variables. There are five main cultural factors that can lead to **discrimination** in terms of physical activity. These are outlined in Figure 7.2.

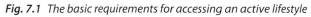

gender

age

ability/ disability

discrimination in sport

social class/ economic status

ethnicity (race and religion)

Fig. 7.2 *The five main cultural factors that lead to discrimination in sport*

Also a number of so-called **target groups** can be identified. These are groups that find it difficult to access sport and recreation. From the list of cultural factors it is easy to identify the target groups of women, those on low income, ethnic minorities, the very young and very old and the disabled.

> ### KEY TERM
>
> **target group**
> a population group that find it difficult to access sport and recreation
>
> **discrimination**
> unfair treatment (to an individual or group) which results in their access to sport and recreation being inhibited

> ### CASE STUDY
> ### DISABILITY SPORT
>
> In March 2007 Oscar Pistorius came second in the 400 metre final at the South African Athletics Championships. This was remarkable since he is an amputee whose legs both end at the knee. Dubbed the 'fastest man on no legs' he runs on blades made from composite carbon called 'cheetah legs'. Initially the IAAF refused his application to run in international able-bodied events since they felt he would have an 'unfair advantage'. However, they later agreed to allow him to run a number of events so that research could be done.
>
> ■ Do you think that athletes with a disability should be allowed to compete alongside able-bodied athletes?

▶ *Oscar Pistorius running on his blades made of carbon fibre*

TAKE IT FURTHER

What are the pros and cons of the debate on athletes with a disability competing alongside able-bodied athletes? Draw up a table that summarises both sides of the argument.

OPPORTUNITY

An individual may feel there are barriers to participation in an activity or sport in this country. In the UK, most sport takes place in clubs run on a voluntary basis, which are often elitist organisations. Clubs work on membership systems and entry is controlled by either the ability to pay fees or, in some cases such as golf clubs, by election to club membership through voting systems. This often limits membership to certain members of the community.

Another consideration for the individual is whether he or she has the time to participate. Women in particular are frequently faced with this problem. The demands of work and family often mean that they have little leisure time, which accounts in part for the low levels of female participation in sport.

PROVISION

Are facilities that allow participation available to you? Living in an inner city area might discriminate against you because there is often little provision for sport and physical activity in these built-up areas. Equipment is also required, which can be expensive. Those on low incomes may be discriminated against unless equipment is available free of charge or available for hire at an affordable rate.

ESTEEM

Esteem in the context of sport is concerned with the views and judgements of society. In many cultures societal values dictate that women should not take an active part in sport and physical activity, or if they do it should be confined to 'feminine' sports such as gymnastics and not 'macho' pursuits such as football and rugby. These judgements are based on the traditional roles that men and women have taken in society and may be very difficult to break.

STEREOTYPES AND SPORTS MYTHS

Often minority groups within a community may be labelled as having certain characteristics or traits, and thus can be steered into certain sports or sporting positions and away from other potentially successful areas. Stereotypical views like this are a form of discrimination.

KEY TERM

stereotype
a widely held series of characteristics or traits, often oversimplified, about individuals or certain groups in society

Stereotypical views may also lead to myths in sport, thereby feeding the discrimination. Common sports myths are that 'black men can't swim' or 'white men can't jump'. Myths are based on very little truth, but often become an over-riding aspect in selection and opportunity.

A good example in the UK is the ongoing lack of Asian footballers. Much research has been done in this area and programmes are now being set up to redress the balance – specifically the Let's Kick Racism Out of Football campaign.

▶ *Let's Kick Racism Out of Football has set out to actively include minority ethnic groups in the game*

Stereotypes and myths can become **self-fulfilling prophecies**. Even the people they discriminate against may believe they are valid and may begin to conform to the stereotype by displaying the appointed characteristics and by choosing the sports that fit these characteristics. In doing so they are unwittingly reinforcing society's view. For instance, older age groups may have been influenced by society's stereotypical views. It is only recently that sports centres have begun to attract older customers, and many now run programmes such as 'Ageing Well' or 'PrimeTime' in an attempt to persuade more people that an active lifestyle can have health and fitness benefits throughout life.

PEER PRESSURE

Peer pressure can also have a negative impact on sport and physical activity participation, especially on young people. Pressure from friends and others at school can make youngsters conform to the stereotypes and myths of society. Unfortunately, peer pressure is probably at its highest during early teens which coincides with the time when most people make key choices about the sport and recreation in their lives.

KEY TERM

self-fulfilling prophecy
a state where people believe a stereotypical view and take on the appointed characteristics

REMEMBER

- Discrimination in sport and recreation arises from socio-cultural variables. There are five main areas of discrimination: gender, race, age, ability and socio-economic background.
- The three elements in sport that are affected by discrimination are provision, opportunity and esteem.
- Stereotypes have an important influence in sport, affecting access and selection.
- Stereotypes in sport often lead to myths and self-fulfilling prophecies.

GEOGRAPHICAL FACTORS

Geographical factors can also affect the opportunity of access to sport and recreation. Where a person lives and the distance to facilities and natural resources will affect their decision regarding which sports to pursue and how often they should participate. Some areas of the UK have large areas of natural resources, such as beaches and lakes, which

facilitate recreation. For those who live in a city there may be parks and open spaces to use and they may have easier access to facilities, such as sports halls and clubs. However, they may have a long way to travel to take part in outdoor recreations.

▶ Outdoor recreations, such as in-line skating, may not be accessible to city-dwellers

EDUCATIONAL FACTORS

Most people first learn to play a sport at school and consequently the type of school and PE experience a person has been through influences their choice of sport and recreation in adult life. School facilities are now being opened up to the public after school and at weekends. The current government policy of extended opening will happen in every school across the country, which means more people will have access to sports facilities.

TAKE IT FURTHER

Can you identify any sports facilities available through schools in your area?

CASE STUDY   HOW MANY ARE PLAYING?

Adults participating in at least one sporting activity	Yearly	Monthly	Weekly	3 times a week
	65.5%	43.2%	31.3%	14.6%

Table 7.2 Participation in sport in the UK   The General Household Survey, ONS 2002

- What do these figures tell us?

TAKE IT FURTHER

Look at Table 7.2. Can you find any comparative figures for other countries? How do the UK figures compare with those for other countries?

KEY TERM

programming
specific sessions and times in a sports facility provided for particular target groups

THE SPORT FOR ALL CAMPAIGN

Originally set up in 1972 and still continuing today, the Sport For All Campaign highlights the value of sport and promotes the idea that sport should be accessible to all members of the community. The campaign initially hoped to increase the opportunities for sport and recreation through developing more facilities and by educating the public on what was available. More recently, the campaign has diversified to target groups of the population that remain under-represented in sport. Campaigns such as '50 and All to Play For' (aimed at older people) and 'What's your sport?' aimed at women have followed.

REFORMATIVE POLICIES

These are the strategies and initiatives put forward to try to encourage people into physical activity. Some national policies have been already been mentioned. Sport England has an Active Places programme which aims to give people access to a web-based database of facilities and clubs in their local area where they can get involved in sport. The PESSCL (PE, School Sport and Club Links) strategy developed by the Youth Sport Trust provides more opportunities for school-aged children to take part in physical activity. It also encourages links between schools and clubs so that there is a natural progression from one to the other and somewhere for young adults to continue playing when they leave school.

TASK

Visit a local sports centre. Can you find examples of concessions and programming in their offer?

Sport England has recently undergone a major reorganisation and has refocused its role into enhancing the opportunity for the whole population to access sport. To facilitate this aim it has launched a range of strategies under the National Framework for Sport in England. In its Active Peoples Survey 2005/6, Sport England has set the strategic aim of increasing participation to 70 per cent over the next four years.

- **Making England Active** – aims to help people of all ages to start and stay active in sport. Sport England sees its role as developing a dynamic network of clubs, coaches and volunteers to increase the opportunities for all to participate in sport and recreation.

- **Multi Sport Hubs** – the development of community sports facilities that offer multiple sport and recreation activities as well as bringing educational, health and social welfare services together under one roof. Sport England sees the development of these facilities as the key to boosting the number of people actively engaged in physical activity.

- **Active Places** – a web-based resource that allows people to search for facilities in their local area. The website gives links to clubs in a local area and the aim is to make it easer for people to get involved in sport and recreation.

- **Public Service Agreements** – the Department of Culture, Media and Sport and Sport England have laid out key public service agreements that schools, local authorities and other local agencies have signed.
  - PSA Target 1: enhance the take-up of sport by 5–16-year-olds; aim is 85 per cent by 2008 having access to two hours of quality PE and sport.
  - PSA Target 3: increase participation in sport and active participation by 3 per cent by 2008 in priority groups.
- **Active People Survey** – Sport England's ambitious targets will be tracked and measured by an Active People Survey undertaken at least every three years.

CONCESSIONS

In the UK most people have to 'pay to play' and the costs of joining a sports club or team and regularly taking part can be considerable. Many sports facilities offer certain target groups cheaper prices or offer schemes that make it cheaper to participate.

Fig 7.3 *Sports facilities run by local authorities very often offer concessions, such as monthly passes at reduced prices*

▶ *Sports centres help promote activities and sports and aim to increase participation in sport*

CASE STUDY
THE COST OF SPORT

Annual membership – usually £40–£60 for a team sport, several hundred for a golf club

Weekly subs or match fees – usually £3–£6 (over the season, total cost approximately £80)

Playing kit and equipment – approximately £50–£100 for boots, training shoes, socks, etc.

Transport costs – approx. £30 (for away fixtures, etc.)

Social costs – approx. £50 (buying raffle tickets, attending fundraising functions, drinks, etc.)

Average cost for senior football/hockey/cricket/rugby/netball club player – approx. £200–£350 per season.

■ Can you identify groups who may find it difficult to meet the costs of playing club sport?

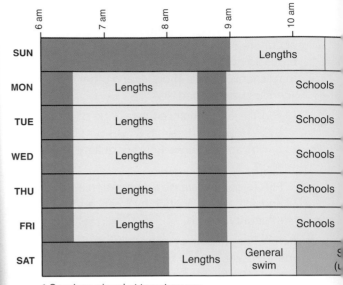

* Sessions aimed at target groups

Fig. 7.4 *Many local sports centres have programmes aimed at promoting participation*

PROGRAMMING

At a local level, sports centres often use a system called programming – a strategy where sessions and deals are allocated to particular target groups, such as women-only sessions, or over-50s sessions. Another programming strategy is to offer concessions to target groups – making it cheaper for particular types of customers.

LOCAL SCHEMES

In many areas local authority leisure departments and local sports clubs have developed their own programmes aimed at promoting participation. Examples include:

■ Sports centres in Derbyshire offering an ironing service as part of an activity price. This was particularly aimed at women at home who reported that one of the main reasons for not participating was a lack of time due to the demands of family life.

■ In Stoke-on-Trent sport and leisure centres provide weekly ageing-well sessions aimed at the over-50s. These sessions offer a range of low impact sports and fitness activities as well as refreshments.

■ Many local authorities also run GP referral schemes, where people visiting their local doctor will be offered the chance to improve their fitness for a limited time at no, or a subsidised, cost at a local leisure centre as well as receiving a prescription for any medication.

TASK

Check out your local sports centres. Can you find any evidence of local reformative programmes aimed at increasing participation?

COUNTY AND SCHOOL PARTNERSHIPS

There are now 43 County Sports Partnerships across England. Their role is to develop and streamline a localised network of clubs, coaches, volunteers and competitive opportunities. To facilitate this County Sports Partnerships have teams of full-time staff who work to develop the links across their county.

There are over 400 School Sports Partnerships in England. They provide the focus for the delivery of the PESSCL project and play a key role in helping young people take their first step towards lifelong participation in sport and recreation (see page 121).

TASK

The Sport England website offers a range of case studies from County Sports Partnerships across the country.

See if any relate to your area.

Swimming: main pool sessions

12 pm	1 pm	2 pm	3 pm	4 pm	5 pm	6 pm	7 pm	8 pm	9 pm	10 pm
General swim		Family fun			General swim		Party hire	Lengths		
Lengths	General swim				General swim				WW	Lengths
Lengths	General swim / **Primetime* (over 50s)**		Staff training			General swim	N.O.A	Swimming Club		Lengths
Lengths	General swim				General swim					
Lengths	General swim					General swim	Aqua natal*	Ladies Only* / WW		
Lengths	General swim / **Primetime* (over 50s)**					General swim		Swimming Club		Lengths
Lengths	General swim					Party hire	Family fun		Lengths	

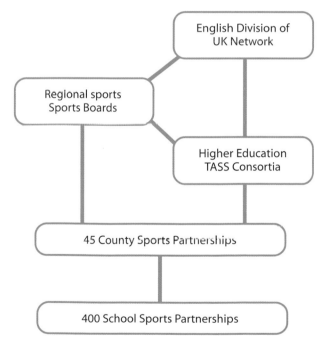

Fig. 7.5 *Sport England's sports network*

- English Division of UK Network
- Regional sports Sports Boards
- Higher Education TASS Consortia
- 45 County Sports Partnerships
- 400 School Sports Partnerships

TAKE IT FURTHER

Which reformative programmes do you think would work best with which target groups? Can you think of any other methods or schemes that would encourage people to participate in sport and recreation?

TECHNICAL DEVELOPMENTS AND CULTURAL TRENDS

There are a number of developments and trends that influence a person's choice in taking up sport and physical activity, such as:

- the recent huge growth in private gyms and health clubs (the issue here is to do with the cost of membership)
- fashion and the role of the media – this can have a positive effect as has been shown by a recent upsurge in both ballroom dancing and ice skating due to high profile TV shows featuring these activities
- technology linked to access – equipment and sports kit is getting cheaper and of a better quality, which in turn has had a positive effect on sport
- adrenalin and adventure sports – there has been a rise in popularity over the last decade, especially in sports labelled 'street' such as rollerblading and skateboarding. This has been facilitated by many local authorities providing nearby skate parks
- the impact of the 2012 Olympic Games being awarded to London.

▶ *London is awarded the 2012 Olympic Games*

CASE STUDY
WOMEN'S FOOTBALL

In the UK there were 11,000 female football players in 1993 and there were 150,000 by 2006.

The Football Association (FA) only began promoting women's football in 2001. An FA survey in 2000 concluded that 1 million girls played football recreationally, but 52 per cent of this number had never had the opportunity to join a club or a team. On the current FA Women's Football Committee there are 10 men and one woman!

- Can you suggest the cause of the rise in those women playing football in 2006?

WORK OF SPECIALIST AGENCIES

WOMEN'S SPORTS FOUNDATION (WSF)

Funded through Sport England, the WSF is the UK's leading organisation dedicated to improving and promoting opportunities for women and girls in sport and physical activity. Since its inception in 1984 the WSF has been involved in a variety of projects to promote women's sport. These have included:

- Women's Sports Foundation Awards, which help female athletes prepare for international competition

- Elite sports workshops and training on dealing with the media, attracting sponsorship and the use of sports science

- National Action Plan for women's and girls' sport and physical activity, which has empowered sports-related organisations to identify target actions that would help achieve sporting gender equity

▶ *The Women's Sports Foundation is dedicated to promoting opportunities for women and girls*

▶ *Children, young people and adults with a disability are campaigning to have equal access to sport and physical activity facilities*

- Women into High Performance Coaching – a project working with four National Governing Bodies in Sport and attempting to develop more women into high performance coaching positions
- Women Get Set Go, which is aimed at getting more young women into sports leadership (this project is run jointly with Sports Leaders UK)
- Women in Sport Resources, which aims to assist schools, clubs and sports organisations.

ENGLISH FEDERATION OF DISABILITY SPORT

This is the national body responsible for developing sport for people with a disability in England. It works closely with and promotes the work of the other five National Disability Sports organisations recognised by Sport England:

- British Amputees and Les Autres Sport association
- British Blind Sport
- WheelPower British Wheelchair Sport
- Mencap Sport
- UK Deaf Sport.

With headquarters at Manchester Metropolitan University the organisation works through a network of nine regions that support national priorities and develop disability sports programmes to respond to local needs. Their mission is to be the united voice of disability sport, seeking to promote inclusion and achieve equality of sporting opportunities for people

with a disability. In practice, this means promoting disability sports events and performers with a disability. Their current high profile programme called 'Count Me In' aims to get 10,000 people to register their support towards children, young people and adults with a disability who should have equal access to sport, fitness and recreational facilities.

KICK IT OUT!

The Let's Kick Racism Out of Football campaign was launched in 1993. It plays a major role in promoting the Football Against Racism in Europe (FARE) campaign. Supported and funded by football's governing bodies, the campaign works through football, educational and community sectors to challenge racism in football.

▶ *Let's Kick Racism Out of Football, a national programme supported by all professional football teams*

LONG-TERM ATHLETE DEVELOPMENT

PHILOSOPHY

The Long-term Athlete Development (LTAD) programme attempts to create clear pathways in sport. The aim is twofold and consists of promoting:

- pathways that introduce people into sport
- pathways that allow people progression in that sport.

The concept of LTAD is credited to Istvan Balyi (2001), the elite sports consultant who wrote an article on the stages in the development of a long-term athlete. Since publication the programme has been used as the model for elite sports development in the UK by UK Sport. The majority of National Governing Bodies in Sport (NGB) in the UK have now produced an LTAD pathway for their sport. The key to the plan is that the pathway is based on the individual maturation of the performer rather than on chronological age. This acknowledges the fact that individuals mature and grow at different rates. In the past this may have meant that late developers would have been missed by the traditional sports pathway.

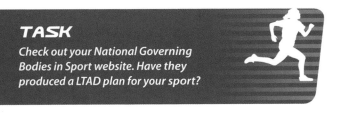

TASK

Check out your National Governing Bodies in Sport website. Have they produced a LTAD plan for your sport?

PRACTICE

The basic LTAD programme identifies six key stages in the development of a long-term athlete:

FUNdamentals – the aim here is for the young performer to learn all the fundamental movement skills and build overall motor skills. This stage is aimed at boys aged 6–9 years and girls aged 6–8 and above all activities should be fun.

Learning to Train – a major learning stage where there is further development of the FUNdamental skills. This stage is aimed at boys aged 9–12 years and girls aged 8–11. During this stage young performers should spend approximately 80 per cent of their time in training and 20 per cent in competitive events.

Training to Train – the objective of this stage is to build an aerobic base, develop speed and strength and further develop sport-specific skills. This stage is

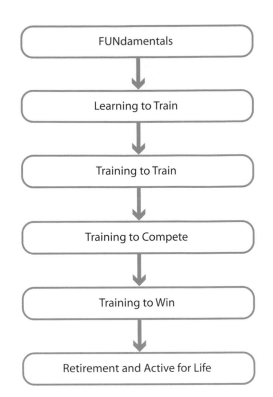

Fig. 7.6 *The six stages in the development of a long-term athlete*

aimed at males aged 12–16 years and females aged 11–15. The main focus is on learning the basics rather than taking part in competition.

Training to Compete – the aim here is for the performers to optimise fitness and develop position-specific skills as well as work on their overall competitive performance. This stage is aimed at males aged 16–23+ and females aged 15–21+. The key at this stage is to give a range of competitive situations in training.

Training to Win – the final stage of athletic preparation where the performer is working towards podium performance. Athletes need to maximise fitness and develop technical and tactical skills including decision making. This stage is aimed at males aged 19+ and females aged 18+.

RETIREMENT AND ACTIVE FOR LIFE

At the end of a performer's playing career the retirement or active for life stage comes into play. This could include:

- moving from one sport to another, for example a sprinter takes up bobsledding
- moving from competitive sport to recreational activities such as jogging and cycling

- moving from highly competitive sport to lifelong competitive sport through age-group competition such as Master's Games

- retiring from competitive sport and moving to sport-related careers, such as coaching, officiating, sport administration, small business enterprises, or media-related activities

- moving from competitive sport to a volunteer role, as a coach, an official or an administrator.

Balyi and Hamilton (2004) described two models for their stages in long-term athlete development – that sport could be classified as either an early or a late specialisation.

Early specialisation – some sports such as gymnastics, swimming, figure skating, diving and table tennis require early sport-specific specialisation in their training.

Late specialisation – sports such as athletics, team sports, combats and rowing require a generalised approach to early training. It is suggested that for late specialisation sports specialist training should not commence before the age of 10.

EXAM TIP

Look for local examples of target-group programmes and reformative policies at your local sports centres. Don't forget to use these in your answers to examination questions.

Early specialisation model	Late specialisation model
1 Fundamentals/Learning to Train/Training to Train 2 Training to Compete 3 Training to Win 4 Active for Life	1 Fundamentals 2 Learning to Train 3 Training to Train 4 Training to Compete 5 Training to Win 6 Active for Life
Sports examples: gymnastics, trampolining, swimming	Sports examples: team games, athletics, rowing

Table 7.3 Comparison of early and late specialisation models

ExamCafé

Relax, refresh, result!

Refresh your memory

Revision checklist

▷ Explain the concepts of sports for all and mass participation

▷ Describe and apply Sport England's participation segments

▷ Explain the constraints of participation and the term target group

▷ Discuss examples of reformative policy

Revise as you go

1. Give examples of the intrinsic and extrinsic benefits of mass participation.

2. Outline some of the constraints on mass participation in the UK.

3. How have changes in lifestyle affected access to sport and recreation?

4. Define what is meant by the term 'target group'.

5. Explain why women may find it difficult to access sport and recreation.

6. Explain what the term provision means in relation to access to sport and recreation.

7. How can sporting myths affect access to sport and recreation?

8. Describe the four Sport England participation segments.

9. Explain and give examples of what is meant by the term reformative policy.

10. Explain and give examples of how sports facilities use 'programming' to increase participation.

11. Give examples of strategies that underpin Sport England's framework for sport.

12. Comment on how technical developments have had an impact on the provision of sport and recreation over the last decade.

13. Describe the role of the Women's Sports Foundation.

14. Explain the four stages of the Long-term Athlete Development model.

Get the result!

Sample question and answer

Exam question

Explain, using examples, what is meant by the terms opportunity, provision and esteem in relation to a person's access to sport and recreation. **(6 marks)**

Student answer

To have access to sport and recreation a person must be given the opportunity in terms of free time and the necessary equipment and cost of participation. They must have the chance to participate regardless of their background. For example, if a person wants to use a local gym they will need to have leisure time to visit and also be able to afford the membership or session fee. Provision refers to the facilities or places where a person can participate in sport and recreation. Is there a sports or leisure centre close to where the person lives or works — how accessible is the facility, do they walk there or do they need transport? For some people such as young or old people this can increase the cost of participating — they have to pay for the sports session as well as a bus or taxi and this can make it too expensive.

If people lack esteem they will not want to participate in sport. Some target groups such as women feel they can not be seen in public swimming pools, they feel uneasy about their body image so will not go and have access to recreation. Some pools try to react to this by having women only sessions to help build esteem.

Examiner says:

This is a sound answer; it works through the question well and covers all that is required. They have explained each of the key terms and then linked this to a specific example. This answer would score the maximum 6 marks available.

UNIT 2
THE CRITICAL SPORTS PERFORMER

PART C
OVERVIEW

The fundamental principle that shapes the work you will undertake in fulfilling the requirements to successfully complete Unit 2 is that you will be engaged in applied coursework tasks that seek to critically develop you as the 'performer in action'.

By *critical* it is expected that you will be willing to analyse your participation in sport or physical activity in terms of both your performance and the context in which it exists. This will require you to understand your own strengths and weaknesses and act to reinforce the former while limiting the negative effects of the latter.

In this unit you will be required to undertake four coursework tasks each of which reflects on the holistic nature of sport and physical activity through applied participation. The tasks are designed to prepare you for a lifelong participation in sport and physical activity focusing on your selecting two defined pathways taken from the three roles common to all sports and physical activities – namely the roles of 'performer', 'leader' and 'official'.

The selection of which roles you undertake is dependent on your own personal preferences, on the alternatives within your institution and in your local community.

SPORT AND PHYSICAL ACTIVITY

By definition sport will include any recognised activity that has an Olympic base, a national governing body, physiological preparation, a local and national structure or meets the specific needs of a local environment and does not involve the intent of deliberate harm to an opponent. Such sports are those in the mainstream school or college curriculum and those undertaken in the wider community.

A physical activity will by definition mean those activities that do have a physiological component, technical merit and tactical considerations but lack a more formal national structure. Examples include rock climbing, dancing or fell running.

CHAPTER 8 THE CRITICAL SPORTS PERFORMER

LEARNING OUTCOMES

By working through this chapter, you should be able to:

■ develop a critical understanding of what constitutes a developing sporting performance in your two prescribed roles

■ understand (through participation) how to enhance your performances

■ build knowledge and understanding of the place of sport, activity and recreation at local and national levels

■ develop applied skills and techniques in the analysis of sport and physical activity

■ become independent learners able to undertake research

THE FOUR COURSEWORK TASKS

This unit is worth 50 per cent of the Advanced Subsidiary award and is marked out of a total of 90.

Task 2.1 **Personal Performance** (30 marks) – participation through two roles from a choice of three

Task 2.2 **Local Study** (15 marks) – based on one sport or physical activity and reflects all three roles

Task 2.3 **National Study** (15 marks) – based on one sport or physical activity and one role

Task 2.4 **Performance Analysis** (30 marks) – dissect one sport or physical activity through five prescribed yet open-ended analysis exercises

UNDERTAKING RESEARCH

One of the biggest challenges to you during the completion of Unit 2 will be the undertaking of independent research. The nature of the four coursework tasks that you will be required to present for assessment allows you to use a variety of methodologies and to use a range of presentation mediums.

HOW TO SUCCESSFULLY COMPLETE MY RESEARCH ...

In order to successfully complete your coursework it will be expected that you will demonstrate the ability to read, investigate and present information – your

independent research. This means using established secondary sources as the principal research method and then piecing together the information you find.

Secondary sources are those that are already written and published, from books and journals to DVDs and newspapers. Primary research on the other hand has traditionally meant finding out something new before anyone else through original research. It is likely that you will produce some 'primary work' for your tasks. This will involve undertaking your own research and then creating a review or collective account of the opinion, data and evidence that you have read or seen.

EXAM TIP

Seek guidance in the first instance from your centre staff on where you may find the information you need.

Construct a writing plan with a timescale that fits in with your centre staff's expectations ... never allow yourself too little time to do your research as this can take longer than the actual writing of the task.

Visit your centre and local library to find the range of material available to you.

Record all your findings as you go along and ensure you keep references to the pages you have read, the authors, the publishers and the date of publications.

Never attempt to hand in a final submission from one attempt. Your centre will expect you to present a 'draft' attempt on at least one, if not two occasions. This will allow you time to make the required corrections before you hand in the completed tasks and gain higher marks.

WHAT ARE THE PRESENTATION MEDIUMS OPEN TO ME?

The variety of presentation mediums open to you are at your discretion and will allow you to follow your own strengths and weaknesses. These include:

■ traditional essay style narrative

■ Microsoft PowerPoint® presentations

■ lecture style delivery with video coverage

■ 'podcasts' with question and answer sessions

■ video footage of performances.

At all times it is important for you to keep records of all your experiences as these are evidence to verify your levels of participation and the standards reached.

RECORDING AND EVIDENCE OF YOUR COURSEWORK – INDIVIDUAL CD/DVD, THE 'E-PORTFOLIO'

In order to satisfy the assessment requirements of Unit 2 you and your centre staff assessors will be required to build a bank of evidence that reflects your achievements. Further explanation of each task and the appropriate methods open to you will be contained in this chapter. Your e-portfolio CD/DVD will live with you throughout the length of the AS course and you will be free to update and amend the content of this as often as you or your centre wish.

The examination board will also provide your centre with formal assessment sheets. These will require you to detail the experiences you have undertaken during the completion of each task and the level to which you have participated for Task 2.1 and depth of your knowledge and understanding for Task 2.4. These assessment sheets help build the e-portfolio that profiles you and as such will help you gain the higher mark bands.

There is no set timescale for the completion of each task and your centre will construct a series of deadlines for you in order to present your e-portfolio for final submission in May of the year of examination.

THE 'E-PORTFOLIO'

Modern recording methods and the use of technology now mean that for the purposes of assessment all the completed tasks for Unit 2 can be saved electronically onto an 'e-portfolio'. The e-portfolio is a CD/DVD that contains all the evidence, including some research where appropriate. In the first instance, this will be standardised by your centre staff and then marked in line with the examination board criteria.

The e-portfolio will then be submitted to a moderation team who will look at the evidence presented to ensure the marks awarded to you by your centre staff are accurate and in line with the expectations of the examination board. Each of the four coursework tasks will differ slightly in their presentation format and you will be allowed to 'mix and match' how you choose to present your coursework for final submission and marking.

EXAM TIP

Never keep a single copy of any work. Back up your e-portfolio with a second copy on a data pen or CD/DVD and on an independent hard drive.

Hard copies may be needed by your centre for assessment as these are sometimes easier to read and correct. Initially, you may find this an easier medium to work with.

HOW DO I FIND THE INFORMATION I WANT?

Research requires investigation – finding out things! You will have a range of avenues to help achieve this. Your centre will have a range of text books, coursework and websites and you can explore journals and magazines with sport and activity coverage. Such examples are:

- The National Governing Body websites, e.g. www.RFU.com
- *Balls Sport* magazine
- PE Review (Phillip Allen Updates).

EXPLANATIONS OF CONSTRUCTING A PLAN, REFERENCING AND PLAGIARISM

OBJECTIVE AND SUBJECTIVE OPINION

The movement into advanced level GCE courses will require you to develop an understanding of your coursework tasks based on the building blocks of:

- research – reading more than one source of evidence
- planning – writing a series of headings with sub-points on which you expect to write
- time management – detail a time framework for the completion of each stage of the task
- presentation – decide as early as possible how you are going to present the information, knowledge and understanding that you have obtained from your research for assessment.

In order to achieve the higher mark bands you will need to focus your knowledge and understanding on **objective** rather than **subjective** opinion.

KEY TERMS

objectivity

the nature of an opinion or study based on fact and evidence and free from personal or emotional distortions or biases of a subjective nature. Examples in terms of human performance could be who is the fastest sprinter of all time as decided by accurate timing technology, or the use of 'Hawkeye' as opposed to the human eye when deciding if a ball is either in or out in tennis. National Governing Body information on participation levels and facility provisions can be taken as 'fact'

subjectivity

the nature of an opinion or study based on personal feelings, interests and prejudices. An example would be how good a performer you think you are or which person you think is the best in your centre in a particular sport

Sports or physical activities that rely on evidence to decide a result, such as the high jump or a swimming race, are objective in nature. Cricket has a third umpire and skiing has electronic timing systems.

In your submission of coursework you must ensure that the basis of your coursework is objective in nature, although by definition if you are to be critical it is inevitable that you will offer some subjective opinion. This opinion can still be formed from a logical and constructive knowledge and understanding. An example of this would be in assessing the local provision of facilities in your school or area. Your opinion may be that the facilities are very good because of their range and quality.

QUALITATIVE AND QUANTITATIVE EVIDENCE

The basis of your research and individual portfolio will rely heavily on both qualitative and quantitative evidence. The move to a more objective e-portfolio will evolve over the length of the AS and A2 courses.

Qualitative evidence is evidence that is dependent on a measure of the quality of a performance. Ice dancing, diving and gymnastics are judged not only on combinations of technical merit and the final outcome achieved but also on the aesthetic beauty, rhythm and the choreography involved, as appropriate. So qualitative evidence is often based on a level of subjective opinion while open to biases. You will be required to amass evidence through written tasks, examination board evaluation sheets, video clips, still photographs and written narratives.

Quantitative evidence is evidence that is based on the recording of numerical data that measures not only the performance but also the outcome of the performance. In sport or physical activities technology now underpins the preparation and evaluation of performances. Removing bias and creating objectivity will provide you with a positive platform from which you can complete your coursework tasks.

TASK

Court Room: Divide the class into two groups. Establish a set of criteria on how you could judge or rate a particular sport or physical activity performance. One half must present the arguments that support the view that a performance of a games player, such as a hockey or tennis player, has a higher value by all established criteria than those of, for instance, a swimmer or a gymnast. The other group presents the arguments against. Such criteria could be the degree of technical difficulty of the performances, the physiological demands placed on the performers and the degree of tactical knowledge required. Your teacher or lecturer will be the judge!

TASK

Class debate: Should all sports or physical activities embrace every aspect of technology in their refereeing or judging process?

List four arguments for and four arguments against this motion before you begin.

THE HARVARD REFERENCING METHOD

The Harvard referencing method or system is now regarded as the universal process for validating work. All published work will be dated, from a named author; in the case of books, DVDs and journals it will have a publisher and where appropriate page or other content identifications. You are advised to present your coursework tasks with full referencing and also to include a bibliography. A bibliography is a list of the resources you have used to complete the task. This is usually the text or specialist books you have read as well as journals, newspapers and DVDs.

When referencing in the text of your coursework tasks use only the author and the year of publication, usually all in brackets or underlined, e.g. (Jens Bangsbo, 1994).

At the end of a sentence or paragraph that you have copied almost directly word for word or when using a direct quote, you should also give the author and date of publication, e.g. (Pereni and Cesare, 1998).

A bibliography comes at the end of your task and it is a list of the resources you have used. These should be listed alphabetically by author. You should include the publisher, the chapter and page references used, the date of publication and book edition. The correct punctuation is important and should be used, e.g. Honeybourne, J., Hill, M., Moors, H., *Advanced Physical Education and Sport* (2nd Edition), Ch9, pp 103–105, Stanley Thornes, 2000.

When referencing information gained from journals, magazines, newspaper articles and CD/DVD the same presentation format must be used. For websites these can be referenced under a sub-title in the bibliography and it is recommended that you include the full website address, e.g. www.teachpe.com

KEY TERM

plagiarism
claiming someone else's work as your own

EXAM TIP

When presenting your coursework for final submission you are required to reference and authenticate the work as your own.
*If you copy other students' work, include direct Internet downloads or 'lift' sentences from secondary sources without reference, you are guilty of **plagiarism**. This will result in your coursework submission receiving reduced or zero marks.*

Never assume coursework can be written at the last minute. View your selected tasks as ongoing working documents building to a final submission and devote sufficient time to your research and preparation.

THE LINK BETWEEN THE AS AND THE A2 COURSES

The tasks in Unit 2, and then in Unit 4 of the A2 course, are designed to be interrelated and as such support the learning outcomes of each unit. The progression from the AS to the A2 course also draws heavily on the theoretical content contained in Units 1 and 3. The links between Units 2 and 4 and the support from Units 1 and 3 are listed in Table 8.1.

Unit 2	Unit 4
Task 2.1 Personal Performance ⟶	Task 4.3 Progressive Participation
Tasks 2.2 Local Study/2.3 National Study ⟶	Task 4.2 International Study
Task 2.4 Performance Analysis ⟶	Task 4.1 The Development Plan
Units 1, 2, 3 and 4 ⟶	Task 4.4 The Life Plan

Table 8.1 Progression from the AS to the A2 course

TASK 2.1 PERSONAL PERFORMANCE – TWO ROLES FROM THREE!

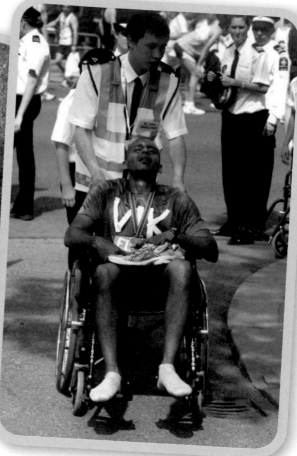

▶ *Performer – this means you select the role of an active participant in a predetermined or prescribed role – a dancer, a tennis player or a climber*

▶ *Leader – this role requires you to select a position of responsibility to work with others in order to enhance both your and their performances – a coach, an instructor, a trainer or a 'first aider'*

REMEMBER

■ Keep a 'scrapbook' of all your performances in both chosen roles. This can include programmes, newspaper reports and school or college reviews. These can be scanned into your e-portfolio and act as evidence of your achievements.

Sports and physical activities do not exist in a vacuum. We all rely on an army of volunteers who contribute to create the structures through which we participate. You will be required to select two performance roles and, through a series of applied development sessions and formal performance opportunities, develop a critical understanding of the technical, tactical, physical and psychological elements that contribute to this participation. Sport and physical activity require these four elements in a healthy combination.

During the course you will be encouraged to develop in all four of the key areas – technical, tactical, physical and psychological components – and include evidence of these on your e-portfolio CD/DVD. You will have a free choice as to which roles you may select and a wide range of sports and activities. You may select both roles from the same sport or physical activity or from different ones.

PERFORMER

A performer may be described as an individual who takes an active part in a sport or physical activity over a period of time, to allow for a minimum of three formal organised performances or planned displays of proficiency at an appropriate level to their abilities. It is expected that you will show application to your structured preparation, that is, you will aim to develop your performances through training and

▶ **Official** – this role requires you to gain experiences in officiating within a formal sporting or physical activity environment – an umpire or referee

practice, and be able to also show improvements in your knowledge and understanding of the performances that you produce.

LEADER

A leader is defined as a person involved in a sport or activity in a role that involves leadership. This may mean that you undertake the role of a coach helping an individual or team to enhance their performances, you may work as a trainer helping to complete the physical preparation of others or you may wish to gain a medical 'first aid' qualification to serve alongside others in a performance environment. You may seek formal evidence of your competencies by undertaking a national governing body award or an award in youth leadership.

OFFICIAL

An official is defined as an individual who seeks to undertake a role whereby they will be responsible for officiating in a performance. You may wish to seek formal governing body qualifications as a measure of proficiency, and for purposes of assessment you will need to be engaged in a minimum of three organised performance situations or a single tournament in line with your confidence and abilities. You will be required to select the role of an official that directly involves decision making and not the simple recording of data, or fact.

ASSESSMENT EXPLANATION

In order to complete the required assessment profile for your two chosen activities, an understanding of how you will be assessed will be invaluable to you. Each of your two chosen roles has a separate set of performance criteria which reflect the application and development that you should make throughout the AS course. The criteria are written in 'bands' and the top band covers marks 13–15. Each chosen role has a top mark of 15 so your total mark for this task could be 30.

YOUR ASSESSMENT – KEY WORDS AND CONCEPTS

Table 8.2 lists the key words and concepts that will be used to both describe and assess the outcome of your work during the AS course. As such, your teachers and the moderation team will use them in their ongoing and terminal assessments of you and in judging the application and progress you have made to your own development during the AS course.

EXAM TIP

Look at each of the applicable key words and concepts for each performance role and consider how you can improve in these areas over the length of the course – by improvement you will gain higher marks.

Performer: As a performer you will be expected to progress through your AS course and focus your developments in the following areas:	Leader: As a leader you will need to become positively involved in a sport or physical activity environment and will need to demonstrate the following:	Official: As an official you will be required to actively officiate at a formal sport or physical activity event and demonstrate the following:
■ *Short-term preparation* – how you prepare for your training, performances and recovery afterwards – warming-up, cool-down and recovery ■ *Long-term training* – the use of planned and systematic programmes designed to enhance all aspects of your ability to participate ■ *Physiological* – the ability for you to maximise the body, its systems and functions – you may be able to improve physiologically by gaining more strength and so possess a high level of 'fitness for purpose' ■ *Technical* – an accepted formal description of procedure in motor skill production – What can I do to improve my technical proficiency? ■ *Tactical* – the ability to construct appropriate plans of action, such as game plans, or interpret and counteract those of others ■ *Psychological* – the ability to maximise the mind in order to produce optimum performances ■ *Dominant performances* – when performing you will be able to produce your typical performance when demanded ■ *The pressure of expectation* – when demanded you will invariably produce a performance in line with your abilities	■ *Applied knowledge and understanding* – using what you know about a sport or activity to influence or change both the physical and psychological behaviour of others ■ *Proficient in communicating* – a measure of how effective you are at making others understand your thoughts, ideas and decisions ■ *Organisational abilities* – a measure of how good you are at managing others and/or completing a task ■ *Motivational skills* – the ability to use methods and strategies to inspire others to produce or give of their best ■ *A knowledge and understanding of health and safety issues* – especially with respect to the appropriate child protection requirements	■ *Extensive knowledge and understanding* – a measure of what you know and can then apply in your selected role ■ *Impose authority* – how well you apply and use the responsibilities and expectations of yourself and others and control both the event, or activity, as well as the participants ■ *Communication* – a measure of your ability to make your thoughts and actions understood ■ *Positioning* – the ability for you to be in the right place at the right time to officiate ■ *Signalling* – a measure of your non-verbal communication ■ *Pre-officiating protocols* – how well you structure the environment to facilitate the successful commencement of a sport or activity ■ *Performance demands* – as an official it is essential you understand the expectations and pressures facing the participant(s) in your sport or activity ■ *A knowledge and understanding of health and safety issues* – especially with respect to the appropriate child protection requirements

Table 8.2 Key words and concepts

HOW CAN I ACCESS THE TOP MARKS?

The development you make in progressing through the course will largely reflect your experiences as you move through the AS course. By using the knowledge and understanding you receive during this period you should focus on the key areas of performance shown in Figure 8.1 in order to progress.

EXAM TIP

Focus on developing high technical accuracy in your core skills and practise these under pressure as realistic to the 'real thing' as is possible.

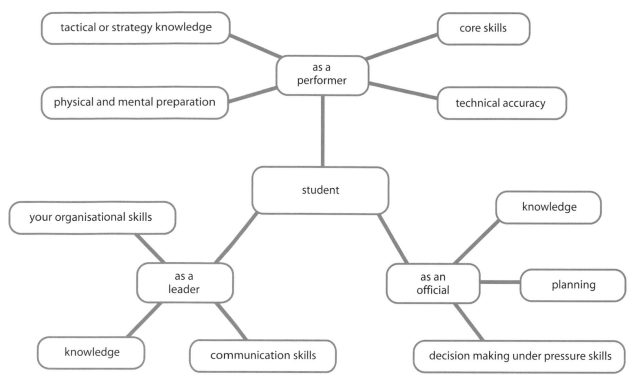

Fig 8.1 *The key areas of performance for performer, leader and official*

TASK 2.2 THE LOCAL STUDY

This task requires you to undertake a single piece of independent research that examines the local provision and opportunities for participation in one chosen sport or activity. In selecting one activity it is recommended that it is your strongest sport or a physical activity that reflects your commitments for Task 2.1.

The task must explore the provisions and organisation at grass roots level and to first-level elite selection. The task will reflect school, college, club and area provisions unique to your locality. The task will contain examination of the facilities, organisations, resources and structures that enable mass participation to begin and personal development to take place. You will be expected to include references to the place of the three performance roles of performer, leader and official and how they combine to enable participation to take place.

The focus of your task will include reference to the provisions of the public, private and voluntary sectors. In addition, it is expected that you will be able to highlight any schemes and funding provisions that contribute to the local provision. Any such provisions may include the opportunities for participants with a disability as well as catering for gender differences.

You will be expected to focus on the development opportunities in one specific role taken from Task 2.1 while also making clear reference to the provisions for the other two performance roles. It is advisable to include an appropriate bibliography reflecting the research that you have completed.

EXAM TIP

'First-level elite selection' means selection of those performers at school or club level who have been chosen to perform above others competing at the same level. When covering this section ensure you clearly explain how the school and club structure form the base for further elite selection and development as appropriate to your chosen sport or physical activity.

REMEMBER

■ When planning your coursework task write a series of sub-headings that will answer the objectives of the task in a list and allocate an appropriate word count to each section in order to achieve a 'balance' to the final submission.

APPLY IT!

Local Authorities, District and Town Councils have funding for coach and performer development.

Make an application and receive funds to complete a recognised sports award or to finance your training and competitive commitments. Your centre will support your application as part of this AS GCE course.

EXAM TIP

Always include a cumulative word count at the bottom of each page to avoid exceeding the word count limit.

RESEARCH

In completing your research you are advised to ensure you have read the appropriate sections of Unit 1 – Chapter 5 'The Development of Competitive Sport'.

Research opportunities for you will centre on the knowledge and understanding you can obtain from such sources as:

- the Internet to search for National Governing Body websites
- sports-specific journals and magazines
- broadsheet newspapers
- local county associations
- local Schools Authority and Area/ County Associations
- local club structure.

REMEMBER

- Research has to be referenced and you cannot guess facts or figures – look them up and check them!
- Use footnotes and appendices to include relevant background information that supports your answer and demonstrates the research you have undertaken.

ASSESSMENT

In order for you to fulfil this task successfully an overview of the assessment criteria will prove useful. This task is assessed in five bands and marked out of a maximum of 15 marks. A knowledge of the key content areas will help shape your final submission.

EXAM TIP

Remember that the local task requires you to include details on all three performance roles – performer, leader and official, although you may specialise in one area in particular while not ignoring the provisions for the other two roles.

KEY CONTENT AREAS FOR THE ASSESSMENT OF YOUR TASK: A CHECKLIST

- Your knowledge and understanding of the local community provisions
- Provision and opportunities at grass roots level
- First-level elite provisions at school or club
- Private, public and voluntary sector involvement
- Funding, agencies and bodies involved
- Additional considerations for gender biases and disabled participants
- Include factual data to support the objectivity of your study
- Be critical in your assessment of the local study

PRESENTATION FORMATS

In completing your local task there is a range of presentation formats open to you. In deciding which format best suits you, your own particular skills and abilities must be considered. You will be able to mix and match these throughout Unit 2. Whichever form of presentation you select, you will record this for moderation purposes on your e-portfolio. If the task is completed in written (continuous prose) format then 1000 words will be considered an appropriate length. Here are some possibilities:

- a continuous narrative or essay style task that can be punctuated with photographs, diagrams or graphs
- PowerPoint® used to accompany a formal narrated presentation
- a lecture given with accompanying notes that is videoed
- a 'podcast' accompanied by details or research.

REMEMBER

■ A plan should be made chronologically starting with the oldest event or item of reference and finishing with the latest. This gives your coursework task an historical perspective.

TASK 2.3 THE NATIONAL STUDY

Task 2.3 requires you to focus on a single performance role selected from those of Task 2.1 – Performer, Leader or Official. In doing so, you will now focus on producing a more detailed review of the developments in a single sport or physical activity beyond first-level elite representation to national selection as appropriate. Your selected sport or activity will also reflect your knowledge and understanding gained in Task 2.2 – The Local Study, and therefore you will be required to base Task 2.3 on the same sport or activity as undertaken for Task 2.2.

REMEMBER

■ The National Governing Body of your sport or physical sports activity will have website information on grass roots sport, on elite development and on disabled provisions and gender differences – use them as a first source of reference.

The pathways you explore will not only include the structures of amateur sport or activities but in addition detail those of the professional provisions available. These pathways should reflect the structure and functions of academies, the training and physical developments available to the performer to move from first-level elite selection to that of national representation. The National Study will include details of any national governing body directives and involvement, not only as a performer but as appropriate to include the provision for coaching awards, the structures for coach development and the official qualifications available.

APPLY IT!

There are over 2700 tennis clubs in this country and 18,000 public tennis courts in the UK, yet tennis remains a minority sport.

Why?

RESEARCH

In completing your research you are advised to ensure you have read the appropriate sections of Unit 1 – Chapter 5, 'The Development of Competitive Sport'.

Research opportunities for you will centre on the knowledge and understanding you will be able to obtain from such sources as:

■ the Internet for National Governing Body websites

■ sports-specific journals and magazines

■ broadsheet newspapers

■ national associations involved in sport such as the CCPR

■ county associations

■ professional sport and physical activity bodies

■ the role of academies and the schools structure from second level to national selection

■ the role of the Olympic associations and the UKSI in performer development.

ASSESSMENT

In order for you to fulfil this task successfully an overview of the assessment criteria will prove useful. This task is assessed in five bands and marked out of a maximum of 15 marks. An understanding of the key content areas will help shape your final submission.

EXAM TIP

Remember that the national task requires you to now specialise in only one of the two performance roles – performer, leader and official that you selected for Task 2.1. You will be expected in most cases to select the dominant sport or physical activity as the basis of the national study.

KEY CONTENT AREAS FOR THE ASSESSMENT OF YOUR TASK: A CHECKLIST

In order to complete the national study you will be required to demonstrate a knowledge and understanding in your final submission of the following areas:

- The structures, provisions and pathways for elite development from first-level elite representation to national selection
- The role and functions of academies
- The processes available for talent identification
- The roles where appropriate of schools, clubs, county and professional bodies and associations
- Schemes, funding and agencies such as the UKSI, TASS and EIS as appropriate
- The provisions for gender differences and athletes with disability
- Factual data to support objectivity
- Critical comment as appropriate

PRESENTATION FORMATS

In completing your national task there is a range of presentation formats open to you. In deciding which format best suits you, your own particular skills and abilities must be considered. You will be able to mix and match these throughout Unit 2. Whichever form of presentation you select, you will record this for moderation purposes on your e-portfolio. If the task is completed in a written (continuous prose) format, then 1000 words will be considered an appropriate length. Here are some options:

- a continuous narrative or essay style task that can be punctuated with photographs, diagrams or graphs
- PowerPoint® used to accompany a formal narrated presentation
- a lecture given with accompanying notes that is videoed
- a 'podcast' accompanied by details or research.

TASK 2.4 PERFORMANCE ANALYSIS

Performance analysis is now fast becoming one of the most important parts of sports and activity development. Both individuals and teams require and demand in-depth knowledge and understanding of all aspects of their performances. Those aspects would include the technical understanding of a skilled performance, the tactical knowledge needed to overcome opponents or needed in problem solving and finally those components central to an individual's development to how best use sports physiology and sports psychology.

▶ *Technical analysis of a core skill (backhand in tennis)*

Analysis is often referred to as the process of dissecting a performance to reveal its strengths and weaknesses. By strengths and weaknesses we mean those components of a performance that have been performed well and those that have been performed not so well. Such areas of analysis may include a detailed assessment of an individual or group's '**fitness for purpose**' or the quality of technical accuracy in the production in a range of motor skills.

STRENGTHS AND WEAKNESSES – SUGGESTED AREAS FOR ANALYSIS

The fundamental requirement of this part of your coursework is for you to work through a series of five performance analysis exercises in order to build a detailed picture of your strengths and weaknesses in one of your chosen performance roles undertaken for Task 2.1. The areas for analysis for the three roles are shown in Figure 8.2. The selected sport or physical activity will be the one that is seen as your dominant performance role.

> ### KEY TERM
>
> **fitness for purpose**
> a judgement on an individual's ability to meet the physical and mental demands of a particular sport or physical activity

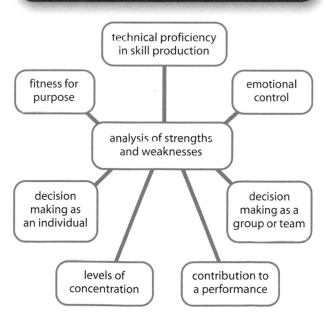

Fig. 8.2 Areas for analysis in determining strengths and weaknesses

These applied exercises are open-ended, which means that while there is an expected outcome to each task they are designed to allow you the freedom to develop, present and refine them to your own sport or activity. In doing so you will understand the need for both short- and long-term development, to support others in developing their performances and to offer pathways for personal development.

The task requirements of performance analysis may be completed during specific dedicated periods or seen as an ongoing process that builds towards your final submissions.

The five component exercises are all worth equal marks, 6 marks each, and in total your performance analysis is worth 30 marks. Each task will be assessed by:

1 The clarity of presentation and technical accuracy   0–2 marks
2 The breadth and depth of information 0–2 marks
3 The relevance to your own development as a performer   0–2 marks

The five exercises are:

1 A technical analysis of four core skills you consider essential to your successful performances in one chosen activity.
2 A tactical analysis to include how you would prepare for and be successful in competition or in the performance environment.
3 Three notational exercises on either a team, an individual or specific techniques.
4 A training analysis that reviews the specific demands and competitive requirements on teams or individuals specific to your chosen sport or physical activity.
5 An analysis of your own and others' strengths and weaknesses in your chosen activity.

THE E-PORTFOLIO

In order to successfully complete Task 2.4 you are able to use a range of presentation mediums. You are free to collate, present and arrange the evidence of your applied research through the following mediums:

- video footage
- written work sheets
- photographic evidence
- charts, diagrams and review narrative
- formal Examination Board assessment profiles.

WHY IS PERFORMANCE ANALYSIS IMPORTANT?

Performers in sport and physical activity will be effective in bringing about positive changes in their performances if they spend time constructing an understanding of what makes the *content* or *elements* of a performance. You will be required to establish a more exact and detailed understanding of your strengths and weaknesses in performances.

The human brain, unfortunately, is limited in its reliability to effectively process and store amounts of **real-time** information, yet we have traditionally relied only upon the human mind for analysis. You will, for these exercises, build a bank of objective data, knowledge and understanding providing performance-related feedback to develop refinement to your performances and in doing so be able to explain this to other people. These include your teachers, coaches and the examiners.

KEY TERM

real time
seeing or viewing something as it happens with no facility to stop the action

ANALYSIS AND IT

Modern sports analysis in seeking objective information in terms of both qualitative and quantitative data has now become an IT-driven and dependent activity. You will have no doubt seen and heard many sports and activity commentaries using computer technology to provide analysis.

TASK

List ten sports or activities where you have seen or heard IT-driven analysis.

HOTLINKS

Tools such as 'Games Analysis' developed by **www.Sportedu.org** in Australia, Dartfish or Kandle and Quintic Sports Analysis software mean sport analysis can become an 'exact science'.

TASK

Can you think of three reasons why sport or activities want to be 'scientific'?

Many sports analysis tools are easy to use and provide a more exact account of the 'action' undertaken. Bespoke software programs for sport enable analysis to become a near 'exact science'. However, you will still be able to complete your five exercises in analysis without the use of IT or sports analysis software by using still photography, hand drawings and data presentations.

WHAT DOES OBJECTIVE DATA AND ANALYSIS PROVIDE?

Objective analysis enables you, with some certainty, to make changes to your performance and this can be drawn from the following sources:

- Past performances – feedback for the correction and reinforcement of technical, tactical, psychological and physiological components

rules structure
(defines the shape and format)
- participation contract by players
- interpretation by officials
- influence of the crowd
- importance of the encounter
- weather
- time factors

scoring systems
(defines the outcome)
- results of previous matches
- cup/league
- size of playing area
- technical merit

Influences on games performances

technique
(defines individual player requirements)
- external factors (pressure/weather/game)
- physical conditioning (state of game – start or finish)
- strategy employed
- strength of opposition
- individual vs collective technique levels
- rules structure/scoring systems

strategy
(defines the way you play)
- weather/playing surface
- decision making/perceptual abilities/anticipation
- opposition's strength
- importance of the contest
- human unpredictably
- physical conditioning
- technique
- previous successes

physical conditioning
(defines the partnerships 'fitness for purpose')
- speed/length/importance of the game
- external influences – size/surface/weather
- opposition
- strategy employed
- training – pre-game preparation
- decision making – perceptual abilities

Fig. 8.3 *Summary of factors that influence games performances*

- During competition – to enable changes to tactics and strategies
- Post competition – to build on the strengths of the performance and reduce limitations on performances through weaknesses in game plans, player development, technical proficiencies and your fitness for purpose.

EXERCISE 1 – A TECHNICAL ANALYSIS OF FOUR CORE SKILLS

The requirements of you in this exercise are to undertake a technical analysis of four core skills in a single chosen sport or physical activity. The selection of which four core skills you will undertake for this exercise will be selected from your dominant performance role undertaken in Task 2.1.

PERFORMER, LEADER AND OFFICIAL – CORE SKILLS

The two selected roles that combine to make your personal performance require you to identify what makes a core skill.

For the performer this is a relatively straightforward process in establishing from a performance a range of skills that form the 'core' of your performance. What core skills do you rely on and use effectively over and over again? If undertaking the role of an official or a leader then core skills do not perhaps so easily present themselves.

It could be suggested that in the analysis of a performance it is very difficult to identify four common core skills and as such, for the purposes of your assessment, it is not important that you get this absolutely correct. You are free to select those core skills that you consider are central to and underpin your performances. Differences in what are the four core skills in a particular sport provide a healthy point of debate.

In undertaking this exercise you will be required to build an e-portfolio of evidence that examines the technical profile of your four chosen core skills. This e-portfolio will examine, in the required detail and as appropriate, four essential components that combine to build the skill (see Figure 8.4).

This profile will enable you to make use of a variety of presentation mediums and analytical tools. You are free to 'mix and match' in this exercise which presentation mediums you employ and the formats

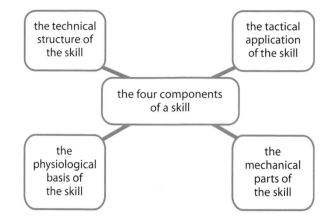

Fig. 8.4 *The four essential components that build a skill*

you decide to use. It is suggested that you could undertake to analyse your core skills by:

- video footage of you in action performing the selected core skills
- still photographs
- diagrams of core skills and their components
- for comparison purposes and thereby analysing your own strengths and weaknesses, both photographic and video footage of elite performers.

PERFORMER – CORE SKILLS

Skills exist in all human activity from eating to writing, from simple running to a back-hand top spin cross-court drive in tennis! Sounds complicated but a skill is to be viewed as the product of a combination of two fundamental processes or applications.

The first of these processes is to learn a 'technique' that defines a movement pattern, for example, the **'Fosbury flop'** in performing the high jump. This technique is different from that of the 'straddle' technique – yet both of these satisfy the requirement to clear the high jump bar. So technique provides the building blocks of a skill and therefore the way you are required to perform a movement or series of movements. Each of the movement patterns acts as a **sub-routine** that can be pieced together in the correct sequence and with the correct timing or rhythm.

KEY TERM

Fosbury flop
a high jump technique developed by Dick Fosbury, 1968 Olympics gold medallist

The second of the two processes is the use of your natural abilities. We all have a range of physiological functions which are genetically given to us and these include strength, reaction times, body somatotype, endurance, agility, balance and flexibility. Through training you will enhance these to a 'maximum' or to your potential.

REMEMBER

■ 'Talent wins games, teamwork and intelligence win championships'
(Michael Jordan)

HOW DO THESE TWO PROCESSES COME TOGETHER?

Skill can be seen as the combination of your fundamental physiological abilities and the use of technique (see Figure 8.5).

Fig. 8.5 *Performance skill is made up of ability and technique*

All performers build 'physical literacy' that comprises a range of skills performed to a degree of competency. It involves a cognitive component and can be measured against both qualitative and/or quantitative statements.

CORE SKILLS – ANALYSIS

In order to analyse core skills a frame of reference needs to be established. It is possible in virtually all skills to achieve production in terms of the intention or successful completion. However, it is not only important to complete a skilled movement or action but to do so by being technically proficient and with the exertion of the minimum of time and effort.

For some sports and activities participants seek perfection in the performance of a skill or range of skills rather than just aiming for the end result. Think of a dancer performing a balance, a gymnast undertaking a vault or a rugby player tackling an opponent – in which of these performances is the core skill a question of technical excellence or the application of the performer's abilities?

Clearly, it is a combination of both as with all **motor skills**!

KEY TERM

motor skill or psychomotor skill
an organised co-ordinated activity in relation to an object or situation which involves a whole chain of sensory, central and motor mechanisms

WHAT FOUR SKILLS MAKE UP A 'CORE'?

By definition a 'core' skill is one that all sport or activity participants will consistently call upon for their position or performance role in a sport activity. Examples of core skills are given below:

■ In gymnastics: the ability to perform a hand stand, a walk over, a backward roll, an arabesque balance, a flick flack.

■ In hockey: dribbling with both open or reverse stick, a push or slap shot, a hit, a scoop or flick, a reverse stick stop.

■ In tennis: a first serve, a forehand volley, a smash, a backhand drive, a drop shot.

Given that core skills are so varied and diverse, it is you, the student who will decide which you consider form your core **skill repertoire**. You may wish to seek advice and guidance from your teachers and coaches.

KEY TERM

skill repertoire
a range of skills, that can be performed proficiently, autonomously and whenever called upon: they form the basis of the performance

TASK

In small groups select one sport or physical activity from the categories of a team, a racket and an individual activity and list four core skills you consider the most crucial to a successful performance.

Compare your thoughts to those of the other groups.

HOW DO WE BREAK DOWN AND DISSECT A CORE SKILL?

Once you have decided upon the four core skills that underpin your performances it will be necessary to think of how you may analyse them. The most logical and straightforward process is to think of the performance of a skill as a series of movements or sub-routines. The sub-routines that you learn, piece by piece, are linked together in sequence in order for a skill to be performed. This in itself is not as easy as it sounds!

> ### KEY TERM
> **sub-routine**
> a separate technical instruction at various points through a movement

A beginner performing in the *cognitive* stage of skill learning will often find the formation of a skill is hindered by their ability to sequence movements in the correct order and more importantly with the correct timing or rhythm. This is why such skill movements often appear uncoordinated and possible 'jerky'.

IS A KNOWLEDGE OF THE STAGES OF LEARNING USEFUL TO ME?

Understanding the stages of learning, or phases as they are labelled, that a performer moves through will enable you to judge the level of technical accuracy you are able to reproduce as you enhance your sporting standards.

It may be possible for a performer, once they have identified their four core skills, to assess if these are all being performed in the 'autonomous' stage. This must be the goal of the performer. It may be possible as a tennis player that you have identified that your game is constructed around the four core skills of:

- an excellent forehand ground stroke
- a very good volley off both wings
- a very good sliced second serve

but

- an inconsistent first serve.

Analysis will reveal the technical make-up of the tennis serve based on the sub-routines that build this motor skill. It would look something like Figure 8.5.

The technical movements needed to perform the serve will only be possible if you have the necessary physical abilities – these will reflect those abilities grouped as either health-related or skill-related components. Health-related components include flexibility, strength, endurance and speed while skills-related components include co-ordination, balance agility and reaction times. It is perfectly possible for you to analyse your technical proficiency in performing the serve as deficient on both a technical fault – poor preparation in the back swing phase – and a lack of shoulder flexibility coupled with a lack of wrist strength. As a consequence of this, you will have a clear target to practise and train on in order to make the required improvements and to move the first serve into the autonomous phase.

The nature of the exercises undertaken for the analysis of performance combine to provide you with a balanced and detailed analysis of your strengths and weaknesses. As part of your examination requirements in the second year of this course, A2: Unit 4, you will be required to undertake a *Development Plan*. The development plan provides you with the opportunity to plan, perform and evaluate a self-constructed programme to improve a weakness in your performance. This can be based on a physiological weakness such as a deficiency in speed or, as in this case, a technical deficiency in one of your identified core skills.

THE LEARNING STAGES OF A SKILL

Fitts and Posner, 1967, saw the learning of a skill as a process through which the performer moved in stages or phases.

The first stage, the cognitive stage, is where fundamental movement patterns are first established,

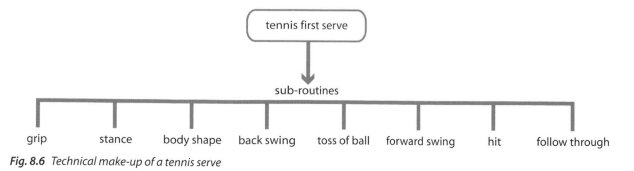

Fig. 8.6 Technical make-up of a tennis serve

learned and then put together with effort and conscious thought. There will be an enormous amount of trial and error and the performer will need to see demonstrations and learn, to some extent, from their own mistakes. Accurate guidance, both verbal and mechanical, is vital to learning.

The second stage is known as the associative stage and this is where the learner is now able to recognise a stimulus and can organise and reproduce a movement, or skill, with reasonable technical accuracy and success. The learner develops a 'feel' for the movement and has control over the outcome if inconsistencies still exist and the speed and power of both the mental processing and physical output need enhancement. The role of feedback here is vital from both internal and external sources. Learning in this stage is rapid and repetition in the form of 'drilling' or fixed practice and 'grooving' can take place. It has been estimated that a 'skill' once learned has to be successfully performed over 120 times in order for it to be 'learned'.

The final stage is where the learner is in autonomous mode where time and effort are not wasted on the thinking involved in forming a skill or on any distractions. The focus is on the tactics and strategies needed as the skill is performed successfully with rhythm and timing and no conscious thought and effort. The long-term memory has stored the components, or sub-routines, and tactical considerations that make the skill and can recall these on demand. Practice has to be continuous to avoid regression and to extend a skill by adding spin or slice, as in the tennis example.

DISSECTING A SKILL FURTHER

Once you have identified the stage of your core skill it can be analysed further into three simple phases:

- preparation
- execution
- result and recovery.

In doing this you will be able to build a simple picture of the sub-routines required in each phase, their order and importance. These foundations are the bedrock on which most of the core skills central to an active performer can be analysed. Therefore a logical sequence will be defined and provide the basis of an analysis framework.

However, what can we do with skills like those performed in athletic events such as the long jump or

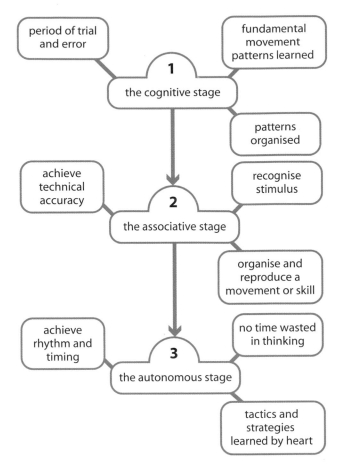

Fig. 8.7 *The learning stages of Fitts and Posner*

a swimming stroke? These sports have a truer base in the analysis of the whole skill through a performance 'timeline':

- the long jump can be analysed through the run-up, take-off, flight and landing
- a swimming stroke can be analysed through body position, arm action, leg action, timing and breathing and the efficiency of the stroke
- a trampolinist can look for the height, shape, control, centring and the aesthetic quality in the movement
- a gymnast performing a vault will look for the approach and take-off, the control of the movement, the repulsion/flight-off, the landing and the overall quality of the vault.

TASK
Can you produce an analysis structure for a shot putter?

Finally, a skill may have its technical structure based on another range of criteria. For cycling, rowing and other continuous skills where skills are performed without a specific start or end and are largely repetitive in nature, then an individual with a unique technical frame can exist. The cyclist will consider leg action, body position, head and arm positioning as well as the movement of the legs as central to any technical analysis.

You are free to construct and use any criteria or frame of reference in your technical analysis. However, you must ensure you provide the evidence in your e-portfolio that is a true representation of the depth of your knowledge and understanding and that you are able to discuss this with your teachers or lecturers.

LEADER – CORE SKILLS

If you select the performance role of a leader in sport the selection of four core skills may not be as straightforward as those of the performer. Nevertheless the core skills of a leader are just as important, and in many ways, just as obvious.

TASK

Working in small groups, can you identify three different leaders in sport or physical activities and agree on four core skills that they all have in common?

You will have perhaps agreed upon the following range of core skills:

- communication skills – verbal
- communication skills – non-verbal
- coaching style
- the application of sport or physical activity knowledge
- motivational skills
- organisational skills.

Leaders in sport and physical activities exist in many different forms and roles. The most obvious leader in sport is that of a coach – a person responsible for improving the performance of others and achieving a specific goal or group of goals. However, a leader may also be any person undertaking a role that by definition assumes responsibility and once again sets a specific goal or goals. This means a sport or physical activity 'trainer' responsible for the fitness and physiological development of others. Another example is that of a sports psychologist who is

responsible for ensuring that the performer produces his or her optimum performance when it is required – ensuring the mind is in harmony with the body and the body in harmony with the mind.

OFFICIAL – CORE SKILLS

An official is defined as any individual who has been given the formal responsibility to perform either an administration task in a sport or physical activity, a referee, umpire or judge, or a role that allows a sport or physical activity to take place. Such roles can include a sports time-keeper, a scorer, a track marshal or a recorder.

TASK

Working in pairs, can you list ten sports or physical activity specific roles that do not come under the heading of referee, umpire or judge?

You must name the role, the sport and an outline of what the official's duties are.

FORMAL OFFICIAL AWARDS

As an official in an active sport or physical activity environment you will be able to undertake formal qualifications that will gain you accreditation. Many of these are awarded from the appropriate national governing body related to your sport or physical activity. Your centre will be able to help you to apply for and undertake these and once completed they will provide you with a lifelong involvement role. Such awards include the first-level referee course in rugby union from the RFU. Your selected official role must be that of a decision maker and not that of a recorder.

The following may be considered as some of the core skills exhibited by officials:

- communication – verbal
- communication – non-verbal
- positioning
- decision making
- sport or activity knowledge.

When presenting evidence in your e-portfolio you may wish to include testimonial evidence from senior officials or your centre staff to validate your competencies as an official.

Performer	Leader	Official
■ ability ■ technique ■ tactical knowledge and understanding ■ psychological control	■ communication skills – verbal ■ communication skills – non-verbal ■ coaching style ■ the application of sport or physical activity knowledge ■ motivational skills ■ organisational skills	■ communication – verbal ■ communication – non-verbal ■ positioning ■ decision making ■ sport or activity knowledge

Table 8.3 Summary of the core skills of the personal performance roles

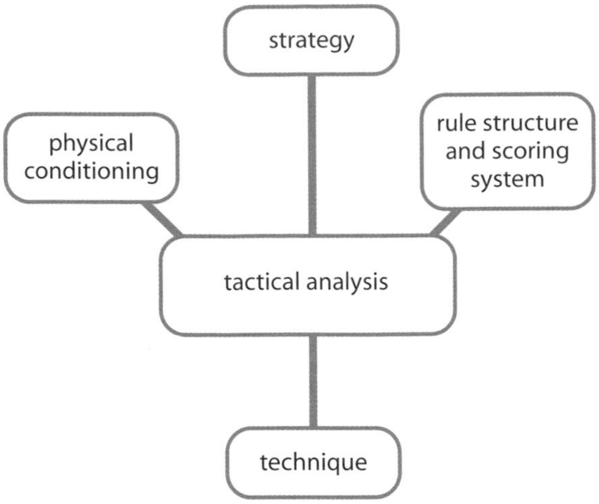

Fig. 8.8 The key factors to consider when analysing tactics

EXERCISE 2 – A TACTICAL ANALYSIS IN PREPARATION FOR PERFORMANCE

The requirement of you in this exercise is to undertake a tactical analysis on your dominant performance role from Task 2.1. A tactical analysis will review how you participate in your selected sport or physical sports activity from the standpoint of how you participate, what **tactics** you employ and the competitive plans you use.

This open-ended task will allow you to fully explore the way both individuals and teams construct and employ tactics. In traditional mainstream sports you may call upon your own experiences as well as studying the tactics of elite performers in highly competitive situations.

One simple way of structuring your analysis on how to construct tactics is to base this on four key factors as shown in Figure 8.8. A full understanding of each factor will enable you to be successful in your own performances. A knowledge and use of tactics enables you to outwit opponents!

- Devising a 'game plan' will be the overall way you can beat an opponent – **strategy**.
- An understanding of where and when to perform a technique will contribute to a successful performance.
- Possessing the correct 'fitness for purpose' enables you to perform athletically with dominance at the right time and in the right areas.
- Possessing a full understanding of a sport or physical activity rule, law and scoring structure will allow you to manipulate an event, competition or game to your advantage.

KEY TERMS

Tactics and strategies often become confused:

tactics
the detailed instructions or plans of action you employ to overcome an opponent or opponents

strategy
the more general or overall game plan employed by a coach

TASK

Using the four tactical consideration factors as headings, can you give a specific sports or physical activity example from a team game, a racket game and an individual sports activity?

An application of tactical considerations:

- Strategy – how do you overcome a bigger and stronger opposition in rugby union?
- Technique – in diving how do I perform a triple as opposed to a double front somersault needed to win a competition?
- Physical conditioning – how do I ensure I do not fall behind the pace setters in an 800 metre race?
- Rule structure and scoring system – how can a detailed knowledge of the scoring system when performing on the Olympic balance beam help me win?

The correct tactics help you structure and shape a performance. Without the correct tactics a performer could be seen as a 'ship without a rudder'. Tactics can help a less talented individual or team overcome and be successful against more talented and higher performing opponents. Tactics should be seen as the guiding principles or rules that you decide to employ.

TACTICAL EXAMPLES – INDIVIDUAL ACTIVITIES, RACKET ACTIVITIES AND TEAM GAMES

In order for you to complete this exercise successfully you may consider some of the tactical examples in Table 8.4. By doing so you may wish to think how many times you have made decisions about

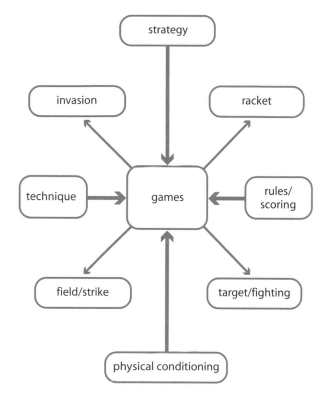

Fig. 8.9 The place of games and analysis components

the structure and shape of your performance and constructed a 'plan of action' or even changed one when things have not gone as well as was planned!

Activities	Tactical considerations
Individual activities	<ul><li>race strategy over 1500 metres</li><li>dance sequence in a competition</li><li>rock face route in climbing a new mountain</li><li>free-style alternatives in a diving competition</li><li>deciding position, when to attack and when to slip stream in the Tour de France cycling competition</li></ul>
Racket activities	<ul><li>when to play a baseline game or a serve volley game in tennis?</li><li>when to change tactics in badminton from rotation to front and back?</li><li>at what stage to attack a player with a weak backhand in squash?</li><li>how to overcome opponents with a greater range of attacking strokes in table tennis?</li></ul>
Team games	<ul><li>how to construct a game plan to overcome a dominant opposition following the first period of play?</li><li>when to change from a kicking to a running game in rugby union?</li><li>how to overcome a well-organised defence when taking short corners in hockey?</li><li>when to change from one formation to another in football?</li><li>what centre pass options to consider in netball to overcome a dominant opposition following the first period of play?</li></ul>

Table 8.4 Considerations when plannning tactics

GAMES EXAMPLE – HOW TO FURTHER EXPLORE STRATEGY?

As a performer in action you will always be asking questions which are in essence what analysis is all about … questions centred on:

- Attack v Defence – are we being outplayed in these areas?
- Anticipation v Deception – can we out-think the opposition?
- Game plans – what if this happens?
- Ongoing evaluation – who or which groups are performing well?
- Response times – are the opposition quicker in their thinking than in their actions?
- Recycle speed – do we hold on to the ball or can we pass it?
- Adaptation to setbacks – can we cope with mistakes or conceding a goal?
- Space – how can we create and deny space?

AN EXPLORATION OF SPORT AND PHYSICAL ACTIVITY STRUCTURES

In order for you to fully understand the specific context of a performance, a wider appreciation of the rationale of sports and physical activities will help. By understanding the context, organisation and structure to a performance you will be able to appreciate tactical considerations. A traditional yet simple way of categorising or grouping sports and physical activities is to place them in three distinct groups based on the performance requirements and thereby determine tactical considerations. The three categories are:

gymnastics – movement replication
athletics – power production
games – coincidence avoidance.

The first group is that of 'movement replication'. This group represents those sports and physical activities that are judged on the performer's ability to reproduce a movement, or series of movements, to an exact prescripted format. Gymnasts, board divers and figure skaters are just some examples. These performers have defined tactical considerations based on their own strengths and weaknesses and their ability to reproduce technically more difficult skills and manoeuvres.

The second group is that of sports and physical activities that are based on 'power production'. This group requires the performer to base their tactics on physiological considerations. The performer will need to plan their training, their competitive selections and their tactics on the ability to perform physiologically at a maximum. This group includes rowing, cycling and athletic events.

The final group, and the most diverse, is the group labelled 'coincidence avoidance'. This sounds very complicated and abstract but represents those sports and physical activities that engage individuals and teams in battles of territory and space or achieve a dominance in competition through the use of an object such as a ball. Invasion game players seek to avoid one another in order to score, tennis players use a ball and tennis strokes to outwit an opponent, wrong-footing them and thus being able to place the ball in open or free space.

PRINCIPLES OF PLAY – INVASION GAMES

Forms of invasion games require structure which can be based on both individuals and teams gaining an understanding of the '**principles of play**' – the

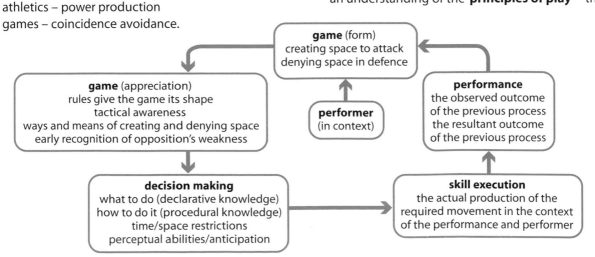

Fig. 8.10 Analysis of performance perspective in games playing

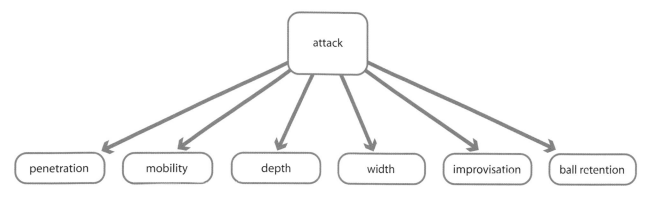

Fig. 8.11 *Principles of play in attack*

first set of tactical principles. Analysis will reveal that performances have to have tactical structure based on principles of organisational play – could you imagine all the players in a hockey team standing on one side of the field or a doubles partnership in tennis where both players always stayed 2 metres behind the baseline?

> ### KEY TERM
>
> **principle of play**
> a rule that guides how you perform. It provides shape and structure to a performance either as an individual or as a team

WHAT ARE THE PRINCIPLES OF PLAY?

The simplest way to view the tactics used in invasion team games is to separate attack from defence. What do we do as individuals and as a team when in possession of the ball and what do we do as individuals and teams when seeking to gain the ball back?

In order to build a tactical platform to win a particular competitive situation the principles shown in Figures 8.11 and 8.12 can be used.

In attack the three main components to consider are gaining then keeping possession, progression on the field of play, and the end product – scoring. When attacking you will need to evaluate the following questions:

- how well you create space moving defenders from good to bad positions
- how good are the players at making decisions
- the quality of technique of the players and their ability to improvise
- the end product of possession, penetration and goal-scoring attempts.

When defending, players will aim to concentrate close to and around their goal areas in order to deny space to their opponents. They will stack with depth – players not standing in a straight line but with others in positions to cover. They will show an organisation and physical strength not only in numbers but individually as well. Delaying the opposition and only tackling when winning back possession is certain are logical tactical principles.

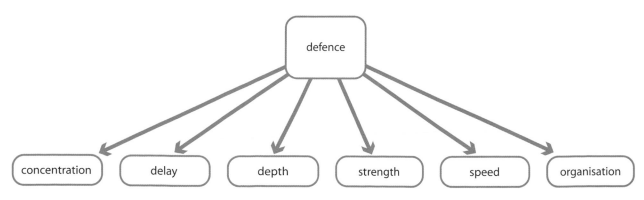

Fig. 8.12 *Principles of play in defence*

EXERCISE 3 – NOTATION

The requirement of you in this exercise is to undertake three notational exercises – these can be completed on your own performance or undertaken on another performer to aid their development.

All sports create passion and opinion – opinion that is often not based on logic, expertise or fact. When analysing sport it is useful to employ 'sports science' to support what is often your 'gut' feeling. One of the methods that you as a student can use is that of **notation**.

The question of credibility in sports analysis and in using notation crucially centres on the now accepted understanding that, following applied research undertaken to study top sports coaches covering a variety of sports, they were only found to be approximately 30–40 per cent accurate in their recollection of key events or conversely 60–70 per cent inaccurate in their recollection of key events (Hughes and Franks, 1997). With the help of notational data and quantifiable criteria-based information you will be able improve a performance.

Performance analysis requires tools, systems and methodologies and it removes conjecture and replaces it with accurate data. Such systems surround us in all modern sports. Cricket now makes use of 'wagon wheels' for bowlers and batsmen while we accept the statistics that reveal the number of tackles made in a rugby match or unforced errors and first services in tennis. Pro-zone now provides professional football clubs and rugby union teams, such as England and South Africa, with player analysis data after each match – but at a price!

KEY TERM

notation
a recording system that employs notes or symbols to record situations, events or points of action on individuals or teams during a performance. Notation was originally used by biomechanics sports scientists

Notation is one such tool that is easy to create and accessible to you, and one that can be designed in your own format to form analysis to your specific

Match Analysis: Gamesheet

Player A _____   Player B _____

		First Half		Second Half		Total
Entries into the attacking third	A					
	B					
Regained possessions in the attacking third	A					
	B					
Effective Crosses	A					
	B					
Non-effective crosses	A					
	B					
Dribbling and turning attempts in attacking and middle thirds — Successful	A					
Unsuccessful	A					
Successful	B					
Unsuccessful	B					
Achieving set plays in attacking third	A					
	B					
Strikes at goal but off target	A					
	B					
Strikes on target	A					
	B					
Goals	A					
	B					

Fig. 8.13 Example of a notation sheet

requirements. Any analysis tool, though, must be both valid and reliable to be of any worth. Does the tool therefore accurately measure what it sets out to, time and time again? What is important for us to remember is that watching a sport or activity performance is different from making an 'observation'. There is a wealth of difference between watching and an observation, where you will need to focus on the performance, not the occasion! You will be required in this and all your analysis exercises to be skilled in observation – notation will help to reduce *fiction to fact*!

TASK

Create a notation sheet on a sport of your choice. This can cover any aspect of team or individual play/performance. Set the parameters, recording style and the objective(s) of the exercise.

As an example you may wish to analyse a tennis match and record unforced errors and successful services or passes by a particular player in a team game.

TAKE IT FURTHER

Carry out the exercise either in a 'real time' situation or by video. What have you proved? List three clear learned outcomes.

ISSUES WITH NOTATION

The major issue is that your notation exercises at GCE level will centre on human recording methodologies and, even in a simplified form, will be subject to errors.

'Real time' versus recorded action also presents us with one of the major drawbacks to the use of notation. Real time can be defined as observation of 'live' events. Observing any sport or activity in real time presents significant problems in detection. The natural speed of a performance, poor viewing angles and complicated action sequences involving many performers make the exercise difficult. The human brain is limited in its reliability to effectively process and store amounts of real-time information.

CASE STUDY
NOTATION IN TENNIS

Let's look at the data collected from a promising player in a quarter final match of an under 17s national tennis tournament.

Shot	Shots played	Points won	Points lost
Serve	98	5 (ace)	12*
Lob	8	3	3
Volley	23	8	9
Smash	6	5	0
Backhand drive	143	21	7
Forehand drive	124	25	13
Chip	5	1	1
Drive volley	2	2	0

NB * represents points lost directly after a serve was made (return of serve).

The data from the volley does not add up to 23 (8 and 9) because the other six shots were in the middle of a rally and were neither winning nor losing shots. This is the same for the other shots.

If we were interested in calculating the percentage of winning volleys, we would calculate:

$$\frac{8 \text{ winning volleys}}{23 \text{ shots played}} \times 100 = 35\% \text{ (rounded up)}$$

- Calculate the percentages won for each shot played (you need the information from the second column only).
- Calculate the player's most successful and unsuccessful shot in terms of the percentages.
- What concerns from a performance analysis perspective do you have with the results you have generated?
- How would you represent this percentage data in graphical form and why?
- As a coach, how could you use this data to aid the player in the future?

Subjective analysis through human processing is problematic and undermines the processes of analysis through a number of factors:

- the length of the observation undertaken
- the passage of time from the real-time event to the video viewing
- observation conditions – indoor or outdoor field work
- highlighting – focusing on specific events rather than general play
- psychological errors – can you cope with the pressure and speed of the exercise?

TASK

Watch the video of any sports event – 15 minutes only. This is called 'real time', or as we know it 'live action' even though it is on a video! Having watched the video construct a notation sheet to cover two key areas of the performance, e.g. in netball, centre passes made successfully and shooting success rates.

Re-watch the video and from your notation sheets record with appropriate marks the number of incidents relating to your specific criteria.

Work in small groups and on completion check with others to validate your findings.

EXAM TIP

Keep your notation sheets simple and focus on two or three areas only, otherwise you will never effectively record in 'real time'.

TAKE IT FURTHER

What were the problems with the notation exercise? List three issues.

EXERCISE REQUIREMENTS: AN EXAMPLE OF WHAT YOU CAN DO

Your three notation exercises will be undertaken on you, or on another, over an appropriate period of time in order to construct a profile on one particular aspect of your performance, e.g. as a hockey player you may wish to measure the improvement in your passing over a three-month period.

Each month a teacher, friend or parent undertakes the same notation exercise on you in action, to record information on passes made, passes that reached their intended target, those that did not and the relevant distances of each. The aim of this exercise is to provide you with data and therefore understanding of your performance to then action appropriate remedial or extension training.

The Russian national team in the 1988 European Football Championships notated on 'active and 'inactive' passes. Active passes were those where the ball went forwards towards their opponents goal, was successful in reaching a team mate and was kept in possession. Inactive passes were those where the ball went sideways or backwards. An active 'pass 3' was one where the ball went forward, where possession was kept and also bypassed three opponents. This helped create a picture of each player's active passes, on passes that 'cut out opponents' and created potential scoring opportunities as opposed to inactive, negative passes.

EXERCISE 4 – TRAINING ANALYSIS

The requirement of you in this exercise is to undertake an analysis of the **training** requirements on your dominant performance role from Task 2.1.

The training analysis exercise will centre on the core performance areas of the tactical, physiological and mechanical/technical components that contribute to enable a performer to participate successfully.

The analysis will take into account the following factors:

- the need to structure training to improve a particular component
- the facilities and time span needed to bring about improvements
- the monitoring and evaluation of such training.

In order to provide depth to this exercise it is suggested that you begin this process as early as is possible in the lifespan of the AS course. By viewing this exercise as a *'training diary'* you will be able to monitor and critically review the various training experiences that you have undergone and to analyse the positive and negative experiences that you have gone through.

The work you undergo in this exercise will help you decide your Development Plan in the A2 course: Unit 4 Task 4.1.

KEY TERM

training
the ability to construct a programme to enhance proficiency in a skill, to improve physical fitness or fitness for purpose and thereby prepare the performer for participation

▶ *Training analysis is used by Paula Radcliffe and other elite performers to improve on previous performances*

TASK

Create a 'pro-forma' training review sheet that enables you to keep an ongoing log of all your training experiences. Share this with other performers and agree a 'best fit' analysis sheet.

You may wish to consider and critically evaluate the experiences and instruction that you have received during the time of the AS course. You are also encouraged to review the training experiences both in and out of your centre:

- Have the training experiences I have been involved in improved my tactical, technical, psychological and physiological abilities?

- Have I benefited from improvements in my competitive performances?

- What qualitative and quantitative data have I been able to establish on my training programmes?

- What changes have I made to my own training programmes in order to progress my performances?

COMPARATIVE REVIEWS – ELITE PERFORMERS

In reviewing the training regimes of first-level elite performers and beyond you will be able to establish the fundamental structures that are in place to ensure your performance expectations are met. Such structures include:

- the quality of coaching you have received

- the planning and monitoring of your physical development

- the evaluation of your tactical knowledge and understanding.

PRESENTATION

Your e-portfolio will now contain a bank of critical reviews of the training experiences you have undergone. These can be presented in any format and can also include still photographs, video footage and written reviews of your experiences.

APPLY IT!

The top 22 players in the 'All Blacks' rugby union team took two months away from playing in order to train specifically to be faster, bigger and stronger in preparation for the IRB World Cup 2007.

Did it work?

EXERCISE 5 – AN ANALYSIS OF STRENGTHS AND WEAKNESSES

The requirement of you in this exercise is to build on your experiences through the completion of all the analysis exercises and to objectively build a profile of your strengths and weaknesses in your dominant sports activity performance from Task 2.1.

This will be crucial to the planning of your Development Plan for Task 4.1 of the A2 course and can be undertaken as the final exercise for you and completed by way of a *'performance review'*. This review will be a combination of both objective and subjective analysis and will draw upon elite performances for comparison.

▶ *Monitoring of personal best results (PBs) is used in analysis of strengths and weaknesses*

Strengths and weaknesses are not always evident or visible to the performer and so your notation exercises, your training and your technical analysis will provide you with the information needed. Objectively you may also draw upon the opinion of others and your centre staff and sports activity coaches will help in this profiling.

Areas and methods of analysis should now be well understood and centre on the four performance components of technical proficiency, fitness for purpose, tactical knowledge and understanding and the mechanical underpinning of techniques. Using these component areas can you honestly assess your own performance?

REMEMBER

■ Never ignore the advice of your coaches. If they spot a weakness in your performances then work hard to correct it – it will gain you extra marks.

CAN I MEASURE STRENGTHS AND WEAKNESSES?

Many sports and physical activities lend themselves both in training and during the competitive performance to measurement. It is logical that during the AS course you will compile a bank of data to support your judgements.

This can be achieved through the following means:

- build a profile of the performance requirements by elite athletes for a comparative exercise
- athletics and swimming allow for 'personal bests' and training times or distances to be logged
- performance records and levels of competition you have participated in
- measurement of physical components through industry-recognised testing
- notational exercises on technical and tactical elements
- a leader may wish to use self-report questionnaires or be observed by an experienced elder
- an official may review a video of their performances.

PERFORMANCE PROFILING

Performance profiling is now well established and a functional part of elite athletic regimes. The long-term athlete development programmes, now commonplace in all sports, have incorporated profiling as the starting point for all preparation and performances. You will be used to hearing the term 'profiling' from your academic studies and essentially it allows you as an individual to highlight your strengths and weaknesses in all aspects of your performances. Those aspects or components

TASK

Carry out an assessment on another performer in the same discipline as you, using the four performance components. He or she can do the same on you and then both of you can compare the results. This may take more than one session to complete. Grading out of 10 is just one, but a common, way of assessing a performance. You can devise an appropriate set of criteria to correspond to the marking.

Can you invent a universal way of measuring the strengths and weaknesses of a performer in your sport or physical activity?

You may wish to consider a scale or list of criteria.

EXAM TIP

From the outset of the course keep a review of all your performances on a pro-forma recording sheet. By reviewing regularly you will be able to make summative statements and include them in your e-portfolio.

of a performance are based on the performer's physiological, technical, psychological and mechanical proficiencies.

TASK

Make a list of the key components of your selected sport or physical activity under each of the following headings: physiological, mechanical, technical (core or fundamental techniques, such as the different techniques or shots in tennis – serve, volley, etc.) and psychological – you may need some help from your centre staff for this. Having listed components relevant to you, now rank order them in their importance to underpinning your own performances. For instance, if maintaining concentration is the major psychological factor in your own performances then this may be ranked number one and therefore the most important to you; strength may be ranked as the number one physiological component for a weight lifter. You can start to build a performance profile.

In order to provide a structure to your profiling each of the four components, while interconnected and dependent on one another, can also be separated and viewed as self-contained components (see Fig. 8.14). Each component has its own sub-components and you will be aware of these from your other experiences in the sport or physical activity environment (see Fig. 8.15).

SPIDERS' WEBS OR WAGON WHEELS

The use of a 'spider's web' or 'wagon wheel' to visualise and structure your performance components allows you, in conjunction with your coach or centre staff, to construct a profile that diagrammatically views those areas of strength and weaknesses in your performance and forms the starting point for development programmes (see Fig. 8.16).

Physiological components can include, as you consider appropriate, strength, speed, acceleration, cardio-vascular endurance, flexibility, balance, co-ordination, reaction times and agility, for example. While psychologically you may wish to consider your levels of motivation, control of anxiety and the causes of stress, goal setting and mental rehearsal, concentration, control of aggression or arousal levels. Mechanically you will be concerned with the technical components that construct a skill, such as the use of levers, the control of force, angles of body limb positioning and **goniometry**, linear motion

and displacement along with the key technical instructions that create the sub-routines and the final overall skill.

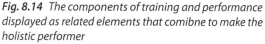

KEY TERM

goniometry
the process of measuring joint angles and therefore gauging flexibility

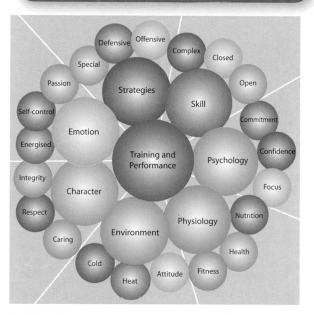

Fig. 8.14 The components of training and performance displayed as related elements that comibne to make the holistic performer

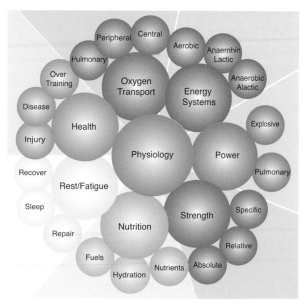

Fig. 8.15 The physiology component of training and performance with its sub-components

(Wenger, 1999)

Recording this analysis exercise on your e-portfolio will allow you to profile and format information on your strengths and weaknesses with notational data, video footage, written review, photographic evidence and observational testimony.

HOTLINKS

A useful source of information on all the exercises outlined here is on the website: **www.teachpe.com**

TASK

Construct a wagon wheel for your chosen sport or physical activity. You will need to construct three – one each for the physiological, technical/mechanical and psychological aspects. Shade in the appropriate segment to the necessary level. While subjective in nature your centre staff or coach will help make a more objective analysis.

Fig. 8.16 *A wagon wheel highlighting the performance components of a footballer*

ExamCafé
Relax, refresh, result!

Relax and prepare

Charlie

'Always use the resources available to you and make sure you hand your coursework in on time to avoid too much work close to exams. For your exams do not leave your revision late – do a bit at a time each day.'

Ed

'Complete your draft coursework early and always ask for help. Use your free time wisely and never put off work that could be done today until tomorrow.'

Harley

'Make sure you do all your coursework to a good standard so you do not have to do lots of re-writing. Hand your coursework in on time as you will get longer to make corrections. If you do not understand something just ask. The same when in class – do not be afraid to ask for help. You can go out with your friends all the time but you cannot complete your school work or exams when you want – do not waste your opportunities.'

Getting started ...

In order for you to successfully begin your coursework tasks you will need to devote sufficient time to plan, research, draft and then submit your work. Aim to find at least three sources of information such as a PE recommended text, an Internet site and a sports journal or periodical. Established texts will contain a very good level of core knowledge and understanding but you will need to 'hunt' out a deeper level of information if you wish to gain the top band marks. Read each source carefully, make review notes of each and always reference the source. Finally, use a few quotations in your coursework that add to the academic standing of your work.

Refresh your memory

Coursework checklist

▷ Seek guidance in the first instance from your centre staff on where you may find the information you need

▷ Construct a writing plan with a timescale that fits in with your centre staff's expectations. Never allow yourself too little time to do your research as this can take longer than the actual writing of the task

▷ Visit your centre and local library to find the range of material available to you

▷ Record all your findings as you go along and ensure you keep references to the pages you have read, the authors, the publishers and the dates of publication

▷ Never attempt to hand in a final submission from one attempt. Your centre will expect you to present a 'draft' attempt on at least one if not two occasions. This will allow you time to make the required corrections before you hand in the completed tasks and gain higher marks

▷ Never keep only a single copy of any work. Back up your e-portfolio with a second copy on a data pen or CD/DVD and on an independent hard drive

▷ Never assume coursework can be written at the last minute. View your selected tasks as ongoing working documents building to a final submission and devote sufficient time to your research and preparation

Coursework tips

The movement into advanced level GCE courses will require you to develop an understanding of your coursework tasks based on the building blocks of:

■ research – reading more than one source of evidence

■ planning – writing a series of headings with sub-points on which you expect to write

■ time management – detailing a time framework for the completion of each stage of the task

■ presentation – deciding as early as possible how you are going to present the information, knowledge and understanding that you have obtained from your research for assessment.

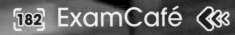

Get the result!

Common mistakes

All students make errors or mistakes when completing their coursework so do not panic if this happens! Your teachers will be on hand to help you. Always remember to keep a record of your work backed up on a disc or data pen. A hard copy is often easier to read and therefore basic errors in spelling and punctuation can be avoided when reading through this copy. Ensure you reference all your sources and quotations using the Harvard method. Do not guess facts as this weakens the quality of your work – spend time researching them. You must avoid plagiarism and never copy from others as you will risk failing the course completely. Many students find it difficult to write to a limited word count – plan each section of your coursework with an allocated number of words from the overall permitted total. This should reflect the Awarding Body mark schemes for each. Do not rely too much on just 'surfing' the Internet or downloading chunks of information – 'hit the text books'!

Sample coursework

Performance analysis: tactical model

<u>Receiving kick-offs</u>

When receiving kick-offs, the catchers should leave plenty of space in front of them to run into (see Diagram 1).

They need immediate support on either side of them. With the formation shown, the three lineout specialists, the locks and the No.8 are in a position to run forward to receive the ball and will have immediate support from one of the front row.

One or both support players can try to get in and support the catcher in the air as if in a lineout. The receiver of the ball is not allowed to be tackled while he is in the air.

When the ball has been brought down, it's a good idea to set the ball up into a maul, this works in a drop-out 22 situation as well.

The options after receiving the ball from kick-off or drop-out and setting up a maul are:

Half-way line

<u>Diagram 1</u>
Formation
for receiving
a kick-off

Key
● = Players   ↖ = Movement of players

Examiner says:

The student has detailed a single tactical consideration for a rugby union side when receiving a kick-off. It is a reasonably short but succinct piece of work for the purposes of this exercise.

Examiner says:

The student could have identified the specific players on the diagram provided with the specific player position number.

- To attack the narrow side (the touch line side) if there is sufficient room.
- To attack the open side if the kick is near the touch line.
- To kick the long, down the tram-lines, deep into the opposition territory and chase.
- If the kick-off has gone long and into the 22m area a kick into touch is another option.

Examiner says:

The student has been successful in being able to suggest solutions to commence an attacking move once the ball has been held in possession from the restart. In doing so he has shown a solid understanding of tactical consideration in one aspect of play for an invasion game.

Local study

My chosen sport is kayaking. The governing body for canoeing and kayaking in the UK is the British Canoe Union (BCU) set up in 1936 to send a team to the Berlin Olympics. To be able to race anywhere you must become a member of the BCU and get issued a licence. There are over 25,000 individual members, 469 associated clubs and 145 approved centres. Kayaking is very much a club sport: some do fun kayaking and others take it seriously in racing. Some schools offer it as a fun extra activity, others take it seriously as a sport. I am going to be talking about the serious aspects of it. More information from the BCU is in Appendix I.

www.bcu.org.uk

Grass roots

My local club would be Reading Canoe Club, more information on this can be found at their website: http://www.reading-canoe.org.uk. This is a typical club for progressing from grass roots to elite. They do Marathon, Sprint, Slalom and Recreational canoeing and kayaking at the club where everyone is welcome regardless of disability or age. Most schools don't offer kayaking but some do; not all take it competitively though. My school does. We do both marathon and sprint and take part annually in the Devizes to Westminster race over 125 miles where there is a school category to win found at http://www.dwrace.org.uk.

In marathon kayaking you do not necessarily need to belong to a club to race, and male and female race together in the same categories. You start in division 9 and work your way up to the highest division 1. In divisions 9–7 you race only 4 miles, div. 6–4 race 8 miles, the 3–1 race 12 miles. Women can not go any higher than division 3 due to the fact that the way they are built will not allow them to. There are no age limits to racing; anyone can enter but you can't be promoted unless you are part of the BCU membership. In marathon you also have "lightning" races for younger beginner paddlers. These divisional races are actually set up by clubs each year and where the National Marathon Championships are held alternates each year.

Examiner says:

The student has been able to successfully review the local provision of their chosen activity and by using factual detail place in context the provisions and opportunities open at grass roots level. In doing so both the differences and similarities between school and club are highlighted along with hyperlinks for reference purposes. This sample text is taken from a minority sport review and as such the factual detail places in context the provisions at grass roots level.

National Study: Talent Pathways

Another method of progressing through the netball system instead of the age related framework. This is called a talent pathway and there are 5 steps within it (see Figure 1).

Figure 1. Talent pathway in netball

Step 1   Satellite/County Academy Development Programme

Within each region, the Regional Head Scout (RHS) is responsible for delivering a Performance Standards Workshop (PSW) for teachers and coaches. Teachers and coaches can then nominate players into Development Programmes, often supported by County Sports Partnerships. This partnership provides an individual development programme according to the Learning to Train stage. A player may spend between 6 months to 2 years at this stage.

Step 2   Regional Talent Development Programme

Each region stages a screening of nominated players from counties. The successful players spend 1–2 years at the Regional Talent Development Programme. Then the regional talent coaches will nominate players within the Regional Talent Development Programme to attend a National Screening Day, which selects players to join their talent squads. The selection panel for the England Netball Talent Squad is comprised of Head of Selectors, U17 and U19 national coaches.

Step 3   England Netball Talent 1 and 2 Squads

These squads are comprised of approximately 20 players that will provide the basis of the England Netball U17 National Squad (Talent 1) and England Netball U19 National Squad (Talent 2). The squads get national training at weekends until selection for the final squads in January. The two squads will compete in the Netball Europe Championships held in March.

Step 4   England Netball Talented Athlete Scholarship Scheme

This scholarship scheme pushes athletes to work towards performances in Super League Squads. To enter the scholarship scheme players who are in the England Netball U21 and U19 squads are nominated along with others involved in the Super League.

Step 5   National Squad

This is where players aged betweeen 16–20 are selected for squads for international events. Here players receive an individual training programme.

Examiner says:

The student has made a good attempt to detail the national structures and pathways open for progression from first-level elite sport or physical activity into higher representation. In doing this the student has covered the selection processes and the pathways that aid performer development. The text contains factual evidence and includes reference to the role of the national governing body and the national squad grouping process.

Performance analysis: technical model

Putting

Before you putt the ball, it is important to take a moment to look at where you are going. The best way to do this is to crouch down behind your ball and to check the line of the put, being closer to the ground and being behind the ball enables you to look at the contours of the ground (i.e. check slopes) and therefore easily visualise how the ball is going to roll. Furthermore you can get a better feel for the distance of the ball from the hole by actually either just standing to the side and looking at the distance or to pace down the line that you wish to putt the ball, this however is optional. After checking your line or put, set up to the ball. Your feet should be just under shouder-width apart and your knees slightly bent, so you are standing fairly tall. Your back should be straight and your left eye should be over the ball (therefore ball position will be left of centre). Your arms should just dangle down and when you grip the golf club, your arms should form a triangle with your shoulders.

There are many variations to the putting grip, but one of the most common ones used is similar to the baseball grip. Hold the putter using a baseball grip and simply slip your left index finger out of contact with the club and place it on top of the fingers of your right hand.

Now that the posture and grip has been established, it is vital to ensure that your shoulders, hips, knees, feet and club head are aiming in the right place (taking into consideration the slopes on the green). The putting stroke is very simple; it is driven predominantly by the shoulders. Your shoulders and arms that form a triangle should move back in a straight line and through the ball in a straight line, simulating a pendulum motion. Keeping your head steady and still is essential as it dictates the movement of the rest of the body, if your head moves so will your body. The wrists should not break during the swinging motion. The actual swing should be the same distance back as through. It is important to make sure that the foreswing is slightly accelerated compared to the back swing, this is to ensure that the ball has enough velocity to reach the hole and, therefore, at least has a chance to go in. If the foreswing is decelerated the ball will not have enough speed to reach the hole and, therefore, has no chance of going in. At the end of the putting stroke your club head should be pointing to the intended target, this is a good indicator as to whether your swing path was straight back and straight through.

Examiner says:

This piece of analysis coursework details the technical elements and mental strategies involved when putting. The standard of information is very good and reflective of the expectations at AS level GCE. By definition the student has identified the preparation, execution and recovery phases with technical detail as appropriate. When using the information contained in the analysis a novice student would, by following the points made in text, make refinements in their technique.

Performance analysis: strengths and weaknesses

<u>French unpredictability</u> — France made six changes for this game and although they are noted for their passion and flair, they do not always show these characteristics. With one of their best back three line up in the world — Sadourny, Bernat-Salle, Dominici — they are always a threat. In the first half France played well with the back three plus the two centres, Glass and Garajosa, being exceptional. France could have been many points in front at half time instead of the 16—13 lead they held.

<u>England's performances</u> — In the first half England were up against a very determined French side but made several errors — Dawson's kicking, from a line out drive in his own 22, straight up into the air from which France collected and Merceron dropped the goal to increase France's lead. Was this because of the long lay off since the last game? However, at half time, the problems were resolved and a much better controlled performance followed. This was a much-improved part of England's game under Woodward. The last time they were behind at half time (Australia) they came out victorious.

Examiner says:

The student has been able to analyse a full International Rugby Union match to good effect. The overview highlights some of the strengths and weaknesses seen in the performances of both sides and details some objective facts that underpin the analysis.

INDEX

Bold page numbers indicate a definition of the term. *Italic* numbers indicate an illustration or table.

ACKNOWLEDGEMENTS

Texts cited in this book are as follows:

American Heart Association, *Circulation*, 2001; 104:1358

Balyi, I., Hamilton A., *Long-Term Athlete Development: Trainability in Childhood and Adolescence. Windows of Opportunity: Optimal Trainability*, National Coaching Institute British Columbia and Advanced Training and Performance Ltd. (2004)

Burns, F., *A History of Robert Dovers Olimpick Games*, Stuart Press, 2000

Department for Culture, Media and Sport (2002)

Department for Transport, *National Travel Survey*, Office for National Statistics, 2001

Department of Health, *Choosing Activity: a Physical Activity Action Plan*, 2005

Encyclopedia, Wikepedia.org, 2007

Fitts, P.M., and Posner, M.I., *Human Performance*, 1967

General Household Survey, Office for National Statistics, 2002

Hughes, M., and Franks, I., *Notational Analysis of Sport*, Spon Press, 1997

Neulinger, J., *To Leisure: An Introduction*, Boston: Allyn and Bacon, 1981

Sheldon, W., *Atlas of Men*, 1940

Wenger, H. *Train to Win*, Sports Coach, 1999

The authors and publisher would like to thank the following individuals and organisations for permission to reproduce photographs:

p3 BL ©PA Photos/ AP Photo/ Victor R. Caivano; **p3 BR** ©Corbis/ Chase Jarvis; **p3 MR** ©Rex Features/ Sipa Press; **p6** ©Rex Features/ Brian Harris; **p11** ©Alamy Images/ Alaska Stock LLC; **p15** ©Rex Features/Voisin/ Phanie; **p21 TL** ©PA Photos/ AP Photo/ Reed Saxon; **p21 TR** ©PA Photos/ AP Photo/ Jason DeCrow; **p22 TL** ©Corbis/ Flint; **p22 TR** ©Corbis / Tim McGuire; **p37** ©PA Photos/ AP Photo/ Itsuo Inouye; **p39** ©Corbis/ Catherine Karnow; **p42** ©PA Photos/ Elise Amendola/ AP; **p52** ©Getty Images/ AFP/ David Boily; **p55** ©Getty Images/ Blend Images; **p71** ©Action Plus / Neil Tingle; **p72 T** ©Corbis/ Fei Maohua/ Xinhua Press; **p72 MR** ©PA Photos/Jon Buckle/EMPICS Sport; **p73 TL** ©Rex Features/ Sipa Press; **p73 TR** ©Getty Images/ Koichi Kamoshida; **p74** ©Rex Features; **p83** ©Photolibrary/ Scott McDermott; **p88** ©Action Plus/ Glyn Kirk; **p99** ©Reuters/ Ian Hodgson; **p103** ©PA Photos/ Adam Davy/ EMPICS Sport; **p105** ©Bridgeman Art Library/ Musée Municipal Antoine Vivenel, Compiègne, France; **p106** ©PA Photos/ AP Photo/ Pier Paolo Cito; **p108** ©PA Photos/ AP Photo/ Douglas C. Pizac; **p109** ©PA Photos/ AP; **p120** ©Alamy Images/ Steven May; **p121** ©Alamy Images/Steven May; **p125** ©Getty Images/ Time & Life Pictures; **p127 TL** ©PA Photos/ Tom Theobald/ Zuma Press; **p127 TR** ©Getty Images/ AFP/ Patrick Hertzog; **p129** ©Action Plus / Neil Tingle; **p130** ©PA Photos/ Gareth Fuller/ PA Archive; **p134–5** ©Rex Features/ Michael Fresco; **p135 BL** ©Getty Images/ Iconica; **p135 BR** ©Action Plus / Neil Tingle; **p137** ©Corbis/ Alessandro Di Meo/ EPA; **p138** ©Getty Images/John Peters/Manchester United; **p139** ©Action Plus / Neil Tingle; **p141** ©Alamy Images/ Matt Fowler; **p144 T** ©Getty Images/ Daniel Berehulak; **p144 BR** ©PA Photos/ Dave Munden/ EMPICS Sport; **p145 TR** ©Action Plus / Neil Tingle; **p145 BR** ©Getty Images/Robert Cianflone; **p156 TL** ©Rex Features/ Aurora Photos; **p156 TR** ©Rex Features; **p157** ©Corbis/ Reuters/ Jessica Persson; **p162** ©Corbis/ Michael Kim; **p177** ©Action Plus/ Mike Shearman; **p178** ©Alamy Images

The author and publisher would like to thank the following for permission to reproduce copyright material:

p5 Fig.1.1, **p12 Fig.1.6** Copyright material is reproduced with the permission of OPSI/HMSO and the Queen's Printer for Scotland; **p6** Logo, **p112** Drug Information Database reproduced with permission of UK Sport; **p141 Fig.10.6** Slice Card (season ticket to sports and leisure facilities) reproduced with permission of Oxford City Council; **p184** Logo with permission of the British Canoe Union

Every effort has been made to contact copyright holders of material reproduced in this book. Any omissions will be rectified in subsequent printings if notice is given to the publishers.